William Edward Jelf

An Examination into the Doctrine and Practice of Confession

William Edward Jelf

An Examination into the Doctrine and Practice of Confession

ISBN/EAN: 9783743390287

Manufactured in Europe, USA, Canada, Australia, Japa

Cover: Foto ©Lupo / pixelio.de

Manufactured and distributed by brebook publishing software (www.brebook.com)

William Edward Jelf

An Examination into the Doctrine and Practice of Confession

AN EXAMINATION

INTO THE

DOCTRINE AND PRACTICE

OF

CONFESSION

BY

WILLIAM EDWARD JELF, B.D.

AUTHOR OF 'QUOUSQUE'

SOMETIME CENSOR OF CH. CH.; BAMPTON LECTURER 1857; WHITEHALL PREACHER 1846

LONDON

LONGMANS, GREEN, AND CO.

1875

PREFACE.

I HAVE not sufficient reliance on myself to put forth a work upon Confession at the present moment, without expressing a hope that any auguries which I may entertain of its acceptance may be realised only so far as the views it contains are in harmony with God's Word and Will; that if, contrary to my own firm conviction, it be otherwise, it may be overruled so as to be of none effect; and with this hope, or rather prayer, I commit it to the judgment of my readers and God's good Providence.

I have thought it best not to load my pages with numerous references to patristic books (not on the shelves of ordinary libraries) in support of facts, the authorities for which can be found almost exhaustively, certainly abundantly and sufficiently, in the pages of such works as Bingham and Usher, and the note in the translation of Tertullian in the Library of the Fathers. I have, therefore, referred my readers to these books, where they will find not only references to the original works, but generally full length quotations of the passages referred to.

I must beg my readers' indulgence for any faults

of style or language which they may discover. Writing on such a subject, it is difficult to be accurate without being tiresome, to be full without overflowing. I am aware that my readers will find occasional repetitions which they may possibly think they might have well been spared: but the matter of fact is, that the subject divides itself into many distinct heads and points of view, and where the same arguments and facts apply to all, or more than one of these, I have preferred to commit an offence against rhetoric by reproducing the link which was necessary to the coherence of my chain, rather than to offend against logic by leaving it incomplete.

40 QUEEN'S GATE GARDENS:
January 1875.

CONTENTS.

CHAPTER I.

PRELIMINARY OBSERVATIONS.

Importance of the Subject—Aspects and Results of the Confessional—Instinctive Aversion to it—Not the Ground of this Treatise—But its Repugnance to God's revealed Word—Urgency of the Question—Indistinctness and Hesitation in dealing with it—Various Grounds of its Acceptance—Necessity for an Examination of it—Conclusion at which I have arrived—The People to whom it is addressed—*A priori* Reasons for doubting its Soundness—Sophistry and Sophistries of its Supporters—Petty Arguments current among its Partisans . . . . PAGE 1

CHAPTER II.

Point at Issue—Not the clerical Commission, but its Nature and Extent—Not whether Men ought to be anxious about their Salvation, but whether Auricular Confession is an appointed Means thereto—Not whether confidential Communications between a Pastor and his Flock are desirable or allowable, but whether formal Absolution is an ordained Channel of Pardon, or a desirable Preparation for the Holy Communion—No Necessity to adduce the extravagant Utterances of the School—The Subject will be treated in its least irrational Aspect—Varieties of Opinion among those who have accepted the System—A Suspicion of Unclearness and Unsoundness created thereby—Not necessary to examine all these in Detail—Some evidently Errors—Some will be touched upon hereafter—Cause of this Inconsistency of View—In the Teachers of the Party—In its Disciples and Partisans—Real point advocated by the Confessionalists—What they mean by Auricular Confession—Notions mixed up in the Term Confession—Confidence and Confession, Absolution and Pardon to be distinguished from each other—Confession in its popular Acceptation, includes *Confidence* and *Confession* in its technical sense—Great Contrast between these—How they are linked together in the Confessionalist system—Points successively advanced—Ending in Auricular Confession, technically so-called—Differing little from the Roman practice—Different in Details—Identical in Error 14

CHAPTER III.

Twofold Plea for Confession:—1. As a natural duty—2. As a divine Appointment—Attempt to identify Confession with the natural Instinct of Confidence by throwing the same Colouring of Duty over both—1. By asserting that they are both commanded in Scripture—2. By Analogies of Lawyer and Physician—This latter Argument examined as used to support Confession—Analogies too far fetched—Do not touch the required Point—Argue from prudential to an intrinsic Obligation—Hence even if they did apply to Confidence, yet they would not apply to Confession—Fail in their Facts—Full disclosure to a Lawyer or Physician often not necessary—Fail in their Relation—One relating to Things natural in which there is generally no Alternative, the other to Things spiritual in which the Absence of an Alternative is the very Point to be proved—These Analogies do not justify special Arrangements for Confession—Betting-houses furnish the closer Analogy on this Point—Question whether Scripture enjoins the Duty of private Confession—Passage in St. James has two possible Meanings—Difference between them—The Confessionalist Interpretation not recognized in the early Church—The Confession spoken of by St. James is Reciprocal—Language of the Homilies on the Subject—St. James is not speaking of technical Confession—If he was, his Language would be more Definite—Confessionalists not to be heard in their Application of this Passage . . . . PAGE 26

CHAPTER IV.

Fallacy of passing from *Confidence* to *Confession*—Gain to the Confessionalist Cause in identifying them—*Confidence* allowable under certain Conditions—Not peculiar to Christianity, though possibly more effective under its Auspices—Arises not from sacerdotal Prerogative—But from the natural Sympathies and Yearnings of Humanity—To be disconnected from sacerdotal Notions—Distinction between Confidences for Relief of Mind, or for the Sake of Advice—The Clergyman the proper Person to apply to, but the having Recourse to him a Sign of Spiritual Weakness—Opportunities for good in such Confidences—Recourse to Clergymen for removal of Doubts of Forgiveness—No Sign of Spiritual Health, but the Reverse—Cure for a morbid State—Any System of Training or Preaching which creates the Need of such a morbid State bears Witness against itself—Confidences to be received under certain Limitations—How they may approach to *Confession*—Care must be taken not to confound these two different Things—Danger at present day in Confidence—Differences between *Confidence* and *Confession*, and between *Pastoral Advice* and *Direction*—Importance of realising these Distinctions—This Confidence only once suggested by our Church to Persons in Health and Strength—Practical Transition from *Confidence* to *Confession* . . 38

CHAPTER V.

Second Plea for Confession as part of a Divine Ordinance for the Forgiveness of Sin—The Theory displays much knowledge of human Nature and human Wants—Might have recommended itself to our acceptance had there been no Revelation—The ignoring of God's revealed Cure for Sin the real Objection to it—No Trace in Scripture of any such Ordinance for Pardon as private Confession to Man, or any such Practice being used, or recommended by the Apostles—Nor yet any Trace of it in the really Primitive Church—Primitive Practices recognised by our Church as a Witness to Facts—Especially valued by Mediævalists—This finds no Place in Primitive Practice—No private Confession practised or recognised except as preparatory to public Discipline, and this not in the earliest Ages—Evidence of Mr. Carter on this Point—Of E. B. P. in a Note on Tertullian—This shows, not only that private Confession was not compulsory as in Romish Church, but that it did not exist at all . . . . PAGE 51

CHAPTER VI.

Further Examination into the Ancient Practice—Both Persuasives to and Dissuasives from private Disclosure of Sin—Solution of this is that Disclosure is recommended in certain Cases with a View to public Confession—Discouraged as a Means of obtaining Pardon from God—Threefold Phase of Sin—Against a Brother—Against the Church—Against God—Threefold Phase of Guilt—Different Means of obtaining Remission of these several Phases of Guilt.

Sins against the Church were Matters of penitential Discipline—Remitted by the Church as the Party offended—Remitted by Individual Christians, when the Sin and Guilt arose from Private Injuries—Sins against God remitted by God alone on Confession to Him—Prominent Place held by Sin against the Church—Afterwards the Notion of such Sin died away, and the penitential Discipline fell into Disuse—Persuasives to disclosure of Sins originally had reference to public Disclosure, Dissuasives had reference to the Requirements of God by Confession to Him alone.

Proofs that public Discipline dealt only with Sins as against the Church—Not with Sins as against God—Line drawn between these—Passage from Cyprian—Differences between Public Discipline and Auricular Confession—Too wide to admit of one being any Warrant for the other. . . 63

CHAPTER VII.

Nature and Decay of Public Discipline—Case of Corinthian Sinner—Developed in the Century after the Apostles—Lapsi—Scandalous Offences—Those which caused no Scandal, left to private Conscience and Discipline—No private Confession, for the Sin was notorious—Public Disclosure of secret Sins for Relief of Conscience—This only allowed on Recommendation of some wise

Layman, or afterwards Priest—Private Disclosure of Sins to such Persons for this Purpose—Not followed by Absolution—Multiplication of such Cases—Appointment of Pænitentiarius—His Office that of '*Juge d'Instruction*'—Advance towards Mediæval System, but not to Absolution—Scandal caused by this Office—Abolished—No warrant for Confession, but the contrary.

Private personal Discipline for Offences not against the Church—Same as that recommended by our Church as Preparation for Holy Communion.

Confidence in Early Church—Primitive Usage retained in our Church, except as regards Public Discipline.

Abolition of Pænitentiarius—Private Confession assumes a substantive Form—Public Confession less frequent—Public Reconciliation for notorious Offences superseded by private—Change in the Notion of Public Reconciliation—Private Confession for notorious Offences authorised—Change of Doctrine as well as Practice—Reconciliation or Absolution still precatory, not indicative, and so up to end of twelfth Century—This is a Matter of Ecclesiastical Arrangement, not of Scriptural Obligation—Hence we must see what is the Practice and Teaching of our own Church.

Attempt to distinguish occasional from habitual Confession—Flaws in the Argument . . . . PAGE 74

CHAPTER VIII.

This a Matter of Canonical Arrangement—Argument from this—Pleas, that this accounts for the absence of Primitive Sanction, and that our Church has a Right to enjoin the Practice—Logical Effect of these Pleas—If so, it cannot be a Sacramental Ordinance of Divine Appointment—Plea, that Language of the Church may indicate a Recognition of its Scriptural Obligation, or makes it binding on us, answered—Effect of such a Plea—Necessity for examining our Church's Language—Positive Assertions of Confessionalists on this Point—Mistaken Proofs they adduce—What it is they assert to be taught by our Church—Visitation Office—Method prescribed—Inquiry into the Fact of the sick Man's Repentance, not any Detail of his Sins—Special Confession—Not necessarily private—Absolution to be reluctantly applied—Pardon not given—But prayed for after the Absolution—This Prayer the Relic of the old precatory Form—Argument of Confessionalists about this Prayer answered—Why it is untenable—Precatory Form up to twelfth Century shows that Forgiveness was held to be a Matter of Petition, not as a '*fait accompli*'—Change to '*ego te absolvo*'—Caution of our Church in this Matter—Instances of the Nature of Absolution in other Passages of our Prayer Book—Morning and Evening Prayer—Must be essentially the same in Visitation Office, differently applied—Not Forgiveness, but God's Promise and Offer to forgive—Difference between Absolution and Pardon—Instances of this in the Prayer Book—In the Visitation Formula—The Special Confession comes nearer to *Confidence*—But at all Events it would furnish no Precedent for Cases essentially different—Certainly not for *Confession* in the only Case in which even *Confidence* is recommended by our Church . 87

CHAPTER IX.

Exhortation to Holy Communion—Wrongly claimed by Confessionalists as decisive in their Favour—The best and indispensable Preparation set forth in the preceding Paragraphs—Case in which *Confidence* is recommended—State of the Man's Mind—What he is directed to do—The Remedy not Absolution, but the Ministry of God's Word conveying the *Benefit of Absolution*—Directions clear and precise, to the utter Exclusion of any Sacerdotal Action—Why and how different Interpretation has been admitted—Counterbalanced by the Fact of the Interpretation put upon it by general Usage. Key of the Confessionalist Position—*Benefit* supposed to be meaningless—Absolution supposed to denote the Exercise of the Power of Forgiveness. Exhortation may be read by a Minister—Confessionalist Argument on the use of this Term—Changes in the Terms in this Sentence—Other Alterations—Prayer Books of 1549 (1552), 1559—As revised in 1662—All these Alterations, Additions, Omissions, Point the same Way—Why '*Absolution*' was changed into '*Benefit of Absolution*'—Attempt of Laud to introduce a Formula of Absolution—Meaning of the Term '*Ministry of Word*'—Language of Homily—Passage tells against the Confessionalists, and not for them—No Clergyman is here authorised to pronounce any Form of Absolution—Canon of 1603—Language of Homily . . . . PAGE 102

CHAPTER X.

Ground of the Discussion shifted to private Absolution—Confessionalist Argument from Ordination Formula—Question at Issue—Relation between our Lord's Words in St. John and the Ordination Formula—Analysis of the Formula—Relation of the third Paragraph to the second—Twofold Power conferred—These were held in Early Church to be exercised by the Dispensation of the Word and Sacraments, and in our own—Not by any Sacerdotal Power or Sentence—This Method exhausts our Lord's Commission as far as private Sins are concerned—No private Power of repelling from the Holy Communion contemplated in the Exhortation to the Holy Communion—Language of our Church on this Point —' Discipline of Church' in the Promise made by the Candidate for Ordination—How limited—These Limitations confine the Exercise of any Power to notorious Sins—Directions before the Communion Office—Summary of the Argument—Practice of our Church—Does not recognise actual Forgiveness as the Result of the Power in any of the Places where it is exercised—Reason and reasonableness of this—Possible Translation of the Formula does not affect this View—What the Power is not—Not judicial—Not operative or effective—Not a Grant of Pardon—Not Supernatural—Not Sacramental—Private Confession to a Priest not necessary to the Exercise thereof—Special Confession in Visitation Office not necessarily Private—Not necessary as giving the Priest Information on the Case—Knowledge of a Man's Sins not recognised as necessary to the telling him ho can be saved—Nor to determine the Amount of Penance or Penitence 119

CHAPTER XI.

Sense of our Lord's Words in St. John xx—Bearing of this Point on our Church's View—Real Question at Issue—Points required to prove the Confessionalist case—Twofold Question—To whom were the Powers given—And what were the Powers—Powers given to those addressed—This assumed to be the eleven Apostles—Admitting this, the Power might have been confined to them—They had Faculties whereby they could pronounce absolute Forgiveness—Which Priests now have not. 'I am with you always' does not carry on this Power—Others addressed besides the Apostles—Others were with him—Power conferred on the Church—This difference Important—What were the Powers given—Clearly the Power of remitting ecclesiastical Offences—But this not exhaustive—Comparison of Accounts of different Evangelists—St. Luke states the Commission to have been preaching Repentance and Remission of Sins—St. Matthew and St. Mark relate the giving this Commission to the Apostles on other Occasions—How the Accounts may be reconciled—Both embodied by our Church—How the Power was exercised in apostolic Age—Confessionalist Assertion—Negatived by Facts—No such Power exercised or claimed by Apostles—Simon Magus—Case of Corinthian Penitent—Tells against the Confessionalists, not for them, even on their own View of it—Literal Meaning of St. John's Words—Not taken by anyone—St. Matthew ix. 8—Practical Test of the Power claimed under this Passage—2 Cor. v. 18—'*As my Father sent Me, so send I you*'—How far the Mission of Church is identical with that of Christ—Confessionalist Position assumes that the Power they claim is the Only Method of exercising our Lord's Commission—How answered—Flaw in the Position that this Way is one out of many—Practical Test of this Argument

PAGE 138

CHAPTER XII.

Witness of the practice of the post-apostolic Early Church as to the meaning of our Lord's Words—As to what was not held—As to what was held—Interpretation put upon our Lord's Words—In their widest sense—Direct remission of ecclesiastical offences—Mediate and indirect commission—By preaching of repentance and remission of sins—Baptism—Intercessory prayer—Result of the power exercised—By the proclamation of God's promises—By baptism—Intercessory prayer—Retaining power—Exercise and results of—Power not to be exceeded—What is absolution—Not mere preaching—Not merely reading the Bible—Proclamation of the Gospel by the Church before the New Testament Scriptures existed—Under our Lord's special commission and authority—This proclamation afterwards embodied in the written Word—Authority of the Church and of the Scriptures—The written Word does not supersede the voice of the Church, but bears witness to it and protects it from corruptions—Essential duty of every Church still to publish the message which our Lord put into its mouth—This prophetic office of the Church exercised in absolution—Conferred in our own Church on the second order of ministers—Couched in a formula of words—Difference between this and preaching on the one hand, and the sacramental theory on the other—Not antagonistic to the written word . 162

CHAPTER XIII.

How this power is exercised in our own Church—In a formula expressing the unlimited mercy of God—In a formula of prayer—In a formula addressed personally to an individual—In the Morning and Evening Service—In the office of the Holy Communion—Confirmed by the comfortable words of Scripture—Visitation Office—State of the man—Nature and result of the absolution—Not granting of pardon, not declaring it absolutely granted—Not a sealed pardon but a sealed offer of pardon—How far it affects the state of the individual—Illustrations—Not required by men of strong faith—Hence only permitted in cases of morbid doubt—How far an assurance of repentance—Doubt of God's mercy not to be suggested—Pardon not to be represented as given through the minister—Not to be suggested with a view to future influence—Absolution not to be pronounced over unconscious persons—Argument thence as to its nature—Confession and absolution not recognised as a preparation for the Holy Communion—Doubts not to be suggested or aggravated—Why absolution permitted on a death-bed

PAGE 175

CHAPTER XIV.

Summary of the proofs and arguments on each side—Case of the Confessionalists—Case on the other side—Practical conclusions—Difference between Rome and Confessionalists one of degree not of kind—Between Confessionalists one of kind not of degree—Powers conferred by ordination—How exercised in our Church—Absolution does not convey pardon—Not even in *I absolve thee*—Confession—Confession as viewed by the Confessionalists and in the Church of England—Special confession in the Visitation Office—Recognised nowhere else—Difference between confidence and confession—Between what is suggested in the Communion Office and that permitted in the Visitation Office—The question is not between habitual and occasional confession—How this notion arose—Flaw in the theory of occasional auricular confession—Solution of the difficulty in which Ritualists plead they are placed by the importunity of applicants—Unreality of the plea—Danger of even confidential consultations in these days—Laity not responsible for the revival of the practice—How clergymen may deal with those who consult them—For relief of mind—For disclosing a doubt—Auricular confession a misuse of the clerical office—Cannot be claimed by the laity as a right—How such an applicant to be dealt with—This method pursued since the Reformation—Distinction between mortal and venial sin—Does not authorise auricular confession—Nor do the Confessionalists confine the practice to mortal sin—Plea for absolution as a restitution to a state of grace . 189

CHAPTER XV.

Catena alleged in favour of it—Value of a catena overrated—Especially when not contrasted with practice—Opposite catenæ—Variety of views in English divines—This caused by the want of a clear idea of truth—By a rapid and fertile thought—Especially under pressure of opposition—This very perceptible in English writers—Passages often taken without the context—Conditions of value for a catena—All authorities to be struck out of the catena who are speaking of something different to the point alleged—And those whose views are based on probably erroneous grounds—Or where they are at variance with the Church of England or with history, or with each other—On the other side, a large catena of practice—Occasional instance of absolution—Not always in harmony with the Church teaching—Catena of authorities on the other side—What the catena is worth at its highest and best—Catena cannot supply evidence—Nor can any amount of vague assumptions—Nor counterbalance the lack of it—Limitations introduced by these divines fatal to their theory—Benefits alleged as arising from the practice—See-saw argument of the Confessionalists—Testimony to its benefits—From personal experience—From parochial experience—Not necessary to parish work properly carried on—Perhaps necessary to public discipline if it existed among us—Possibly useful for direction, but this not recognised in our Church—Confidential intercourse admits neither sacramental confession nor direction—Confession and absolution are not to be directed as a condition of pardon, or used to get the secrets of a man's soul—Alleged benefits counterbalanced by known evils—Question whether it is not an intrusion on the revealed scheme of salvation—This the great question—The evil of this not counterbalanced by any great benefits—What God has given us is exhaustive and sufficient—Clergy not physicians, but only errand-boys of the Great Physician—Have no licence to alter or add to His panacea—Certainty of methods prescribed by God—Danger of human devices—Auricular confession implies disbelief in God's promises—The importance of this principle makes me defer the consideration of the benefits of confession—Argument for toleration is a sign of conscious weakness—Not likely to succeed—Apathy on the point quite unintelligible—Important results of the confessional : Theologically—Evangelically—Ecclesiastically—Religiously—Personally—Nationally—Socially—Danger of again allowing it to take root . . . . PAGE 209

CONFESSION.

CHAPTER I.

PRELIMINARY OBSERVATIONS.

Corrigenda.

Page 69, line 3 from foot, *for* son *read* sun
,, 70, ,, 18. *for* remitted *read* not remitted
,, 130, ,, 8, for *there* read *here*
,, 135, last line, *for* Christ *read* church
,, 136. ,, ,, after *penitence* insert, that is, bodily punishment exacted by a priest before he will pronounce the pardon he professes to grant

the day from which it is impossible to turn in silence: and this all the more as its advocates boast of the strides which it is daily making among us. In whichever of its manifold aspects it presents itself—whether theologically, or politically, or socially, or individually—it is a principle and a power which must be regarded either with dread or with hope, certainly not with indifference. The total change it introduces into what may be called the machinery of the spiritual life, as administered by the Church; its invasion of many of those principles and rights which we and our fathers believed ourselves to have recovered at the Reformation, as essential points in

<small>Aspects and results of the Confessional.</small>

ceptible in English writers—Passages often taken without the context—Conditions of value for a catena—All authorities to be struck out of the catena who are speaking of something different to the point alleged—And those whose views are based on probably erroneous grounds—Or where they are at variance with the Church of England or with history, or with each other—On the other side, a large catena of practice—Occasional instance of absolution—Not always in harmony with the Church teaching—Catena of authorities on the other side—What the catena is worth at its highest and best—Catena cannot supply evidence—Nor can any amount of vague assumptions—Nor counterbalance the lack of it—Limitations introduced by these divines fatal to their theory—Benefits alleged as arising from the practice—See-saw argument of the Confessionalists—Testimony to its benefits—From personal experience—From parochial experience—Not necessary to parish work properly carried on—Perhaps necessary to public discipline if it existed among us—Possibly useful for direction, but this not recognised in our Church—Confidential intercourse admits neither sacramental confession nor direction—Confession and absolution are not to be directed as a condition of pardon, or used to get the secrets of a man's soul—Alleged benefits counterbalanced by known evils—Question whether

CONFESSION.

CHAPTER I.

PRELIMINARY OBSERVATIONS.

Importance of the Subject—Aspects and Results of the Confessional—Instinctive Aversion to it—Not the Ground of this Treatise—But its Repugnance to God's revealed Word—Urgency of the Question—Indistinctness and Hesitation in dealing with it—Various Grounds of its Acceptance—Necessity for an Examination of it—Conclusion at which I have arrived—The People to whom it is addressed—*A priori* Reasons for doubting its Soundness—Sophistry and Sophistries of its Supporters—Petty Arguments current among its Partisans.

THE progress of the doctrine of Confession—the revived use of the Confessional as a channel of pardon and a means of grace—is one of those remarkable features of the day from which it is impossible to turn in silence: and this all the more as its advocates boast of the strides which it is daily making among us. In whichever of its manifold aspects it presents itself—whether theologically, or politically, or socially, or individually—it is a principle and a power which must be regarded either with dread or with hope, certainly not with indifference. The total change it introduces into what may be called the machinery of the spiritual life, as administered by the Church; its invasion of many of those principles and rights which we and our fathers believed ourselves to have recovered at the Reformation, as essential points in

_{Importance of the subject.}

_{Aspects and results of the Confessional.}

the Charter of Salvation, which God has given us through Christ; the retrogression it marks towards the Mediæval phase of Christianity, from which the Reformation set us free; the power it will give to the clerical caste, which is almost sure to develop itself all the more rapidly under its auspices; the new element it will introduce into the closest relations of life; the new spring it will create in politics; the fresh barrier it will set up between the Church and the Nonconformists; the new aspect it will throw over the spiritual energies and growth of each individual—combine to give it an importance which can be claimed by scarcely any, if any, other point of religious controversy. It is not merely a part of the programme of the school which is opposed to the Reformation and protests against the Protestant character of the English Church, but it affects the whole of the inner and outer state of the Church and Churchmen. It is simply a revolution. If it is true, we have nothing to do but to accept it, with shame and sorrow for the short-comings and the loss of our forefathers and ourselves; if it is false, we have nothing to do but to oppose it with the energy of men who are indisposed to accept a new religion, in the place of that which our forefathers recovered and handed down to us.

It is a revolution in religion.

The advocates of the Confessional sometimes pretend that it is the tremendous character of the practice which makes people shrink from it, and therefore condemn that which they afterwards approve and value. In the book circulated for the guidance of the clergy in the London Mission[1] it is said that 'it is the instinctive consciousness of the divine power of the priesthood which makes Confession such a dread reality.' It may be true that there s much about it which is repulsive, and that people shrink from it without exactly knowing what it is; we

Instinctive aversion to it not unreasonable.

---

[1] 'Parochial Missions.' page 92.

have reason to thank God that it carries with it this providential safeguard against itself. It may be true also, on the other hand, that when persons under the influence of excited or morbid feeling look upon it as it is painted in false colours by one of these men—as a special means ordained by God, and entrusted to his ministry—they may, deceived and seduced by his apparent earnestness and confident assertion, be induced to catch at this straw, which he holds out to them, after having, by concealing God's covenanted promise of forgiveness, persuaded them that they are as drowning men without any other means of escape; but this does not prove that the original repulsive instinct was not well-founded, or that the changed view is reasonable. With this instinctive aversion to the Confessional, however, I have nothing to do, beyond thanking God that it exists, and praying that it long may exist. I am not going to found my case against the Confessional upon it; its only relation to what I am going to write is, that I trust the following pages will, among other results, prevent its being overpowered or extinguished by the fallacies, the sophistries, the misrepresentations, the unauthorised promises, sometimes the falsehoods—one does not like the word, but truth compels one to use it—with which some of its advocates are trying to impose it on the religious yearnings, on the awakened consciences of our people. The repulsive character of the Confessional is not my reason for condemning and opposing it. I condemn it —I oppose it—because, while in practice it is an act of disbelief in God's revealed promises, in theory it is a superseding God's ordained means for the forgiveness of sin and restoration to a state of grace: placing instead thereof a human, unrevealed device, not to be found in Scriptural Christianity, not known in the primitive Church, struck out of our own Church system at the Reformation—a system and a practice which it is wickedness to attempt to

But not the ground for opposing it.

But because it supersedes God's revealed promises and methods.

re-introduce, and madness to permit its introduction; seeing that it was in its earliest existence the offspring of a debased Christianity— afterwards the parent and the nurse of a Christianity still more debased.

Present state of the question.

The state of the question, too, forces it upon us. It is not merely that it is pressed more eagerly than ever by the small but energetic school of Mediævalists, but that even some of those who are most opposed to it seem to have more difficulty in treating it than they had when it was first mooted. As long ago as the Nottingham Congress, I heard it remarked, that the utterances for it, though studiously moderate, were bolder and more decisive in tone, the utterances against it more hesitating, than on former occasions; and though popular feeling has at length most justly, and not one hour sooner than was needed, roused itself against it, yet it must be confessed that the utterances and actions of many of our spiritual guides are marked by an indistinctness and hesitation, of which, I suspect, they are themselves painfully conscious. Those who broadly abjure it in one sentence, partially admit it in another, seemingly shrinking from denying in its details that which they condemn in theory, without being exactly able to define the grounds of their condemnation. The aim of those who do not condemn it seems to be the limiting it to certain occasions, thus admitting a principle of which they cannot define satisfactorily the limitation.

Prevalent indistinctness and hesitation on the subject.

This difficulty, which is felt in dealing with it practically, is one of the points which convinces me that the matter is very imperfectly understood, sometimes purposely mystified: that it has been subjected to very superficial tests by a large number of those who have, either actively or silently, given it countenance. This is explained by the fact, that till within a very few years men, not being obliged to look at it practically, were content to

Causes of these.

adopt what certain writers had said before them, or to state loosely what seemed to them at first sight to be the theory of the Church, without caring to look into it more deeply. It was not of any practical importance either in the teaching of the Clergy, or in the use of the Laity; and hence, now that it has been revived among us in its practical bearing on everyday life, it is accepted very differently, and on very different grounds, by different people—the natural result of its having existed among Divines in the shadowy form of *posse* and very rarely, if ever, in any well-defined reality of *esse*. By some it has been accepted on the authority of one or two great names, without any real examination into its intrinsic merits and claims and history; by others it has been adopted as part of the system of a school; by others, again, as holding out a prospect of that personal influence over their people, which is so great an object with every active clergyman, whether his aim be personal success or the salvation of souls. Others, again, look at it as a means of stemming dissent and recovering dissenters; others have taken it up on the show of reason which has been cast around it by the mis-statements and sophistries of its champions; others, again, have been won by specious statements of the practical blessings which, it is asserted, experience proves it to possess. It seems to me that those who look at it with dislike and suspicion (and these are very far from being exclusively what are called Low Church or Broad Church) hardly know how to deal with the audacity, with which its advocates assume that their case is self-evident, or with the portions of the Prayer-book which are alleged as putting the matter beyond doubt or dispute.

The *onus probandi* should, indeed, rest with those who are endeavouring to introduce in a greater or less degree Auricular Confession, as a means of grace more or less indispensable: but the argument and proofs they have put

<small>Reasons for the present treatise.</small>

forward have met with a sufficient degree of acceptance to justify, and indeed to necessitate, a searching examination into their validity and value. I should have been thankful if I had found this done to my hand as fully and satisfactorily as I believe it admits of being done; but as I have not, my apology for coming forward is, my having, after a long, careful, and thoughtful consideration, come to the undoubting conclusion, that neither in Scripture nor in the early Church, nor in our own Church, is there anything to justify its being placed in the position, in which even the most moderate of its advocates seek to place it, far less in that which is claimed for it by the extreme partisans of the so-called 'Catholic' revival. This conclusion, and the grounds on which I have come to it, I submit to the judgment of my readers. I can scarcely hope that what I urge will be generally accepted by those who are pledged to the practice. There are some, doubtless, whose honesty of character and purity of conscience, and love of truth, will induce them to abandon even a favourite system if they see that it is baseless. But, generally speaking, it would be too much to expect that men, whose professional position rests mainly on the success of what they have advocated so warmly and so confidently, will kiss the axe which professes to be laid to the root of their self-esteem, and to convict them of being misled and misleading. It is not to, or for, such men that I am writing. I am convinced, however, as I said above, that there are many who have adopted, or approved, or not opposed, this innovation, in consequence of being unable to see their way out of the arguments, which were presented to them as self-evident propositions, admitting no denial and needing no proof. There are a still larger body, who have an instinctive repugnance to such a system, as well as rational doubts of its being part of God's will for the salvation of man, and yet scarcely know how to maintain their position in

People to whom it is addressed.

the face of so aggressive an enemy. Many, for instance, especially in holy orders, have been perplexed by being told that sacramental confession is expressly ordered by the Church, and implied in their ordination vows. And I cannot help hoping that some benefit will result to the Church and to Religion, if it can be shown that this dogma has in it nothing more substantial than the colouring which a sharp-dealing sophistry throws around it; that the statements whereby men have been perplexed are inaccurate, not to say false; the reasonings totally inconclusive; that the injunctions of Scripture, the witness of antiquity, the voice of their own Church, are so far from lending it any countenance that they are decidedly and directly opposed to it.

I confess that I have been very much surprised at the singular poverty and shallowness of the grounds and arguments alleged in support of so weighty a matter; a poverty so transparent and so striking, that it is almost incredible that those who use them can possibly believe in their depth or force. And it is quite in harmony with this, that the tone they adopt with their opponents is often that of rude arrogance and impertinent surprise at their differing from them.[1] I have been struck, too, with the sophistry with which some minor detail of the system is elaborately discussed, as if the main point were confessedly true. Thus one divine of note among them writes a thick pamphlet to show that every man may choose his own father confessor, as if this was the only point that remained to be settled. Others, again, will discuss the question whether auricular confession is voluntary or necessary, as if it were admitted on all sides that, within certain limits and in certain cases,

Sophistries of supporters

Passing by the point which requires proof: ignoratio elenchi.

---

[1] I recollect a man younger than myself, to whom I was personally known, on my expressing an opinion such as I have given above, sneeringly saying, 'I suppose you have been ordained'? as if it was possible that a reasonable man should express so decided an opinion on a *vexata quæstio* without having thoroughly weighed a point which lies on its very surface.

it was established beyond a question. In this as in most other parts of the Mediæval system, one of their most usual fallacies is passing over the point to be proved, and enlarging on some general principle, which, however true it may be, does not hold good for their purpose until they have proved the point that they have passed over. Thus, for instance, Mr. Carter attempts to show that the great promise of immediate forgiveness from God Himself may be reconciled with his theory of the necessity or benefit of a deferred forgiveness by sacramental confession, on the principle that two contradictory doctrines or truths may co-exist. He ignores the equally undoubted principle, that this does not hold good except where each of the opposed points is expressly and unmistakably revealed in Scripture. He ought to have proved that this deferred forgiveness is revealed in Scripture, instead of arguing that, if it were so, the two must be held together. Any mere rationalising deduction from a Scripture word or phrase in favour of deferred forgiveness — any plea resting merely on its benefits real or assumed — cannot neutralise or weaken any definite proof against it, drawn from its being a negation of a clearly revealed fact of the Gospel scheme, or from there being no pretext furnished by Scripture for withholding or deferring God's mercy for a moment from anyone who really seeks it. And even if deferred forgiveness could find any warrant in Scripture, it would not follow that it would depend on the sentence of the Priest—it would not sanction the Confessionalist theory.

Unwarranted conclusions. Another of these fallacies is the drawing, as if from preceding pages, a conclusion which is not contained in them, and is utterly unsupported by the statements from which they quietly pretend to deduce it, or place it as if it were a deduction from premises.[1]

[1] This may be instanced by the assumption from private Confession not being compulsory in the Early Church, that it was recognised as an optional

It would be impossible to go through all the petty arguments in the use of which the rank and file of the Confessionalist party are so carefully drilled by their leaders. It will, however, I fear, be necessary from time to time to deal with them, as this or that part of my subject, with which they are specially connected, brings them on the tapis. Some, however, of the more prominent may be touched upon at once: it is like the clearing away the rubbish from a building, the true proportions of which it is sought to discover and restore.

Petty arguments in defence of it.

Thus, the attempt to identify the revival of the Confessional with what they call the deepening of the spiritual life, as if this were an undisputed argument in its favour, is sophistical. This assumed coincidence fails in more points than one. There is much dispute, and much greater doubt, whether what they call deepening the spiritual life is not rather filling it up and choking it with rubbish. Sisterhoods, they say, attendance at communions, and the like, are coeval with the revival of confession, therefore confession is a spiritual good; they beg the question whether the perversion of the Lord's Supper to uses for which it was never designed, the turning it into a Culte—function for high days and holidays—the clothing it with powers and attributes of which there is no trace in Scripture, be not rather a detriment to Christianity than the contrary: whether the clothing the spiritual sacrifices of prayer and praise with a Mediævalistic formality, ceremonial, and routine be not rather a deadening of spiritual devotion; whether the restricting the religious life to special vows, special dress—the identifying it with the monastic institutions of sisterhoods—be not rather a narrowing, and contracting, of the powers and

From the assumed deepening of the spiritual life under its influence.

ordinance; or from public Confession not being required for certain sins, that private Confession was necessary to their forgiveness. Both of these arguments are found in Ritualistic authors.

sphere of Christianity: whether the divorcing of religious life from the ordinary life of a faith be not rather a death-blow to religion than the revival of it; in which case, the coincidence they remark between the progress of Confession and the progress of Mediævalism is an argument against the former, and not for it—an argument which is confirmed by the known results of Confession in every country where it has obtained. Where Confession has most had its own way, there is least of spiritual life in any real sense of the word—more of vice, superstition, and infidelity. This fact they pass over *sicco pede*.

Abstract arguments in favour of it.

Under the same head we must place the use of arbitrary deductions, from facts known or assumed, to establish this or that ordinance or doctrine; such as all abstract arguments in favour of Confession, resting on the nature of man, or the nature of sin; or in favour of penance from the way in which God dealt with our first parents after their first sin. It may be true, that if confession and penance were established on sufficient grounds of Revelation, then facts in natural religion, or Scriptural instances of God's method of dealing with His people, might be alleged as harmonising with, or illustrating, the points so established by Revelation, or as answering objections against them; but they cannot supply the want of definite evidence, or give to a passage an interpretation which it could not otherwise have. Such arguments are really the same as those of rationalising scepticism or heresy, only with a different application—the one arguing that this or that doctrine, though not definitely revealed, must on rational grounds be admitted into revealed truth—the other, that this or that doctrine, though clearly revealed in Scripture, must on rational grounds, be rejected.

Arguments from Scripture.

Nor are they more fortunate in their arguments from Scripture. Such an argument, for instance, as I have met with, to the effect that though there is no precept to confess sins to God, yet there is one to confess sins to men, rests on a misinterpretation of two texts, and an illogical deduction from them even so misinterpreted; for the text 'Confess your sins one to another,' even if the way in which they take it were the true one, does not contemplate absolution, conveying, or declaring judicially, an actual forgiveness of sins, but by prayer, regarding the forgiveness as a thing not yet in *esse* but in *posse*. And even if it were true that there were no text enjoining confession to God as a condition of forgiveness, yet this would not give any sanction for confession to a priest.

Again, the scanty passages adduced by men of the weaker sort from the historical books of the Old Testament only show, that in order to find any Scriptural support of their system, they are obliged to let themselves fall into misrepresentations of the facts they quote; for instance, Achan's confession was public and not private; and Achan had been already miraculously convicted of his sin. David's confession was not of sins poured secretly into Nathan's ear, but the acknowledgment of the sinfulness of an act which Nathan, already knowing it, had brought home to his conscience. Nathan in a figure told David the nature of his sin, David did not tell Nathan; besides which, unless I am mistaken, Nathan was a prophet and not a priest. It would be easy to go through them all with the same result, but I am unwilling to waste my space in disproving arguments (if it be not a misuse of the term), which even instinctive logic will feel to be fallacies. It really is not too strong to say that they are nonsense—simply insults to our understanding. *From Cases in Scripture.*

Another instance of this inherent feebleness is the attempt to neutralise the almost universal instinctive feeling against Confession, or even to convert it into an apology and support of it, not by showing that this feeling is based on unreal grounds, or embodies nothing but unfair *Argument from preju dice against it.*

prejudices: but by a vague reference to the fact that a popular feeling is *sometimes* an unfair criterion, founded on prejudice, not experience: whence they argue that adverse popular feeling is a proof in favour of their system. But if being spoken against is no proof of this or that thing being bad, still less is it a proof that it is good. Where it is not mere prejudice—where the feeling is based (even though perhaps unconsciously) on experience or history— then such an attempt to evade the witness which it bears against the practice is but to acknowledge its reality and force. I confess that to my mind such reasonings are like the dummies in a druggist's shop, which betray the emptiness of the stock, as well as the poverty of the man's resources.

<small>Such arguments signs of weakness,</small>

They have, however, an argumentative value, though not exactly of the sort which they were designed to have. When a system is obliged to rest on false assumptions, inaccurate quotations, wrong interpretations, illogical deductions, obvious fallacies, indistinct views, it creates a strong suspicion against itself: betraying at the same time a logical incapacity in those who use such arguments without discerning these flaws, which accounts for the phenomenon, so puzzling to some people, that men with some reputation for ability are found among its partisans. The fact is, that such logical incapacity is not unfrequently accompanied by a certain superficial acuteness, which invents or adopts a shadowy reasoning, without sufficient judgment to detect the want of substance which makes it, for the purpose of argument or truth, worse than nothing. Men thus endowed are very apt, especially under the pressure of a favourite crotchet, to rest on grounds, which turn out to be mere quicksands, the positions which self-esteem or obstinacy forbid their abandoning as untenable.

<small>but have a logical value.</small>

Under the circumstances of there being so much

sophistry and unclearness hanging about this subject, I trust I shall not be held guilty of unpardonable presumption if I confess that I have been induced to put forth these pages in the hope of being able to place it before my readers in the light which has been thrown upon it in my own mind, by a somewhat patient study of what is claimed for the system, and on what those claims rest. I feel myself more imperatively called upon to do this from having found, on communicating to others what has been developed in my own mind, that I have been able to relieve them from what seemed insurmountable difficulties in rejecting and opposing Auricular Confession.

CHAPTER II.

Point at Issue—Not the clerical Commission, but its Nature and Extent—Not whether Men ought to be anxious about their Salvation, but whether Auricular Confession is an appointed Means thereto—Not whether confidential Communications between a Pastor and his Flock are desirable or allowable, but whether formal Absolution is an ordained Channel of Pardon, or a desirable Preparation for the Holy Communion—No Necessity to adduce the extravagant Utterances of the School—The Subject will be treated in its least irrational Aspect—Varieties of Opinion among those who have accepted the System—A Suspicion of Unclearness and Unsoundness created thereby—Not necessary to examine all these in Detail—Some evidently Errors—Some will be touched upon hereafter—Cause of this Inconsistency of View—In the Teachers of the Party—In its Disciples and Partisans—Real Point advocated by the Confessionalists—What they mean by Auricular Confession—Notions mixed up in the Term Confession—Confidence and Confession, Absolution and Pardon to be distinguished from each other—Confession in its popular Acceptation, includes Confidence and Confession in its technical sense—Great Contrast between these—How they are linked together in the Confessionalist system—Points successively advanced—Ending in Auricular Confession, technically so-called—Differing little from the Roman practice—Different in Details—Identical in Error.

<small>Real points to be considered.</small>

THE perpetually recurring attempt to put the question on a wrong issue makes it at the very outset necessary to state very clearly the point which is to be submitted to my readers' judgment.

<small>As to the clerical office.</small>

Be it then borne in mind, that the question is not whether the clergy do, by divine appointment, intervene in any way between God and the sinner; not whether they are, or are not, intrusted with a ministry of reconciliation; but whether that intervention is to be exercised, and that reconciliation to be effected, in that particular way which the Confessionalists hold; so the extent and nature, and not the fact, of the clerical commission enter into the discussion. Again, the question is, not whether the clerical office is of divine or merely of human appointment—not, whether ordination does or does not confer a certain commission and authority from on high—but whether this divine appointment and commission invest the clergy with the powers which these men profess to exercise in the confessional—with the power to forgive sins by private and personal absolution. Nor yet whether remission of sins is brought about by the exercise of the clerical office, but whether it is to be sought and ministered in that particular way which is known by the name of Sacramental or Auricular Confession, or, to call it by its proper name, the sacrament of penance.[1]

In many cases the advocates of the system take the first point in each of these questions, as if this, being established, compelled the admission of the second point, whereas in reality it is the second point in each question which they have to prove. The first may be and is held by very many who absolutely deny what is sought to hang upon it as inevitably implied in, or following on it. *Wrong point proved.*

So, again, in the exhortations wherewith Confessionalists press their system, when they urge the salvation of the soul as the reason for acceptance of it—assuming that those who will not listen to them are indifferent on the subject—the practical question is not between an anxiety to be pardoned and an indifference to pardon—not between a man's allowing his sick soul to go on without seeking any remedy, and the availing himself of a remedy ready to his hand; but whether God has ordained that health and pardon should come to the soul through Auricular Confession—whether God has provided such an ordained means of pardon at all, or whether what they prescribe may not be called a quack remedy, more likely to kill than cure. To urge anxiety for one's soul as an overwhelming reason *As to anxiety for salvation.*

[1] It is so called in the Intercession paper of the notorious Confraternity for February 1873.

for adopting Auricular Confession, is much the same as if anxiety for our health was held to oblige us to the use of some of Culpepper's prescriptions.

Confidential communications to a clergyman.

And most particularly it is necessary to point out that the question I am considering is not primarily, whether certain confidential communications on matters of conversation and conduct between a pastor and members of his flock, in certain cases, are or are not desirable and spiritually beneficial, but whether the confessing sins privately to a priest, and receiving from him, as a priest, his formal absolution, is an ordained means of grace, in itself an ordained means of recovery from sin, or of obtaining pardon, or a recognised and desirable preparation for the Holy Communion. The first point may be—nay, is—perfectly true, and all the rest utterly false. I think, before I have done, it will be seen that the difference between these is not one of degree, but of kind.

Extravagancies not noticed.

It will not be necessary to place before my readers, for the purposes of refutation, the extravagant utterances of those among the school who carry their doctrine out to its legitimate conclusion; such as those who talk of Confession as the cleansing stream. These, indeed, may fairly be used as arguments against that of which they are the legitimate conclusions; and as such I may, perhaps, use them in the way of *reductio ad absurdum*; but I am not desirous to prove my case by disproving notions which to most thinking minds carry with them their own refutation. I am willing to take the system in its best and least irrational phase, as of course these ultraisms fall to the ground if that whereof they are the ultraisms is displaced.[1]

[1] Some of these extreme views must be read before it can be believed that clergymen of our Church can put them forth as the doctrines they are bound to teach. In a small tract, in the series of 'Books for the Young' (Palmer, 2 Little Queen Street), called 'Confession,' it is broadly stated '*Our Lord Jesus Christ commands us to confess to His Priests all the great sins we have committed.*' Is it too much to say that this is an unmixed falsehood?

It is, however, necessary to say a few words on the differences of view on the subject, not only because this sort of haziness creates a reasonable suspicion of the theory round which it hangs, but also because it is in a great measure the cause of the modified acceptance which it finds in some minds, and because it undoubtedly increases the difficulty of dealing with it; indeed, the first thing which will strike anyone who sets about treating the subject scientifically, must, I should think, be the variety of notions which in theological as well as in popular thought and language, have been, and are, mixed together in the term CONFESSION, as if they were essential parts of a whole, one of which could not be denied without denying the others, or as if one being admitted the rest must be admitted also. This, though perpetually assumed by the Ritualists, is very far from being the case.

Differences of view must be considered.

Thus some writers in defending Confession content themselves with proving absolution. Some maintaining absolution, think their point is established if they believe that they have shown confession to be useful or necessary to the spiritual life. Some identify absolution with the absolute forgiveness of sin, or a judicial power of forgiveness; others speak of it as having the promise of forgiveness of sin, or as an assuring or absolving grace, or grace of absolution, or an authoritative grant, or assurance of forgiveness; others, as the channel through which forgiveness *ipso facto* flows; some as the application of the Blood of Christ to the soul for the remission of sins. Some call Confession a divinely appointed means of cleansing the soul; others, a divinely appointed condition of pardon; some hold it to be indispensable, others only beneficial; some universally obligatory, others universally optional; some as obligatory only in some cases, optional in others—some, as beneficial only to persons of a peculiar temperament, or only for grievous sins; others, for all persons and for all sins—some hold

Instances of these differences.

C

that every sin must be laid before the priest; others, that only particular sins must be disclosed—some hold Confession to be an essential part of the forgiving ordinance; others, only as necessary to it, either for a complete repentance, or for the assurance of a complete repentance, or as enabling a priest to judge of the sincerity of a repentance necessary for forgiveness—to fix the amount of penitence to be gone through before absolution, and the amount of penance to be appointed after it, so that he may be able to arrange the terms on which God's mercy may be obtained! Some learned men say the difference between Confession in the Church of England and the Church of Rome is, that in the latter it is habitual and obligatory, and in the former occasional and voluntary; laying especial emphasis on its not being compulsory in the Church of England, as if anything of the sort could be compulsory in our Church, except in proportion as people were told that they could not do without it. In fact there are not many of its advocates or apologists who do not at one time advance one thing, and at another something else.

It is unnecessary now to go into all these in detail. There are probably few of my readers whose acquaintance with the Christian scheme is not sufficient to enable them, with very slight reflection, to see that some of these notions are more or less intrusions on, and innovations in, the Gospel scheme of mercy; for instance, the notion of an exact arrangement of the terms on which pardon can be obtained, of some proportion to be laid down between the sin committed and the satisfaction to be paid by the repentant sinner, would strike most people as being, in more regards than one, a simple and direct denial of some of the most distinctly revealed features of the Gospel. Others, less self-evident, will be treated of in their proper places as far as they deserve separate notice.

In the case of the teachers this inconsistency seems to be caused by the difficulty of finding or framing a definition, which will not be too openly opposed to plain statements of Scripture on God's mercy and the forgiveness of sin, to allow its passing muster even for a time; while in the case of some who are rather passively its partisans than actively, it is mostly an indistinctness arising from the circumstance of a matter of great importance and greater interest, both in a religious and social sense, having been suddenly and unexpectedly brought forward at a time of somewhat feverish excitement, in a fashion which almost precludes the possibility of more than a superficial acquaintance with what is thus presented for the immediate acceptance of those, who had hitherto formed no conceptions upon it, and in whose religious training and education and practice it had been hitherto unknown. In some cases, I suspect, a misty indefiniteness has been purposely thrown over it by the leaders or the partisans of the pseudo-Catholic revival, in order to elude the grasp of those who by their natural logic, or common sense, would be able to grapple with and overthrow the system, were it presented to them undisguised by words and inconsistencies. A conscious runaway often assumes disguises in order to escape detection. *Whence proceeding.*

The first step towards a clear understanding and a logical treatment of this tangled subject is, to keep steadily before our minds that which, even amidst all this variety of view and discrepancy of language, it is not difficult to discern, viz. that the Auricular Confession which the sacerdotal party really advocate, is composed of two elements, private confession, and private absolution, each, in their creed, essential to the other; and though either of these may be viewed independently, yet when so viewed, it is very different from what it is when combined with the other: so that no recognition, no case of private con- *First: real view of sacerdotal party.*

fession alone, or of private absolution alone, if any such can be found, necessitates the admission of what is commonly called Auricular Confession, or can be alleged as furnishing any authority or precedent for it. Thus all those views which do not recognise absolution as a necessary part of the practice—in which Confession is rather pastoral than sacerdotal—are not really admissions of the Confessionalist system within certain limits, but of something distinct and different from it.

Next: the necessity for distinguishing different senses of the word.

Hence we shall be naturally led to distinguish between the several notions which have, especially of late years, been jumbled together under the name of Auricular Confession, or wrongly identified with it. Thus Auricular Confession will be distinguished from the public confession of ecclesiastical offences, or of offences viewed as such in the early Church, which, though it is sometimes adduced as furnishing a precedent for the modern system, has nothing to do with the question, except as far as it may explain certain terms and practices, and give the key to certain patristic passages, loosely and inaccurately adduced in favour of the auricular confession of the present day. Perhaps there is nothing which will throw more light on the confusion which at present prevails on the subject, and lead us to a clear understanding of it, than to recognise the difference between Confidence and Confession, Absolution and Pardon; which, though commonly spoken of as identical, and comprehended under the term Auricular Confession, are, in reality, very different in their nature and results; and I think that such an analysis of the system will enable us to recognise the value and extent of that which we may see reason for admitting as true, and to mark it off by essential differences from that which we reject as false. As we proceed we shall, I think, see that the term Confession, in its present theological sense, cannot properly be applied to pastoral confidences, and throughout these pages, the essential differences between them will be marked by terming one **Confidence** and the other **Confession**; and I would suggest that the term might be advantageously adopted; at all events those who admit and approve of Confidence would be able to mark, without any explanation, that they do not intend to give the least approval or sanction to Confession. *(Confidence distinguished from Confession.)*

Taking, then, this term Auricular Confession as representing in its technical, as well as its popular, acceptation, the two elements of confession and absolution, there is a further distinction to be drawn between two phases which the former may bring before the mind. One of these, and that the simplest, is nothing more than a confidential intercourse between a father and a child, or between a pastor and any of his flock who in times of doubt and difficulty come to him for comfort or counsel: and this is a loose and inaccurate use of the word. The other, and that the extreme phase, is intimately joined with sacerdotal absolution; and this is its proper technical sense, representing it as a part of an ordained means of obtaining pardon of sin from God. *(Different phases of Confession.)*

When we put these side by side, the difference between them is so great it is at first difficult to see how the one could be engrafted on the other, or be signified by the same term. Look at the girl who goes to her clergyman to ask his advice how to meet a particular doubt, or temptation or weakness, and then turn to the penitent, prostrate on the chancel floor of a ritualistic church, till a priest in full costume comes to lift her up, and lead her into the vestry to receive her confession, to give her his absolution, and to appoint her penance. How great the contrast between them; it is a difference, not in degree but in kind; and yet, in this age, the one is often but the first step to the other. It is one of the evils of *(Difference between these.)*

this system, that what may be useful and innocent in itself becomes, under its auspices, dangerous and suspicious.

As we, however, look into the matter, it is not difficult to see how the advocates of the system manage to intertwine progressively the several notions and practices, so that they become links in the chain whereby feminine consciences learn to rest their hopes and peace on a priest — feminine wills to submit themselves to him in obedience. The voluntary disclosure of a mental difficulty to some one who, from position or experience, is fitted for the giving of counsel—the disclosure to a priest of some particular sin as the source of the difficulty, the knowledge of which is, therefore, necessary to its solution—the full disclosure, still voluntary, of all the sins and secrets of the heart, as a matter of prudence—the full disclosure of these to a pastor and guide, as a matter of obligation— the obligation of confession to a priest—its necessity as a preparation to absolution, and as a condition of forgiveness—the inherent and talismanic efficacy of the exercise of a sacerdotal power in the formal absolution pronounced by a priest—the saving and healing virtue of penance as a reparation for forgiven sin—all these are links in the chain, steps in the ladder. Each of these challenges examination, both in itself and in its relation to the link which precedes and follows it in the chain; and I am much mistaken, if my readers will not be convinced, not only that each point as maintained by the Confessionalists is, more or less, unsound in itself, but that even where it is not so, it is only by a series of sophistries that the last stage in the system is represented, not merely as the accidental development and consequence of the first— which, unhappily, I fear, thanks to these pseudo-Catholics, it is—but the legitimate and logical development, which happily it is not.

How they are linked together in the Confessionalist system.

Let us first look a little more closely into these points as they are successively advanced. The Confessionalists generally begin by introducing us to that confidential intercourse which would naturally exist between a person in spiritual difficulties and one older and wiser than himself: to this they presently add the notion of the disclosure of sins to some one—a father or mother, perhaps—as sources of these spiritual difficulties, making it out to be a matter of obligation, by virtue of a special command in St. James v. 16, the full consideration of which must be deferred for the present (see page 33). They next put the case of the father or mother being persons in whom the girl can have no confidence, and there being no one else among her friends or family to whom she could have recourse: then she naturally turns to her clergyman to help and guide her out of her difficulties. My readers will see how the clergyman is introduced, not by virtue of that sacerdotal right which is presently to be assigned to him, but in the lack of anyone more fitted for the purpose. The next step brings the clergyman before us as being professionally, apart from the above-mentioned lack of others, the fittest person to be consulted, as a lawyer in matters of law, or a physician in matters of health. Then by degrees this fitness is to be looked at as official and supernatural, not arising from his character or knowledge, or experience of spiritual things, or even from his pastoral position, but by virtue of his having received the Holy Ghost for this especial purpose; as having a commission and authority from God in this matter, which gives him a right to be consulted and listened to, and imparts to his advice a weight, and wisdom, and power which it has not in itself. Here the act first approaches the character of sacramental confession; that is, the act of confession is viewed as attended with some talismanic grace as being made to a priest, besides and beyond the benefit derived

Arguments successively advanced.

from the opening out the heart to a sympathising friend, whether lay or clerical, and receiving from him the comfort and counsel he is personally or professionally fitted to give. I must beg my readers to mark the chain of the sophistry; the sympathising pastor sliding quietly and noiselessly into the Mediæval priest, pretending to represent the person of God. Then comes in that which the Confessionalists allow, or rather maintain, gives a completely new character to all that has gone before; namely, the personal exercise of a sacerdotal power of forgiving sins confessed, by the pronouncing certain words uttered over the person confessing, as being expressive of that power. The moment absolution (in their sense of the word) comes in, there is a difference in kind—the theory is different—the practice different—the aim different—the means different—the agency different. It will probably have struck my readers, without my calling attention to it, that the change introduced by this new element is so great as to draw a marked line between it and what has gone before it; unless, perhaps, the line should properly be drawn at the earlier stage in which, as I have pointed out, the priest is first introduced in place of the pastor. However innocent and useful the act may have been up to this point, it does not follow that it is so after it, any more than the fact of a river being pure at its spring implies that it is pure and wholesome at its mouth.

Auricular Confession. We have now arrived at what is technically called Auricular or Sacramental Confession, that is, confession received by a priest in the exercise of his sacerdotal office with a view to, and to be followed by, a formal and personal forgiveness of sins, in the exercise of a sacerdotal power attached to that office, but which, in the parlance of the school, is generally called Confession, without any addition to distinguish it from the earlier and more innocent stages; to confound it with which is the result, if not the design, of this usage of the word.

My readers can scarcely fail to see that, while this differs essentially from pastoral intercourse, it differs little, at least in its extreme development, from the pseudo-sacramental Romish practice; that the change from the one to the other would be little more than nominal and accidental. I say 'in its extreme development,' because there are varieties in the mode of administration of this so-called ordinance, corresponding more or less to the externals of the Romish rite, as there is a greater or less identity in essentials. Sometimes I believe the penitent, to use a *verbum artis*, simply kneels down after he has confessed his sins to receive absolution; sometimes the confession is made kneeling, the priest being clothed in his sacerdotal garments; in some few churches the confessional-box has been added. Sometimes the 'Confiteor,' in its longer or shorter form, is used: sometimes confession is made to God, and 'Thee, O my Father:' sometimes there is a mere disclosure of sins. Perhaps the most ultra of all is where the form is gone through, though there are no definite sins to confess.[1] But in all these varieties of development, differing, as I have said, more or less from the Romish externals, the same doctrine is at work; there is at bottom the same misapprehension of the Gospel scheme, the same error of belief and practice on which this stronghold of Romanism is built.

Different modes of ministering it

[1] 'Mission Book,' p. 09. 'There are some persons who make this excuse' (that they have nothing to confess) 'with sincerity—but then they will not be afraid to go through the form of Confession.'

CHAPTER III.

Twofold Plea for Confession:—1. As a natural duty—2. As a divine Appointment—Attempt to identify Confession with the natural Instinct of Confidence by throwing the same Colouring of Duty over both—1. By asserting that they are both commanded in Scripture—2. By Analogies of Lawyer and Physician—This latter Argument examined as used to support Confession—Analogies too far fetched—Do not touch the required Point—Argue from prudential to an intrinsic Obligation—Hence even if they did apply to Confidence, yet they would not apply to Confession—Fail in their Facts—Full disclosure to a Lawyer or Physician often not necessary—Fail in their Relation—One relating to Things natural in which there is generally no Alternative, the other to Things spiritual in which the Absence of an Alternative is the very Point to be proved—These Analogies do not justify special Arrangements for Confession—Betting-houses furnish the closer Analogy on this Point—Question whether Scripture enjoins the Duty of private Confession—Passage in St. James has two possible Meanings—Difference between them—The confessionalist Interpretation not recognized in the early Church—The Confession spoken of by St. James is Reciprocal—Language of the Homilies on the Subject—St. James is not speaking of technical Confession—If he was, his Language would be more Definite—Confessionalists not to be heard in their Application of this Passage.

I THINK that my readers will have gathered from what has been said above, that the case for confession rests upon two grounds or pleas, (1) its own independent claims and merits—that such a disclosure to our fellow-men is a natural instinct, elevated into a moral duty by the analogies of the lawyer and physician, and recognised in Scripture, especially in the words of St. James: (2) As a corollary of absolution; that it is a necessary part of a divine ordinance for the pardon for sins, which makes it according to some in all, according to others in some, cases a matter of divine appointment and obligation.

The attempt to confound Confession with the human

yearning after sympathy and the out-pourings of a burdened spirit—so that the *soi-disant* religious duty may seem to be but the development and perfection of the natural instinct, and the confidential disclosures of difficulties or doubts to a friend or pastor, which are admitted by all, may be identified with the formal confession of sins to a priest, which is denied by most—is so transparent a fallacy, that it may be safely left to the judgment of common sense, and the common knowledge of human nature. It will be sufficient to place before my reader, as I shall presently do, the differences which exist between that pastoral *confidence*, which is the development of the natural instinct, and that *confession*, which they profess to derive from, and to fasten on it. I must, however, first call attention to their no less fallacious endeavour to bring the two nearer together by professing to prove that this simple instinct is a moral duty.[1] This they do by the same analogies of the lawyer and physician, and the same words of St. James (see page 23), which, as I have said above, they also erroneously apply to confession. So that the validity of these pleas in both cases may be

<small>Attempt to identify Confession with natural yearning for sympathy.</small>

---

[1] I will *en passant* call attention to an argument which is sometimes used to throw the desired colouring of duty over the disclosure for sympathy or advice. It is said that those who thus consult others are bound to make a full disclosure of all the circumstances of the case. Whether this is so or not will be touched upon presently: suffice it now to say, that supposing that such a full disclosure is matter of obligation, it does not prove that the disclosure itself is obligatory. This is the point which they ought to prove, but which their proof does not touch.

Another method which is sometimes used to throw the notion of duty over these disclosures, is to insist on the necessity of following the advice given (see p. 45). Of course if a man discloses a pressing difficulty for the sake of being relieved from it, it is so much his wisdom to follow the advice given that it may be loosely spoken of as his duty. And the notion of duty being thus vaguely thrown over the last part of the transaction, it is still more vaguely reflected back on the first part; the notion of duty is thus connected with the whole matter in hand, and minds with not very acute powers of distinction—and these are the minds whom the Confessionalists generally lay wait for—accept this confused notion into which the Confessionalists wish to lead them.

disposed of together. These analogies of the lawyer and physician play so important a part, in all apologies for the Confessional, recurring in almost every book or tract on the subject, that they require a longer examination than they are intrinsically worth, and I will first dispose of them.

<small>Shadowy character of the analogies adduced.</small>

I will not, however, weary my readers with the process which I have myself gone through in testing this favourite weapon of the revivalists, but merely give an outline of the considerations which have led me to the results at which I have arrived. The great difficulty in dealing with such arguments is their impalpable nature. One is compelled to analyse these shadows to see what they really mean, on what they really rest, and what is their real logical force and value; to reduce them, in short, to something like a substantial form which admits of their being grasped by logic, or tested by the touchstone of common sense. It is harder to fight with shadows which assume the shape of realities than with realities themselves.

<small>They are indirect.</small>

At the very first glance it seems strange that so weighty a theory should be made to rest on grounds so indirect as the analogy of these two arts in a completely different subject matter; in itself it creates a suspicion that it is unsound; and such a suspicion is in no way removed by the fact that it is not shared by those who, having pledged themselves to the system, are glad to catch at anything which seems to provide a ground for it to stand upon.

<small>Do not touch point required.</small>

And when we come to look into the matter, we find that the analogies, even if correct, would fall far short of a satisfactory proof of the point required; or rather, they would leave this point altogether untouched. For, as I said before, what the Confessionalists have to prove is, that it is obligatory to have recourse to a priest; what they do prove, assuming that they prove anything, is that if such recourse is had, the disclosure must be full—a proposition which would be equally true (that is, as far as it is true at all), of a voluntary disclosure, and therefore can have no bearing on the point of the disclosure itself being obligatory.

Again, they argue from a prudential necessity in the case of the lawyer and the physician to what they assert to be a religious, and therefore intrinsic, necessity of confession to a priest. It is true that they sometimes pretend that confession is prudentially needed in order to give the priest the information necessary to judge of each man's particular case; but this is very quickly seen to be a mere pretext: and that the real value of the necessity of a full disclosure arises from the theory, that it is part of a religious ordinance and act, and not from any merely prudential motives. And hence we may see that, even supposing these analogies did establish this duty in Confidence, it could not be passed on to Confession in its technical sense; for this would be to argue from a prudential obligation depending upon circumstances to an intrinsic obligation not depending upon circumstances; so that I think my readers will agree with me in the conclusion to which I have arrived, that the alleged analogies fail in their application—that they are not applicable in the shape of proof to the point which they are alleged to establish—not to Confidence, because at the most they only prove the prudential duty of a full disclosure, if any disclosure at all is needed—not to Confession, because a prudential obligation does not imply an intrinsic obligation.

Argue from a prudential to an intrinsic obligation.

Next, the analogies fail in their facts. Total disclosure is not always necessary in applications to a lawyer or a physician—in irrelevant or unimportant particulars, for instance, or particulars already known; or where the

The analogies fail in their facts.

question submitted is merely an abstract one; or where the medical man may be in possession of some panacea which is applied irrespectively of particulars—such as the celebrated root which in India is the unfailing specific for the bite of a snake—and in no case is total disclosure necessary for its own sake, as it is held to be in the case of Confession.

And in their relations

Again, everyone knows that an analogy—especially a positive analogy[1]—requires an identity of relations between what may be called its two sides; but here one relates to the body, the other to the soul; one to things natural, the other to things supernatural; one to matters in which, ordinarily speaking, there is no alternative, such as matters of health or legal affairs—anyone who wants to be cured must, ordinarily speaking, apply to a physician; anybody who has law business must apply to a lawyer—to assert such a necessity of applying to a clergyman in matters of spiritual health or spiritual interest is simply assuming the very point to be proved: it certainly cannot be allowed by those who maintain only the occasional use of the confessional. This may be illustrated by referring to the exceptional cases, either in law or physic, where people can manage to settle their private affairs without the aid of a lawyer, or cure themselves without

---

[1] By positive analogy I mean an analogy used to establish independently, as here, some fact or phenomenon, as distinguished from an analogy used to obviate objections to a fact, resting on other grounds. The use of positive analogy is more restricted and uncertain than of the other sort. For instance, it cannot be argued from some fact in the rational creation to the same fact in the irrational creation, without first showing that they stand in exactly the same relations to Him who created them. But if this same fact has been established on other grounds in the one order of Beings, the analogy might be used to prove that there is nothing incredible in the notion of all created beings, and therefore the irrational creation, being thus constituted—I have always thought this distinction very necessary in estimating the value of analogical arguments—it is clear that the positive analogy is much inferior to the other, both in its use and its force.

the aid of a physician: such persons might, without any violation of prudence, have recourse to neither.

Nay, these analogies do not even furnish justification for the assigning a particular time or particular place, in defence of which our Confessionalists are never tired of alleging them. It will be seen in a moment that these arrangements of the lawyer or physician arise from the ordinary and necessary requirements of their profession; and this cannot be assumed in the case of the clergyman without, as before, assuming the very point to be proved— that the hearing confessions is an ordinary, necessary, and legitimate exercise of the office; for such arrangements for private interviews can only be held to be justifiable when the object for which they are held is in itself justifiable. Supposing a lawyer was detected in arranging private interviews for the purpose of organising a rebellion, he would hardly escape the penalties of treason on the plea that such arrangements were as natural as those of his ordinary business; or if a physician were to advertise appointments for some illegal branch of his profession, the case against him would be none the weaker for his being able to show that such interviews occurred in his ordinary business. It occurs to me that the betting and gambling-houses present truer analogies to the private interviews with the priest, than the office of the lawyer or the consulting-room of the physician, with which the Confessionalists try to identify them. The law recognises single bets, and views them, in certain cases, as binding between man and man, but prohibits the setting up betting-houses for the systematic transaction of such business, as temptations and steps to evil and ruin. So the Church recognises confidential communications as extraordinary resources in religious matters, without recognising arrangements which represent a system of confession as part of the ordinary exercise of the ministerial office: or even confidential

Do not justify special arrangements for Confession.

Betting-houses more analogous.

communications as everyday incidents in pastoral work: for such an arrangement would represent as a universal or a usual practice that which is only an exceptional remedy; a practice, moreover, which, however innocent in itself, is in the present day suggestive of, and a step to, if not an actual opportunity for, the confessional, with which it is so studiously confounded by the Confessionalists.

How far these analogies apply to Confidence.

The conclusion to which I think we may come is this: that this Confidence, and these confidences, even in the definite phase of pastoral intercourse and influence, may be possibly justified, or perhaps illustrated, by the analogy of the lawyer and physician as far as they are voluntary and prudential, but no further; as far as they are not recognised as acts of religion or devotion, or as a supernatural means of grace or pardon, or as a necessary, or even healthy, stage in progress heavenwards, but as differing herein from the confession of the Confessionalists not in degree but in kind; as long as they are not recognised as necessary for all, or binding on any, nor even as desirable or advisable for most, nor yet as the surest way for relieving and guiding the conscience.

Scripture passages alleged.

We must now turn to the question whether Scripture contains any mention of the general duty of private confession to men, whether clergy or laity, of sins committed against God. The Confessionalists adduce St. James v. 16, 'Confess your faults one to another, and pray for one another that ye may be healed.'

Language held on this text.

The very way in which they treat the text is almost sufficient evidence against their interpretation of it. On the warrant of this text it is stated, by one whom I should hardly class with the most advanced of his school, that those, who refuse confession, would do well to acknowledge that they only obey so much of the Bible as is not unpleasant to them—that they have an expurgated Gospel of their own. Of course this piece of verbiage is merely an assumption, somewhat childishly and insolently expressed, that the passage can only mean what the writer says it does, and nothing else. The writer does not seem conscious that, if it has any other meaning,[1] then the charge, thus brought against others of expurgating their Bible, changes into the fact of the interpolation of the Bible by the Mediævalists; nay, even if the text is fairly capable of another interpretation, the charge has no logical foundation: it is merely an impertinent piece of rhetoric.

It may, I think, be admitted that *primâ facie* there are two possible meanings for the passage. <small>Its two possible meanings.</small>

1. A command to confess all offences against God to one another, naturally implying equality and reciprocity between the parties, as such offences must exist on both sides.

2. A command to confess our offences against our brethren, each to each, naturally implying equality and reciprocity between the parties.

The difference between the two is, that the offences <small>Difference between them.</small>

---

[1] The words 'confessing their sins' in St. Matthew's account of the Jews flocking to John the Baptist, as well as those in Acts xix. 18, 'and many that believed came and confessed and shewed their deeds,' can scarcely need any argument to show that they have no bearing on the Confessionalist theory of confession being enjoined as a duty. In the first place both are stated as facts, not as injunctions or even exhortations; in the next, there is no proof that in either case the act was private. In the case of St. John's baptism it could not have been so; in fact it is more than probable that what is meant is that the Jews were baptised as a confession of their sins. The original certainly is capable of this meaning, and the Baptist could hardly have heard the individual confessions of all those who flocked to his baptism; at all events there is no injunction. In the Acts the passage evidently alludes to the pretenders to, or believers in, supernatural powers, who, warned by the fate of Sceva's sons, came publicly forward, confessed publicly their faults and (some of them) their *deeds*, and showed the tricks and juggles whereby they had deluded the public (ἐξομολογούμενοι καὶ ἀναγγέλλοντες—both of these words imply publicity), some even burning their valuable books; here, again, there is no injunction; on the contrary, it is a single occasion under peculiar circumstances; so that it cannot establish even the practice of confession, much less the duty thereof: still less of private confession, as a preliminary or part of sacramental forgiveness of sin, consummated by formal absolution.

D

differ in kind, or at least in relation: the one including all offences against God, the other extending only to those that are not only against God, but also against some definite person, and in relation to him. These differ also in the persons to whom confession is to be made: in one, it is to each other indiscriminately, or as some of the school, in defiance of the original, construe it, 'to others;' in the second, only to those to whom offence has been given or injury done.

Meaning of the passage.

The first of these interpretations places the text up to a certain point on the side of the Confessionalists—*valeat quantum*; the second deprives it of the bearing they wish to give it.

The Confessionalist interpretation not practically recognised.

Which of these is the true or the probable one must be decided by the terms of the passage, and the light thrown on it either by the context, or the practice in Apostolic times, in which we may assume the true meaning to have been reflected. I think that a sufficient clue to a sound judgment upon it will be found in the consideration, that if it expresses universal obligation applying to all sins, we shall find such private Confession universally taught, enforced, and practised, as an essential duty of common Christian life; if it only applies to individuals under exceptional circumstances, we shall be prepared to find little or no mention of it as a matter of public interest, but only under the peculiar circumstances to which it refers. Now, as a matter of fact, it is not spoken as of universal obligation (see page 56 *sqq.*), or recommended except under peculiar circumstances, of which instances will be given hereafter (see page 68), while almost side by side with any persuasives to it, there exist the strongest dissuasives from it, which could not have happened had it been recognised as obligatory.

The confession spoken of is reciprocal.

Again, it is evident that if the passage contains an injunction to general confession, the duty is reciprocal—the priest must confess to the penitent no less than the penitent to the priest—as is observed in the Homilies,[1] speaking of this passage—and this is inconsistent with the Confessionalist theory. But if we take it to mean that one man is to confess his sins to another, whom he has injured—and *vice versâ*, if the case so require—this interchange of confession and forgiveness does not involve any difficulty; for whether a priest injures a layman, or a layman a priest—a beggar a prince, or a prince a beggar—there is the same duty in both cases: Christian charity, as well as the Apostle's command—as well as the higher instincts of humanity—enjoins upon the greater the duty of thus reconciling himself to the less, quite as much as if their respective relations were reversed.

The language, which is found in the second Homily of repentance on this passage, embodies the general views of the ancient writers on this subject: '*As if he (St. James) should say, "open that which grieveth you that a remedy may be found; and this is commanded both for him that complaineth and him that heareth, that the one should show his grief to the other;" the true meaning of it is, that the faithful ought to acknowledge their offence, whereby some rancour, hatred, grudge, or malice have arisen among men, one to another, that brotherly reconciliation be had, without which nothing will be acceptable to God as our Saviour, Jesus Christ, doth witness. St. Matt. v. 23. It may also be thus taken: we ought to confess our infirmities one to another, that knowing each other's frailness we may the more earnestly pray Almighty God our Heavenly Father that He will vouchsafe to pardon our infirmities.*' This latter interpretation I

Language of Homilies.

---

[1] Second Homily on Repentance. 'Then the laity hath as great authority to absolve the priests as the priests have to absolve the laity.' In the Romish Ordo Missæ the priest confesses to God &c., and the ministers—'*Confiteor Deo &c., et vobis fratres,*' the ministers then answer with the precatory form of absolution, which is not, however, termed absolution in the rubric. The ministers then confess to God &c. 'and to thee, O Father.' The priest then uses the same precatory form, which is then termed absolution.

think must be held to be the less reasonable of the two; but whichever of the two be taken, there is not thrown upon Confidence, nor upon Confession, that shade of obligation and duty which the Confessionalists try to extract from the passage. If the first be true, then because the class of offences is different: if the second, because such intercommunication is not spoken of as a duty enforced, or arising from a positive command, but only as a voluntary act recommended to those who desire a particular benefit, namely, intercessory prayer, under particular circumstances.

Even if a command, no sanction to Confession, technically so called.

At all events, the apostle is not speaking of Confession in the technical sense of the word. Even if St. James were enjoining, as a duty, mutual disclosure of sins against God, as Augustine takes it,[1] it would not go further than that *Confidence* among Christians for mutual edification and counsel and prayer which is practised, I believe, in some Nonconformist bodies in the present day; it cannot be carried on to a system, the two essential points of which find no place in it, viz. private confession to a priest, and private absolution by a priest. The object of the confession here mentioned is not absolution, but mutual prayer. Nor is the disclosure spoken of as private: in the circumstances of the context the elders or presbyters of the Church, and not one single presbyter, are spoken of as present; and 'others,' even if we suppose that this is a possible translation, is not singular, but plural. Nor is modern Confession sanctioned by the language of those Fathers who, on the authority of this text and of that in which our Lord directs His disciples to wash one another's feet, speak of Confession being made, not to a priest, but to one another.

St. James' language indefinite.

Further, had the Confession which they advocate been

---

[1] Augustin, Tract lviii. in Joannem; cf. Bingham vi. 481.

known in the early Church, it is impossible to believe that St. James, who gave such straightforward directions for the anointing with oil as the means of miraculous cure, would not have written with equal plainness, 'Confess your sins to a priest, and receive absolution for them,' instead of using words which can only assume the Confessionalists' meaning by a degree of twisting and squeezing, which is in itself sufficient to show that the meaning is not the real one.

The Confessionalists, too, generally speaking, allow that this apostolic command, supposing it to be such, would be satisfied by a girl making a confidant of her father or mother—an acknowledgment which at once bars its application as a command to the far weightier matter which they rest on it. If a command is satisfied by going to a certain point, it cannot be a command to go any further. If the command to confess is satisfied by doing so to a layman, then it cannot carry any obligation to confess to a priest as such.

I think my readers will now be satisfied that the Mediævalists are not to be heard when they try to throw around the simple instinctive practice of one man opening his heart to another the religious obligation of a definite command of Scripture; or carry it on to that system which they pretend to trace back to these simple beginnings, so that their auricular confession may present itself for acceptance, only as the natural growth of a practice scripturally enjoined, innocent in itself, and universally recognised and adopted in the everyday affairs of life: in other words, this passage furnishes no foundation or apology for that in justification of which it is alleged.

Confessionalist use of the text not tenable.

CHAPTER IV.

Fallacy of passing from Confidence to Confession—Gain to the Confessionalist Cause in identifying them—Confidence allowable under certain Conditions—Not peculiar to Christianity, though possibly more effective under its Auspices—Arises not from sacerdotal Prerogative—But from the natural Sympathies and Yearnings of Humanity—To be disconnected from sacerdotal Notions—Distinction between Confidences for Relief of Mind, or for the Sake of Advice—The Clergyman the proper Person to apply to, but the having Recourse to him a Sign of Spiritual Weakness—Opportunities for good in such Confidences—Recourse to Clergymen for removal of Doubts of Forgiveness—No Sign of Spiritual Health, but the Reverse—Cure for a morbid State—Any System of Training or Preaching which creates the Need of such a morbid State bears Witness against itself—Confidences to be received under certain Limitations—How they may approach to Confession—Care must be taken not to confound these two different Things—Danger at present day in Confidence—Differences between Confidence and Confession, and between Pastoral Advice and Direction—Importance of realising these Distinctions—This Confidence only once suggested by our Church to Persons in Health and Strength—Practical Transition from Confidence to Confession.

Attempt to identify Confidence with Confession.

To adduce arguments in favour of this pastoral Confidence and then pass on to Confession as if it were the same thing, or to allege *confidence* as sanctioning *confession*, is a mere fallacy; the same in kind as the attempt to identify it with a natural instinct, and no less transparent. But transparent as it is, it is insisted upon with the most confident pertinacity by the Confessionalist School, for the simple reason, that if they could establish this identity by sound argument, they would gain a position, which would not only enlist on their side the sympathies of our moral nature and the facts of our moral life, but would make it impossible to object that it is alien to the mind of our Church. For when we proceed to analyse Confidence, and determine its nature and claims, we find

Confidence natural and allowable.

that the seeking counsel and aid in spiritual or mental difficulties from others to whom, from their natural relations to us, or from their superior age and wisdom, we look up, is a good deal more than allowable; provided that it is clearly kept in view that it is no part of the supernatural scheme of Christianity for the salvation and comfort, and forgiveness of sinners, but flows directly and simply from the natural yearnings for sympathy—the natural recourse of the weaker to the stronger, whether physically or morally—which are instincts of humanity, energising in all states, all religions of the human race. It is not specially connected with Christianity except so far as the desire is heightened by the stronger sympathies of Christian love, or by the greater amount of benefit which may be expected from Christian wisdom, or which may be won for the sufferer by Christian prayer. In the case, indeed, of a clergyman being the person to whom recourse is had, doubtless there comes in the feeling that he, whose aid we are seeking, has received by his office a special obligation to aid and comfort those who come to him; and that, *cæteris paribus*, an especial blessing may naturally be expected from the aid and sympathy of one whom God has appointed to watch over our souls; even apart from any superior qualifications for the office of comforter, which may be supposed to arise from his especial professional knowledge of religious needs and difficulties; and so far, the aid of a clergyman in such cases may be superior to that of a layman. But this arises not from any special prerogative, attached to his offices of hearing and forgiving sins, but from its general character and duties, and opportunities of showing men, as a minister of the Gospel, how doubts may be solved, difficulties removed, despondency corrected, and faith increased: in short, it is pastoral and not sacerdotal. That this is so, is clear from the fact that it is admitted

Its nature. to be in the power of a layman to perform this office, so that it cannot arise essentially from any prerogative in the clerical commission. It must be carefully disconnected in our notions from forgiveness of sin, except so far as a soul may be thereby led to comprehend its need of God's mercy, and accept the pardon which God promises on the sole conditions of repentance and faith. Keeping this in mind and speaking generally, it may be said that our Church tacitly, if not expressly, contemplates this communication between the pastor and his flock at all times; not, as I said before, as anything peculiar to Christianity; far less as a sacramental or definite ordinance of grace, but as a practice almost co-extensive with human nature, which there is nothing in Christianity, but the contrary, to forbid or discourage: for which the peculiar relations existing between the clergyman and his flock present the same opportunities and facilities which exist, not only in Christianity, but in all religions, or rather so-called religions, between the wise and the ignorant, the teacher and the taught, the priest and the people. To say that the Church does not, generally speaking, exclude or discourage such confidential intercourse between the pastor and his flock, is simply to say that it does not discourage one of the simplest instincts of thoughtful minds.[1]

Confidences for relief or for advice. We must distinguish too between confidential communications made for the relief of a burdened conscience by another's sympathy, and those made for the sake of spiritual advice, how to meet a temptation, or how to get rid of a habit. In both these cases, certainly in the last, the clergyman is generally—nay, were it not for personal

---

[1] I say 'generally speaking,' because it is perfectly conceivable that a bishop might recommend abstaining from such confidential communications with a clergyman whose known opinions and tendencies made it likely that he would abuse such communications to the gradual introduction of the system of Confession.

circumstances, always—the most proper person to have recourse to: and recourse to him is in itself a wise and good method—the wisest and best for those who do not, for some reason or other, find guidance and help from above in the ordinary means of grace. The having such recourse to a clergyman, though indicating a certain amount of spiritual feebleness, is not, in itself, an indication of spiritual disease, nor likely to produce any spiritual evil, provided that care is taken that it does not pass into Direction.

Such confidences may open to the pastor great opportunities of promoting the spiritual progress of those whom it is his business to guide, so long as his guidance is not carried so far as to destroy the personal energies of the individual conscience, or to deaden or blind the power of personal moral perception; but it must not be forgotten that the love of power and personal influence will often, if not generally, present a strong temptation to a clergyman to disregard in practice the moderation which he may profess in theory. *Such confidences beneficial.*

A third sort of this confidential communication is for the solution of a doubt as to the forgiveness of this or that sin, or course of sin. This, we must recollect, is not a sign of spiritual health, nor yet a healthy stage in spiritual progress; it is not, I think, to be recommended as such to either young or old: far less ought the young to be trained in, or habituated to it: for it arises from that lack of perceptive faith in the soul, which is able to see and comprehend the unlimited and always ready mercy of God; able to read the word 'pardon' in the promises and invitations in which God's Word abounds; a lack of that receptive power of faith which apprehends and appropriates that mercy. It is easy to form a notion of such a spiritual state by bodily ailments—blindness, deafness, paralysis; none of these are states of health; no one would think of representing them as states of health, *For solution of doubts of pardon. Is a cure for a morbid state,* or bringing a patient to health through them, or speaking of relief from them as preferable to the ordinary exercise of the ordinary powers of the physical frame. And so if a boy is induced to believe that a spiritual state, which is really a state of morbid incapacity, is an exhibition of spiritual life, then I think he is misled rather than led; and any preaching, or teaching, or training, which results in the production of this morbid state, whether chronic or intermittent, is not healthy teaching or training, in accordance with God's will, but unhealthy and contrary to it; and if the result of any preaching or teaching, is that, while consciences are awakened to a sense of sin, there are not almost at the same moment awakened those perceptive and receptive powers of faith of which I have spoken above, then I cannot help thinking that such preaching must have been radically wrong, or singularly powerless and unfortunate. Nor do I think that any man may dare to bring a redeemed soul to such a state; yet if, from some cause or other, a soul has brought itself into this state of incapacity, then a minister of God's Word may be sure, not only that he may receive, but that he may not refuse, such confidences, in cases where the person offers them, not with any notion of their being acts of obedience to an ordinance of God; or as being beneficial as acts of obedience to God's will; or as acts of humiliation to another man; or as having in themselves any talismanic power of deepening the spiritual life; or as being acts of religion spiritually beneficial for their own sake; or as being the better for being made to a clergyman, except so far as they are means for removing those doubts and difficulties which stand in the way of the acceptance of that pardon, of which the clergymen are the authorised ambassadors. Provided too that from these communications is excluded the notion of their being anything but wholly voluntary; that they are neither given or received under the impression that they are the only, or the safest, or surest means of pardon or escape from sin, or of leading a religious life; in short, there must be a total absence of any of those notions which distinguish Confession, and whereby the Confessionalists manage to destroy the practical voluntariness of the action, while they make it in words to depend wholly upon the free will of the agent. If any of these notions are allowed to insinuate themselves into the confidential communications between a pastor and any one of his flock, they either become Confession in its technical sense, or approach more or less nearly to it. And we may observe that it does come nearer to this confessional system, as it is founded on, or encourages, that superstitious regard for the priesthood which is common to all the phases of imperfect or false religion. I must again repeat that in all cases the distinction between this Confidence and that Confession must be carefully kept in mind, by the clergyman and the people alike; both to prevent the misuse of what is right, and to get rid of the notion that he, who admits the usefulness and blessedness of the one, is bound consistently to admit the practice and the claims of the other. Care too must be taken by the pastor to mark the differences between such Confidence and Confession, and to make the applicant understand that it is the former and not the latter to which encouragement and response is given, so as not to lend any sanction to the Mediævalists, when they try to lead weak minds into the fallacy of arguing from one thing to another, from which it differs in the most essential points: into arguing from the Church's sanction of pastoral confidence followed by advice, to confession to a priest as a devotional exercise and discipline, and an ordained means of grace; the first step in an act of religion, of which, according to them, absolution and direction are the conclusion and consum-

How they may approach to Confession.

Care to be taken

Danger of it.

mation. For there is in the present day a danger even in Confidence, which must limit its use, viz., that the Confessionalists take advantage of it, both in theory and practice, as an introduction to, and apology for, that confession with which it has no connection, save nominally and accidentally, however perseveringly the school try to connect the two essentially together.

Recapitulation of differences between Confidence and Confession.

This makes it, perhaps, all the more necessary to state at once the difference between Confidence and Confession, in the technical sense of the word: they are clear and marked enough. In the former the applicant addresses his pastor and guide, the minister of God's Word; in the other, he is supposed to address himself to the priest as God, or to God in the priest; he kneels before the priest, as a being of another mould to himself, vested in sacerdotal garments, as emblems of the sacerdotal power with which he claims to be clothed. The notion of discipline is wholly excluded from Confidence; it is an essential notion in Confession. In the former the applicant does not confess, but consults; he opens his grief, but not necessarily his sin; in the latter it is the reverse; he does not consult, but confesses; it is a list of sins which he details, not a grief which he opens. The subject-matter of the one is a difficulty, or doubt, or danger, to be solved or set at rest, or met; of the other, sins to be forgiven by absolution, and atoned for by penance. In the one, there is an affectionate trust in the sympathy and wisdom of the pastor; in the other there is a superstitious submission to the power and will of the priest. The end of the one is the quieting of the conscience, or the receiving that advice and counsel which may lead to freedom, the soul yearning to be free, by the acceptance of pardon from God Himself; the other is the receiving pardon from the judicial fiat of the priest. The conditions of the one are a full, unreserved disclosure for its own sake, as an act of duty or as an act of humiliation and penitence; in the other there is no condition of its effectiveness, save that the difficulty or the doubt should be stated as far and as clearly as the circumstances of the case require. It is not the better in itself for being unreserved, nor the worse for not being so.

Nor must we omit to notice the difference between the advice following on Confidence, and the Direction and the Penance which are parts of the supposed sacramental ordinance of Confession. In Direction the benefit follows chiefly from the act of submission to the supposed divine authority of the priest, standing in the place of God, the same in kind as that which is paid to God Himself—no matter whether the act enjoined over-rides the commands of God, or the dictates of conscience, or the laws of man. The pastoral advice is followed not as an act of obedience, but as an act of prudence, subject to the dictates of conscience, and the known principles of right and wrong. I do not say that in Direction the advice given is generally contrary to morality;[1] but unless I am much mistaken, sometimes it is purposely made so, in order to test the completeness of the obedience of the penitent. To think whether direction is right or wrong, or whether it shall or shall not be followed, is in itself a sin to be confessed. Nor do I say that sometimes the advice given in Confidence may not have the force of command, when the person is deeply impressed with the superior wisdom or experience of him whom he consults; in both cases the advice may be sought and implicitly followed in faith; but this does not do away with the essential difference between

Between pastoral advice and sacerdotal direction.

---

[1] I have heard of a case in which, to a girl's plea that to do what the priest ordered her would involve disobedience to her parents' wishes, it was answered that this would make it all the more meritorious, according to the well-known passage, 'He who loveth father and mother,' etc. Those who thus use this text forget that it is not duty to parents, but earthly affection to them, which is contrasted with the heavenly love of God—in fact, obedience to parents and duty to God are, speaking generally, coincident.

the one, as an act of unreasonable submission, and the other, as an act of reasonable prudence. And hence care must be taken also that compliance with advice given is not represented, or understood, as being in itself an act of ordained obedience to the will of God or of the pastor consulted, but adopted by the reason of the recipient, either on its own merits as a recognised injunction of Scripture, or as the opinion of a wise man, whose judgment on such matters must have weight with a person less learned or experienced; in short, that the advice be received and acted upon as it would be if read in a book written by a person of valued wisdom.

Importance of keeping these differences in view.

It is all the more important to realise these distinctions because it is this Confidence which so many divines have meant, and do mean, when they speak of Confession being retained in the everyday system of the Church of England. I do not mean that this holds good of all who assert or have asserted this; most, if not all, of our Mediæval school contend for Confession in that technical sense of the word in which it is distinguished from Confidence; but I believe that a large number of divines of the present day have hesitated, and still hesitate, to denounce this Confession, because under this term is included in their mind that Confidence, the usefulness of which they cannot and do not wish to ignore, either in itself or as recognised by the Church; the reasonable practice of which, it would be a misfortune, if not an impossibility, for any Church unreservedly to exclude from its system.

Confidences only once suggested by the Church.

It must moreover be remembered that though our Church does not discourage these confidences, yet in one case alone is the expediency thereof suggested, at least to persons in health and strength;[1] and that only as a last resort, after the ordinary ways of quieting the conscience

---

[1] The case of the Special Confession in the Visitation of the Sick will be treated of hereafter.

have failed to produce the blessed result of a full trust in God's mercy.

I am of course aware that the passage in the exhortation to the Holy Communion, to which I am alluding, is claimed by the Confessionalists as unmistakably and decidedly in favour of Confession with a view to absolution—that is, Confession Proper. I shall defer the full consideration of this to the time when I shall have to weigh and test the arguments of the school in support of that Confession. For the present, I will content myself with asking my readers to turn to the passage, work out carefully the meaning of each word and sentence, and see whether they cannot discern the fact, that what is recommended to the doubting soul, and the method prescribed to the minister, not only do not authorise the method recommended and prescribed by the Confessionalist, but do positively and definitely exclude it. *Passage in the exhortation to the Holy Communion.*

The transition from these confidences, which may exist between the pastor and his flock, to the mutual benefit of both, into Confession, is easy enough; especially when a notion of obligation, both as regards the act and the matter, has been cast upon them. I must request my readers to bear in mind that by Confession Proper I mean that which in connection with absolution, commonly so called, is viewed as preparatory to, and necessary for, that forgiveness of sins, which the Confessionalists assert is to be obtained—some of them only, others most safely and surely—through that channel, by virtue of words of absolution pronounced by the priest; the necessity of which is especially insisted upon as a purification of the soul before the Holy Communion. It is in this connection that Confession acquires its peculiar characteristics and importance and value in the sacerdotal system; so that the whole relations between the pastor and his flock are, as the Confessionalists themselves assert, completely *Transition from Confidence to Confession.*

altered. The clergyman is no longer the friend, from whose mouth words of wisdom and peace are looked for, but the judge, by whose fiat we learn whether our sins are, or are not, forgiven; no longer the ambassador, who proclaims to sinners God's free mercy, and persuades them to accept it as freely as it is offered; but he is the agent for God, who is to arrange the terms on which a sinner is to be pardoned, to settle the exact price which is to be paid for each sin, and to keep out of sight the sinner's free discharge, till he has made him feel that it is not free. It is not that ministry of reconciliation which says to the trembling soul, 'Throw aside your doubt, tarry not: there is Christ calling you; go to Him while he may be found;' but it is the stern minister of justice, speaking to the soul, who with trembling steps is drawing near to the Father's house : ' Whither so fast, my friend? are you sure Christ will receive you? beware of drawing near to Him without my countersign; wait awhile, till I can weigh your sin, and see at what price God's justice estimates it; till I can see how much of the price you have paid, and how you may be able to discharge the remainder.' If this is Christianity, then the Bible is false. Practically, it is pretended that our Lord has delegated His prerogative of forgiveness in favour of certain men whom He has appointed personally to represent Him on earth; and such a pretension, by its very audacity and weight, presses itself on the acceptance of those who are tender and fearful of heart. The process is easy enough: it is only to bid us shut up the page of the Bible, where we may read the parable of the prodigal son, or any of the parallel illustrations of God's unlimited and unconditional mercy—to bid us lose sight of such passages as, ' Come unto me all that travail, and I will give you rest,' as not adapted or intended for us; and then to open it at the passage, ' Whosesoever sins ye remit, they are remitted,' as giving the only hope of remission of sins—and the formal part of the work is done. It only remains to create and encourage in what has well been called a feminine heart in either sex—but let us take the most common case—to create or encourage in the heart of some pious girl, a doubt of God's willingness and readiness to pardon her sins committed since baptism, or, in her daily life—to keep out of view God's, so to say, impatience to forgive her—to throw cold water on any hopes of forgiveness she may have found, or be trying to find, in Christ's own words—to check any step she may have been by Christ's own invitation induced to take towards Him—to bid her stop outside her Father's house, and to shrink from His loving presence till they, the hired servants, have found out whether she may venture in—to make her doubt whether her repentance is such as God will accept—to suggest sins she may have committed without knowing them—to enlarge her knowledge of sin, and sins—to represent Christ as deaf and unsympathising towards those in whose favour they have not exercised their priestly power and privilege—to create a yearning for some more tangible and material grasp of forgiveness than that which faith can find in the revealed love of God, and the revealed efficacy of Christ's atonement as set forth in the Gospel, preached in the Church, and sealed in the Sacrament of Baptism—and then to offer her at their hands that forgiveness which she is desiring above all things, in the tangible form of absolution, addressed by them as priests personally to her as penitent; to encourage the vine-like instinct of clinging to something seemingly stronger than herself, and then to offer her the aid of their supernatural agency; and she will soon be brought to the feet of her Father Confessor, even though at first she felt some repugnance to the notion.[1]

Leading a girl to confession.

---

[1] I shall never forget overhearing at one of the Congresses a notorious Confessionalist speaking of the Cardiff mission as a great success. 'There

And these are the triumphs which these men pride themselves upon, and boast of; this is the work which is being incessantly, actively, though often covertly, carried on by men, who either really believe that they are doing God's work therein, or who have rested their own personal prestige on bending souls to their views, and securing the triumph of their party.

were,' he said, 'some fifty cases of confession, all most satisfactory. One in particular, a girl, came to us (*i.e.* the mission priests); we told her there was nothing for it but confession. She kicked against it at first, but she was soon brought to.' The impression produced on my mind by this, which was spoken on a public platform loud enough for those around to hear, was deepened when I found, from the bishop of the diocese, that these mission priests had given him a pledge that confession should not form part of their mission teaching.

CHAPTER V.

Second Plea for Confession as part of a Divine Ordinance for the Forgiveness of Sin—The Theory displays much knowledge of human Nature and human Wants—Might have recommended itself to our acceptance had there been no Revelation—The ignoring of God's revealed Cure for Sin the real Objection to it—No Trace in Scripture of any such Ordinance for Pardon as private Confession to Man, or any such Practice being used, or recommended by the Apostles—Nor yet any Trace of it in the really Primitive Church—Primitive Practices recognised by our Church as a Witness to Facts—Especially valued by Mediævalists—This finds no Place in Primitive Practice—No private Confession practised or recognised except as preparatory to public Discipline, and this not in the earliest Ages—Evidence of Mr. Carter on this Point—Of E. B. P. in a Note on Tertullian—This shows, not only that private Confession was not compulsory as in Romish Church, but that it did not exist at all.

I WILL now turn to the second plea for Confession, in its connection with Absolution, as an essential part of a divine ordinance for the forgiveness of sin. It need not be said that this is its most important aspect, both in its nature and bearing. Nor can it be denied that the system exhibits much knowledge of human nature, much familiarity with its secret impulses and instincts; and were there no such thing as a revelation of that way and those conditions of obtaining pardon, for which these men have substituted this *soi-disant* ordinance, it might be accepted as an effective device for gaining control over the unruly wills and affections of sinful men; for relieving guilty consciences from the burden and distress which the fear of unforgiven sin must always cause, even to the natural man, unless he has lost all religious feeling, and all sense of a future state; and for which so many remedies were by men invented in the various religious systems in order to supply the lack of that revealed

Counsel and Method of God, which they had been ignorant of or rejected. The fact, indeed, of that pardon depending on, that control being irresponsibly exercised by, the wills of no less sinful men, would create a doubt of its substantial value, even though we were without the witness which the history of the world for many ages bears against it. This witness alone would be enough to make us hesitate before we allowed it again to take root among us; but still the main objection—the real objection—against it is, that it forms no part of the scheme revealed by God for the salvation of the world; no part of what is revealed by God as the rule for making that salvation our own, or working it out; that in the very presence of the heavenly, it is of the earth, earthy; that it ignores or contravenes some of the leading features of the Gospel as given us in the writings and practices of those whom the Holy Ghost led into all truth.

Revelation furnishes the real objection to Confession.

Had it been otherwise, I should not have been now writing what I write. Whatever has been revealed by God, I feel myself bound to accept, not merely from religious sentiment or moral considerations, but because I should feel it to be a negation of my rational being to deny or refuse it. The Word of God stands alone in the world, firm, as demanding rational acquiescence and belief. It is indeed an essential requisite to such trust in Scripture, that great pains and care be taken to ascertain what the sense of Scripture really is, in other words what God really tells us; and it is part of our intellectual trial not to allow mere human conceits and theories to set us upon squeezing out of Scripture what is not of God, or getting rid of what is; if we do so, it is on our own responsibility and peril. This is no place to enter into the principles which ought to guide us in our interpretation of Scripture, and must guide us, if we are to pass through our trial safely; suffice

If Scripture had been in its favour, nothing could have been said against it.

it to say, that we are not only permitted but entitled—and more than that—expected by God, to use our reason; nor is there any limitation to this, provided that it is used reasonably: that it is not allowed to exercise a final judgment on matters which are beyond its sphere, but is confined to enquiring and deciding whether this or that point is or is not revealed. On matters beyond the sphere of sense and reason (and these include the whole world of supernatural and spiritual being and agency) the Word of God claims, on rational grounds, our assent to whatever we find written in it, interpreted by other passages of Scripture: (as the passage of St. Paul where he explains the words of our Lord's institution by telling us that the bread is the Communion of the Body of Christ), or by the facts of history which are, *ipso facto*, an interpretation (as in the case of the prophecies fulfilled in the fall of Jerusalem), or by the facts of science (such as expressions which imply that the sun goes round the earth). If then the Confessionalist system had been revealed—if we found in Scripture what the Confessionalists teach—such as, 'if anyone wishes to be forgiven, or wishes to be sure that he is forgiven—or is travailing and heavy-laden—or if any man sin—or if any man wishes to come to the Holy Communion—let him confess his sins to a priest, and have pronounced over him the words of the formal remission of sins by that priest,' then these questions would be settled. Whatever objections might present themselves in the abstract, whatever evils might seem to have practically developed themselves from, or attached themselves to, this system, it would to me matter not at all.

DEUS EST LOCUTUS, CAUSA EST FINITA.

My main objections then to Confession are not founded on any abstract dislike or practical suspicion, nor yet on the evils flowing from it in various ways, but simply that it is not of God. It is true that the evils flowing from it would suggest and demand a most careful enquiry into the fact of its having been revealed and ordained by God; but this fact being ascertained, no other objections would hold good: all we could do would be to consider how far the evils introduced into even a divine ordinance by human perversity might be guarded against, avoided, remedied; but against the thing itself I, for one, should not dare to speak.

Question settled as far as Scripture is concerned.

It will be necessary then to consider the question whether private confession to men of sins against God, as held by Confessionalists, is a revealed and appointed ordinance for obtaining pardon for sin; whether there is any promise attached to it, as there is to confession of such sins to God. The answer is clear; There is not a single trace in Scripture of any such practice by the Apostles; there is not a single instance of their requiring such Confession, or of their encouraging it or receiving it, or apparently being aware of its existence, though the occasions where they must have done this, had they known of it as ordained of God, occur in almost every chapter of the Acts of the Apostles: and I need hardly point out to my readers how conclusive an answer this total absence supplies against all abstract probabilities of its having formed part of the Gospel scheme. Those who say the contrary have only to give the chapter and verse where it is plainly commanded or recognised by the Apostles; till this is done, in harmony with the ordinary rules of interpretation, so as to recommend itself to learning and common sense, the matter may be considered settled as far as Scripture is concerned.

Has it any claim as a part of early discipline?

But though it may have no claim upon us as a Scripture ordinance, it may have a claim, though a less decisive one, as a point of early discipline—a point of accidental, though not of essential importance and obligation—on which every branch of the Catholic Church has a right, as far as its own members are concerned, to make what rules and requirements it pleases, provided that there is no interference with any doctrine or duty laid down in Scripture, or any ascription to God of what He has never said, or any limitation or alteration in the scheme and terms of salvation which each branch of the Catholic Church is commanded to proclaim and minister in its own sphere. Generally speaking, those particular Churches act most reasonably and prudently, who conform themselves to the really primitive Church, except where changes in domestic or social life make so manifest a difference in the Christian's relations to those around him, that what was practicable and desirable and edifying in the first centuries is no longer so now; or where the errors, superstitions, scandals of later ages can be reasonably traced to their rise, in certain notions, opinions, usages which recommended themselves to the uninspired judgment of early Christians: for we must bear in mind that such notions, even when harmless or even edifying, are recommended to us on the score of prudence, not of obligation. The authority is human, not divine—it cannot contradict facts, or neutralise the witness of experience or history. *Importance of this question.*

We therefore have next to consider the practice of the truly primitive Church, and the mind of our own Church in the matter. The first point is all the more important because our Church recognises primitive antiquity as a witness to the teaching of Scripture,[1] with the limitation that the writers of those times must not be so understood as to contradict the sense of Scripture ascertained by sound reason and legitimate interpretation. *Primitive antiquity recognised as a witness to the voice of Scripture.*

---

[1] It is important to recollect that the negative witness of antiquity is more valuable than the positive. If there is no evidence of a certain doctrine or certain practice in the Early Church, there is the highest degree of probability that it is not Scriptural. A far higher degree than can be derived from the mention of a doctrine or practice in primitive writings, for there is always the possibility of its having grown up from human fancies, in post-revelation ages.

And not only so, but the Mediævalists carry this principle to such an extreme, that the records of the Church, after the Canon of Scripture was closed, and the writings of men far more removed from the Apostolic Church, are to them of equal, nay, almost of greater value than Scripture: for if any trace of a favourite doctrine or usage can be found in these writers, they force the sense of Scripture to harmonise with this presumed witness of antiquity, instead of allowing Scripture to mould and correct their notions of the meaning of these writers: Scripture is interpreted by the Fathers, not the Fathers by Scripture. Therefore they above all others are bound to admit and abide by the witness borne by the early Church in this matter; and it will be a most decisive argument against there being anything in Scripture which can either directly or indirectly give countenance to Sacramental Confession, even in its modified form, if no such practice is traceable in really primitive antiquity—if the date can be fixed at which it was introduced.

And the mind of our own Church is scarcely less important, because of course men who receive their authority to teach and feed the flock from that Church, can hardly reasonably or honestly think themselves justified in teaching what it does not teach, or claiming for themselves an authority different in kind from, or exceeding in degree, that which it has commissioned them to exercise.

We will first consider the first point, whether private Confession finds any place in the practice of the primitive Church. In the early Church—that is, the Church of the first three centuries—there is not to be found the smallest real reliable recognition of the system which they so confidently, or rather audaciously speak of, as if it were *e confesso* a primitive Catholic practice. It is true that they can find a few sentences, expressions, phrases, which at first sight seem to be in their favour; but when these are

Confession in early times unknown, except in connection with public Penance.

compared with the context, and interpreted by the known realities of the Christian life of the age, they are found to denote, or refer to, something so essentially different from the thing they are brought to support, that they cannot honestly, or reasonably, be alleged or accepted in its favour. This fact is admitted by leading men among themselves, but seemingly without any consciousness of its bearing on their own position. Mr. Carter quotes approvingly from Marshall, '*that in the earliest times there was no private confession except in connection with public discipline;*' which is to say, in other words, that modern confession, which has no reference whatever to public discipline, did not exist in the early Church; '*it was made either because the sin needed public penance, or to relieve the mind of the penitent from the fear of having committed such a sin.*' What is meant, I suppose, by this somewhat awkward sentence is, that when a man was in doubt whether his sin did or did not require public penance and reconciliation, he consulted some learned and discreet person, in most cases probably a presbyter of the Church, on that point; if it was decided that it did require such penance, this was the remedy prescribed to him; if it was decided that it did not, he was relieved of the apprehension of having committed such a sin, and it was left to his own conscience and faith to do what was needful for the obtaining pardon of his sin. But it does not require much exercise of the logical faculty to see that the voluntary communication of a sin or sins to a priest, in order to be satisfied whether the character of some sin or sins is such as to require public confession and public penance, as an offence against the Church, with a view to obtain the Church's forgiveness, is quite a different thing from the confession to a priest of sins against God, as a religious act and a religious duty, with a view of obtaining remission of sins from God, by an

_{Admitted by Mr. Carter.}

_{This totally different from modern confession.}

act and sentence of forgiveness announced by the aforesaid priest. Of this we shall have to say more presently.

The Editor also of the notes on Tertullian in the 'Library of the Fathers' (Oxford, 1842), whom, from the initial letters E. B. P. affixed to the preface, I take to be Dr. Pusey, not only admits, but very ably maintains, the same view.[1] After having set forth from the ancient Fathers the nature and object of public discipline, and having proved by a vast array of authorities, that for sins between a man's own conscience and God, confession to God did in the usage of the ancient Church alone suffice, he goes on to complete his case with the following remarkable passages: 'Even negative evidence has much 'weight when the materials are adequate; if, under 'parallel circumstances equally detailed, and in a suffi-'cient number of instances, mention is uniformly made of 'a religious practice at one period, while it is omitted at 'another, it does imply a different view as to the virtue of 'the practice. Religious persons would not, without some 'adequate ground, *uniformly*[2] neglect at one period what 'was practised at another; and such ground is furnished 'by the different view of the Church respecting it; at the 'one time, when recommended by the Church, they per-'formed it; if, at another, they neglect it, when obedience 'to the Church was equally recognised as a duty, it would

Positive evidence.

Negative evidence.

---

[1] Notes on the Translation of Tertullian, 'De Penitentia' (Library of the Fathers), vol. i. pp. 379–407. The note begins by the following statement of the difference between the Romanists and the writer on Confession: 'The 'point at issue relates not to its general advantage, or its necessity in particu-'lar cases, or its use as a means of discipline, or to the desirableness of public 'Confession before the whole Church, or the great difficulty of true penitence 'without it, or the duty of individuals to comply with it if the Church requires 'it, but whether Confession to man be so essential to absolution that the benefits 'of absolution cannot be had without it.' It will, I think, be seen presently that the real question raised in this most remarkable dissertation is, whether private confession, except for the purposes of public penitence, existed at all in the early Church, and that the negative conclusion must be drawn.

[2] The italics are mine.

'be because the Church did not require it.' I must just interrupt E. B. P. for a moment, to observe that if it had been a Divine ordinance, the Church must have required it, and that he might have added '*or recommend it.*' 'The instances, then, being in each case very 'numerous, *the absence of any mention of Confession in the* 'early Church under the following circumstances does, 'when contrasted with the uniform mention of it in the 'later, put beyond question *that at the earlier period it was* '*not a received practice.* The evidence is given at great 'length by Daillé.[1] 'Secret Confession has, among the 'modern Latins, a chief place in the religious acts of 'the faithful; clergy, monks, lay; princes, private persons; 'nobles, people; men and women; but *nowhere in the* '*ancient Church*' (Daillé iv. 3); 'especially at the close of '*life, as a bounden duty, it is universal among the moderns,* '*unknown among the ancients*' (ib. c. 5); '*or in* '*sudden perils, as sickness, wars, shipwrecks, journeys, &c.,*' (ib. c. 6); '*in persecution or by martyrs*' (c. 7); '*at great* '*festivals*' (c. 8); '*and certainly the details are given so* '*fully, that it is inconceivable that the practice of Confession* '*should have been so uniformly mentioned with praise in the* '*later, and wholly omitted in the earlier Church, had the* '*practice of the earlier been the same as that of the later.* '*An argument of the same sort is deduced from the body of* '*writings, the great number and variety of questions and dis-* '*cussions, to which the modern Confessional has given rise,* '*and from its very nature must give rise.*' (Daillé iv. 14.) 'It again is inconceivable that with the large remains of 'antiquity which we have, and the notices of lost works, 'there should be no vestige of anything corresponding to 'all this, *had the practice which occasioned it existed.*' Again, E. B. P. adopts Daillé's observation that 'penitence' in the early Church signified '*public penitence,*' because public

Quotations from Daillé.

---

[1] Daillé, 'De Confess. Auricular,' note to Tertullian, *ut supra*, p. 406.

penitence alone existed—then when penitence was either public or private, it was distinguished accordingly—and when public penitence had been dropped, the word signified private penitence, without any distinguishing epithet; whence he draws this most decisive conclusion, 'This variation would not have been had *the modern private penitence existed in the early Church.*'[1] The argument seems to be, as E. B. P. says, 'unquestionable,' no less so in 1874 than in 1842.

Conclusion drawn by E. B. P.

In the conclusion which E. B. P. draws from this, which I subjoin below,[2] two things are observable; first of all, that he limits the application of his argument to obligatory Confession, whereby he gives the direct negative to the position now advanced by Confessionalists that their Confession is enjoined by Scripture; for had it been so, it would have been obligatory in all circumstances which gave occasion for its use, just as any other enjoined ordinance; and further that it is not easy to see by what legerdemain of logic the argument is limited to obligatory Confession, and not extended to the voluntary phase; for voluntary Confession to men of private sins against God finds no more place than obligatory Confession, unless, indeed, it is meant to be inferred that the negative argument has a positive side, and that, because obligatory Confession was not recognised in the early Church, such voluntary Confession was; an argument from contraries which is not only unwarranted by the rules of formal logic, but contradicted by the facts of his case; for this turns on the total absence of any mention of private

Cannot logically be limited to obligatory Confession.

---

[1] Page 406.

[2] 'Although, however, it is certain from the above evidence that the early 'Church had no obligatory Confession except that of overt acts of sin with a 'view to public penitence, and consequently that Confession as now practised 'in the Roman Communion is not essential to the validity of the general exer-'cise of the power of the keys, still as a matter of discipline it belongs to the 'Christian prudence of any Church to imitate or lay it aside, &c.' See page 407.

Confession whatever, not only on the absence of obligatory Confession. My readers will observe that E. B. P.'s premiss goes a good deal farther than the conclusion drawn from it; I simply take his premiss, which is the conclusion I want. It is the verdict of the early Church— not only against its absolute necessity, but even its general advantage, and its use as a means of discipline, or the notion of true penitence being very difficult without it— which is read clearly enough in the fact that 'there is no vestige corresponding to all this,' 'that it was wholly unknown among the ancients,' 'wholly omitted in the early Church,' 'that in the earlier period it was not a received practice.' I do not know how the case against the Confessionalists, in respect of the witness of antiquity, could be more decidedly expressed.[1]

Does not go so far as the Premiss.

The writer says, indeed, that as a matter of discipline, it belongs to the Christian prudence of any Church to imitate or lay aside the practice.[2] Are we then to believe that the early Church judged rightly in these matters? if so, the Romish practice, even if not enforced, is contrary to the judgment of the early Church, and cannot be adopted by those who defer to that judgment; if not, the argu-

---

[1] This note is much prized among Confessionalists as establishing their case against Rome's enforced confession; but they cannot evade as against themselves the condemnation which they insist upon as against Rome; for those who are acquainted with the manuals of Confession circulated by the Mediæval Clergy, will see how little their system differs from that of Rome, except in the point of not being, professedly at least, enforced. And this is not the point in which the Romish system fails of finding any warrant in antiquity. The Confessionalist writers, indeed, argue as if its being enforced was the only point treated of, whereas it does not enter specially into the discussion at all. The bearing of the note is to prove the total absence of any recognition of any of the points in which E. B. P. says (see above, p. 58, note) there is no difference between him and Rome. And the witness of antiquity being against Rome in these points, they must admit that it is equally so against themselves.

[2] I conclude that the practice of obligatory private Confession in the Romish Church is what is meant; it cannot mean 'private Confession as in antiquity,' for what has been proved not to exist cannot be imitated: but the sentence is not easy to interpret with any certainty.

ment from antiquity, as regulating the practice of after-ages, fails altogether, and Mediævalism and Romanism collapse at once. Is it not rather manifest, that it cannot enter into any Church which fashions itself on the injunctions of Scripture and practice of genuine antiquity; and that the practice of Confession, as held by the Confessionalists, invalidates, so far, the claim of any Church to be called Catholic, just as Mariolatry excludes, so far, the Romish Communion? It may, perhaps, occur to most minds, as it has to my own, that the reasonable dictates of Christian prudence would lead a Church in dealing with a practice never sanctioned in Scripture, unknown to antiquity, to lay it aside if it had been introduced, rather than introduce or imitate it; especially one which has produced so much domestic, social, and political evil, that even those who have drank it in with their mother's milk are now striving to get rid of it.

Auricular Confession excluded by antiquity.

CHAPTER VI.

Further Examination into the Ancient Practice—Both Persuasives to and Dissuasives from private Disclosure of Sin—Solution of this is that Disclosure is recommended in certain Cases with a View to public Confession—Discouraged as a Means of obtaining Pardon from God—Threefold Phase of Sin—Against a Brother—Against the Church—Against God—Threefold Phase of Guilt—Different Means of obtaining Remission of these several Phases of Guilt.

Sins against the Church were Matters of penitential Discipline—Remitted by the Church as the Party offended—Remitted by individual Christians, when the Sin and Guilt arose from private Injuries—Sins against God remitted by God alone on Confession to Him—Prominent Place held by Sin against the Church—Afterwards the Notion of such Sin died away, and the penitential Discipline fell into Disuse—Persuasives to disclosure of Sins originally had reference to public Disclosure, Dissuasives had reference to the Requirements of God by Confession to Him alone.

Proofs that public Discipline dealt only with Sins as against the Church—Not with Sins as against God—Line drawn between these—Passage from Cyprian—Differences between Public Discipline and Auricular Confession—Too wide to admit of one being any Warrant for the other.

WITH this proof of the fact that Confession, as advocated and practised by the Confessionalists, was unknown in the early Church, my readers might dismiss from their minds this part of the case. It will, however, I think, be more satisfactory to go into it a little more in detail, and bring forward a little more clearly and logically the points of distinction between the modern system and the primitive practice with which they endeavour to connect it, or rather with which they have of late years assumed off-hand its connection. *Question though settled must be gone further into.*

It must first be observed, that one of the phenomena to be accounted for is the existence, almost side by side, in early writers, of the strongest persuasives to, and the strongest dissuasives from, the disclosure of secret sins to *Contradictory language of ancient writers.*

men,[1] and I think it will be felt that no exposition of the system will be satisfactory which does not furnish a solution of this contradiction. Nor is this, I think, done by supposing that the persuasives refer to auricular Confession as voluntary, the others to it as obligatory: for Confession would be beneficial, if beneficial at all, to the person using it, though he took doctrinally a wrong view of it; the dissuasives would have taken the shape of pointing out the doctrinal mistake of supposing it obligatory, not of forbidding or disparaging what would have been otherwise beneficial. Both persuasives and dissuasives are didactic not doctrinal; they are quite general and absolute, and do not enter into the points of difference, optional or not optional—this person or that; so that the difference cannot be that the one is viewed as applying to those who want it for its own sake, the other to those who do not. The persuasives are worded as if disclosure of secret sins was necessary for all under certain circumstances; the dissuasives, as if it was necessary for nobody. I think the solution may be found in the difference between certain sins and certain other sins, and the aim and result of the disclosure of each respectively. The disclosure of certain sins is enjoined under certain circumstances, with a view to certain results (see page 77 *sqq.*): where the character of the sin is different, and there are no such circumstances or results, then confession to God alone is enjoined—confession to man forbidden. The question is, can such a difference between sin and sins, and their circumstances, be established?

Solution of this.

The Note on Tertullian recognises such a difference when it is said that there was no private Confession, except with regard to public penitence: we shall see hereafter that Confidence (not Confession in the technical sense), was, in certain cases, recommended and practised. But we may go further than this.

[1] See Bingham, vi. 469-485. Usher, 83. Note on Tertullian, 388-520.

THREEFOLD PHASE OF SIN.

We shall scarcely form a complete notion of the ancient penitential discipline, and the position which it held in the Ministry for the remission of sins, unless we take in the fact, that most sins have a threefold phase of offence, and taint of guilt. First, they are transgressions of God's holy law and will—simple offences against God; secondly, they are injuries done to a brother Christian, as well as offences against God; thirdly, they are scandals and dangers and injuries to the Christian commonwealth, the Church. Corresponding to this triple aspect of sin, there are three acts of forgiveness mentioned in Scripture, whereby the guilt attaching to each phase is severally and separately remitted. When a sin is not only against God but also against a brother, the forgiveness of the guilt attaching to such a sin in this aspect or relation—the loosing the sinner from his sin—is procured by the condonation thereof by the injured person, on the acknowledgment, and, if possible, the reparation thereof, by the person injuring; and where such an offence is thus forgiven by the injured person, this forgiveness is ratified in heaven, and the guilt belonging to it in that relation blotted out, according to our Lord's promise given in St. Matt. xviii. 18.[1]

Ancient penitential discipline.

Threefold phase of sin.

Sin against an injured person.

But if a sin is not only against God and against a brother, but against the Church, as causing scandal without, and evil within, then such a sin requires the forgiveness of the Church,[2] in this aspect and relation, and public

Against the Church.

---

[1] See Bingham, vi. 578, note s; Usher, pp. 110, and 130. This interpretation of the promise given in this passage is as old as Origen (see Bingham, vi. 579), and it is found also in St. Augustine (see Bingham, vi. 578, note u) and Chrysostom, *ad loc.*; Jerome also, *ad loc.* 'Si peccaverit in nos frater noster, demittendi habemus potestatem—si autem in Deum quis peccaverit non est nostri arbitrii,' quoting 1 Sam. ii. 25. It is the one which the context suggests: the whole chapter from verse 15 treats of the duty and the benefit of the forgiveness of private injuries on repentance, and the danger of refusing personal reconciliation.

[2] See Fell's note on Cyprian de Lapsis, p. 136, given in Bingham, vol. viii. 414, note q.

reparation, provided the Church chooses to demand and exact it; and this the early Church judged it necessary to do with ever increasing severity. The sin of the Corinthian, for instance, was a sin against God, as being a violation of the seventh commandment; it was a sin against his father: it was a sin against the Church as bringing scandal upon it: and it was probably in this last aspect and relation that St. Paul took cognizance of it; first, punishing and excommunicating the sinner, then forgiving him and re-admitting him on his public confession and repentance.

Public Discipline and reconciliation.

Now, it pleased the early Church—with what reason or with what views we need not stop to enquire—to devise penitential discipline as a means whereby satisfaction was made to the Church for sins against herself—the scandal removed, the evil remedied, and the dangers, which threatened the communion therefrom, prevented. This was analogous to the acknowledgment and reparation which passed between private individuals. Such sin in this aspect was remitted when the offender was reconciled to the Church by the public laying on of hands by the priest, always followed by a prayer (see p. 165), and re-admission to the Holy Communion, as soon as the severity of his penitence seemed not only to have testified and tested his repentance before man, but also to have counteracted the evil to which the commission of such a sin might, in the way of evil example, have exposed the community. Doubtless, another object in inflicting this discipline was to awaken the sinner to a sense of his sin as in God's sight and against God, and thus to save him from the destruction of impenitence; the sin, however, was viewed as a sin against the Church, visited with Church censures and deprivations, and forgiven by a formal public act of reconciliation and re-admission to Church privileges. Such public discipline has been adopted by Churches most hostile to private Confession, and therefore cannot be identical with it. And where such sins in their ecclesiastical relation were thus remitted by the offended party—the Church—it was part of God's promise to the Church that such remission of what may be called the ecclesiastical guilt should be ratified by God; while the guilt belonging to the sin, as an act of disobedience against God, has the promise of forgiveness on simple repentance or change of heart, and confession to Him. Hence, the work of forgiveness being between God and a man's own conscience, when God was the offended party—and between the offender and the Church when the Church was the offended party—or between brother and brother when individual Christians were the offended parties—it naturally happened, that ecclesiastical or canonical discipline held the most prominent place in the public life and public ministrations of the Church. The peculiar position of the Church in early days increased its prominence and importance: for in the times when the Church was on its probation before the world, this aspect of sin in its relation to the Church was of more vital consequence than afterwards; hence the offences against God's moral law for which ecclesiastical discipline was enforced, were those sins which most directly and seriously affected the character and progress of the Church in the world at large, such as apostacy; while the sins which either in their own nature, or from their not showing themselves in outward acts, did not affect the character and interests of the Church in the world, were not taken cognisance of by the Church, but left as matters between the sinner and God, such as envy, covetousness, pride, and even carnal lusts, lasciviousness, drunkenness.[1] As time went on, and Christianity became identified with civilised society, the injury done to the Church by such heinous sin was seemingly, and

Prominence given to it

---

[1] See Bingham, vi. pp. 471 and 478 and note v. Note on Tertullian, pp. 392 and 394.

perhaps really, less, inasmuch as both the scandal and the danger were diminished; and this being the case, it followed that, as soon, and in proportion, as the inconveniences and the scandals and abuses of this public penance, were felt to be greater evils than those which they professed to remedy, it was, partly by canonical authority, and partly by spontaneous disuse, allowed to pass away, except on a few extraordinary occasions, from almost the whole of Christendom; but it does not follow that what was substituted in its stead can claim the sanction of the previous practice from which it differs so essentially.

Difficulties in ancient discipline explained hereby. I venture to ask my readers whether a good deal of the indistinctness and contradiction which mark most dissertations on the ancient discipline, is not got rid of by what has been suggested above on the phases, or threefold relations of sin to the several parties who are, or who may be, offended by it; to each of which three different methods and conditions of forgiveness, were severally attached. In this light the penitential discipline, with all its adjuncts, will be viewed as the condition imposed by the Church to obtain condonation of an offence committed against the body politic; while the forgiveness for sins committed against God's will and law, which belongs to God to give, as the party offended thereby, was to be sought for, and obtained by other methods ordained and required by God Himself. This at once accounts for the earnest exhortations to disclosure of sin where necessary, as in the case of known sinners who refused to submit to the discipline of the Church—or salutary, as in the case of men whose consciences might be relieved by public Confession (see page 76), or where it was desirable to ascertain, by disclosure of sin to a fit person, whether such discipline was necessary; that is, whether the offences were such, in kind or degree, as to require ecclesiastical condonation as against the Church. It accounts too for the no less earnest declarations that confession to God alone was the method to be pursued, and not Confession to man; that is, for offences in their relation to God.[1] At the same time we can see why, and how, the forgiveness of sin by God, and the forgiveness of sin by the Church, are spoken of as not identical, nor even always coincident.

That public discipline had to do with sins in their relation to the Church, and was founded on considerations of the common weal, is clear, from the limitations affixed to the condonation, even on repentance, of certain offences, or the repetition thereof. In such cases, the ecclesiastical forgiveness was withheld from men even though they were held to have been pardoned by God;[2] or men were encouraged to seek from God that pardon which the ecclesiastical system forbade them to hope for from the congregation.[3] Here we see a distinct recognition and distinction of sin in its relation to God, and pardoned by Him, and against the Church, and not pardoned by the Church. This, too, appears in the fact that such sins as drunkenness, covetousness, &c. (see above, p. 67),

Distinction between sins against God and sins against the Church.

---

[1] It would be difficult otherwise to account for the utter repudiation of the Mediæval notions of confession, penance, and absolution, which we find in passages of ancient writers, of which the following are specimens: 'Neither do I constrain thee, to discover thy sins unto men, unclasp thy conscience before God, show thy wounds unto Him, and of Him ask thy medicine.' 'Do I say confess them to thy fellow-servants, who may reproach thee therewith? confess them to God who healeth them.' 'Confess thy sins to me (God) alone in private.' 'He commandeth us to give an account thereof to Him alone.' 'To Him to make confession of them.' (Bingham, vi. 469.) These words of Chrysostom leave untouched public discipline as required by the Church; he had in his eye sins for which no such satisfaction was demanded by the Church, sins between God and the sinner alone. My readers will see in a moment that such passages could not have been written, if confession to, penance from, absolution by, a priest, had been an ordained or recognised method for the remission of sins, as sins against God.

[2] 'Augustin, Epist. liv. ad Maced. (Bingham, vi. 475). He is speaking of those who after public reconciliation had fallen again, 'Even over these God makes His son to rise, and gives them the gifts of life and salvation no less than he did before.'

[3] Bingham, vi. 475, and viii. pp. 408 and 409.

which are the gravest sins against God, were not regarded as sins against the Church.[1]

Passage in Cyprian.

A passage in Cyprian is still more explicit.[2] Certain 'Lapsi' had obtained from martyrs, or confessors, mandatory letters for their restitution to Church fellowship, and presumed on them as superseding the necessity of anything more. Cyprian protests against the notion that such men's sins are pardoned before they had gone through the discipline required by the Church for the sin as committed against it, and the method ordained by God for the sin as committed against Himself. 'Let no one deceive himself, He who bore our sins can alone forgive those which are committed against Himself: the servant cannot forgive the heavier sins committed against the Lord: it is written, Cursed be he who puts his hope in man: the Lord must be prayed to, the Lord must be appeased by our satisfaction.' Hence it would seem that the sins which a man commits against God were remitted, as against Him, in the Church.[3]

Summary of what has been said.

On the whole, I think we should gather from the practice of the early Church, and the passages in the patristic writings which bear upon it, that God has appointed repentance and confession to Him, as the sole means and conditions of obtaining the pardon of sins as against Himself. That the Church, acting upon the powers and constitution which Christ gave it, appointed penance, public confession, public reconciliation, for sins against the Church. That individuals were taught to forgive sins against themselves on the acknowledgment and repa-

---

[1] It must be confessed that the estimate of sin in God's sight, where the inward source of the sin is more sinful than the sin itself, contrasts strangely with the theory of ecclesiastical discipline, where the inward sin is not taken cognisance of, unless it shows itself in some outward action injurious in some way or other to the Church in its relation to the world.

[2] Cyprian de Lapsis, Ed. Fell. p. 129.

[3] See also Cyprian, Test. iii. c. 28.

ration thereof. Further, the forgiveness granted by the Church of sins against the Church, or by an individual of sins against himself, carried with it pardon from God of that degree of guilt attaching to them in these several relations. And the expressions which recommend disclosure of private personal sins to a brother Christian, or to a priest, refer to public Confession, as the satisfaction to the Church, as the party offended, and not to any requirement of God, for the pardon of sin, as against Himself.

But if we throw aside these distinctions, and hold that penitential discipline had direct reference to sins in their relation to God, still the difference between the ancient ecclesiastical discipline, and the modern system which our Confessionalists advocate, is so marked and distinct, that the one can afford no argument or precedent for the other. It is mere waste of time for our Confessionalists to prove the penitential discipline—this is an undoubted fact, indisputable and undisputed—but it does not prove their position; and to argue from one to the other is at once a sophistical attempt to impose upon the careless, and a logical confession of weakness. No amount of invariableness in exacting this public satisfaction for notorious sin gives the slightest sanction to private confession of secret sins with a view to the forgiveness thereof pronounced privately by a priest. No opinion entertained of the necessity of such public penance and absolution for notorious offences, proves any necessity or benefit of private confession or absolution for secret offences. No confession to the Pœnitentiarius for the purposes of ascertaining the nature of a sin in its relation to ecclesiastical discipline, can prove the practice of confession to a priest of a sin as a means to, and a condition of, forgiveness from God. No amount of inexorable severity enforced by the Church as a satisfaction and security to itself, on offenders against the public weal, can jus-

Essential difference between public discipline and Mediæval Confession in theory.

tify or excuse the placing a single hindrance in the way of God's mercy, or attaching even a feather-weight condition to what is laid down in Scripture as sufficient to obtain forgiveness of sins against His Divine Majesty; to what our Lord Himself, by promises, and doctrines, and prophecies—by parables, and miracles—so constantly and clearly set forth. That which was required *in foro ecclesiæ* to satisfy a nescient Church of the sincerity of a sinner's repentance and the reality of his amendment, proves nothing as to anything of the same kind being required *in foro cœli* to assure an Omniscient God of a repentance, or to make it such as to obtain His forgiveness. Such a necessity may, or may not, exist, but it cannot be argued from the public discipline which the Confessionalists assume as the undoubted proof—the exact exemplar of it.

<small>And details.</small>

And when we come to look into details the differences and distinctions stand out still more intelligibly. The acknowledgment of the sinfulness of notorious sin differs essentially from the disclosure of secret sin. The acknowledgment of sin against the Church, as a party injured, differs essentially from the disclosure of sin to a priest by whom the sin is to be forgiven, as the *soi-disant* representative of God. The acknowledgment of a notorious sin in order to obtain public reconciliation from the Church as the act of the whole Church through the agency of its officials, is different from the disclosure of secret sin, in order to obtain forgiveness from God, through the private exercise of a power for life or death supposed to belong to every priest. The disclosure of a secret sin in order to be satisfied, whether from its kind or degree it requires public confession, is different from the disclosure of secret sin as for its own sake, a necessary element of repentance, the surest method of obtaining forgiveness from God. An act of reconciliation given by a bishop or priest, as the official representative of the Church, is essentially different from a grant or sentence of pardon by a priest pretending to act as the representative of God. So that even if all these practices were taken as having existed from the beginning, they would furnish no warrant for a practice which is essentially different from them—one and all—in spite of the assumption of their identity; the antiquity of the one, however conclusively proved, does not prove the antiquity of the other.

<small>*The one no warrant for the other.*</small>

CHAPTER VII.

Nature and Decay of Public Discipline—Case of Corinthian Sinner—Developed in the Century after the Apostles—Lapsi—Scandalous Offences—Those which caused no Scandal, left to private Conscience and Discipline—No private Confession, for the Sin was notorious—Public Disclosure of secret Sins for Relief of Conscience—This only allowed on Recommendation of some wise Layman, or afterwards Priest—Private Disclosure of Sins to such Persons for this Purpose—Not followed by Absolution—Multiplication of such Cases—Appointment of Pænitentiarius—His Office that of *'Juge d'Instruction'*—Advance towards Mediæval System, but not to Absolution—Scandal caused by this Office—Abolished—No warrant for Confession, but the contrary.

Private personal Discipline for Offences not against the Church—Same as that recommended by our Church as Preparation for Holy Communion.

Confidence in Early Church—Primitive Usage retained in our Church, except as regards Public Discipline.

Abolition of Pænitentiarius—Private Confession assumes a substantive Form—Public Confession less frequent—Public Reconciliation for notorious Offences superseded by private—Change in the Notion of Public Reconciliation—Private Confession for notorious Offences authorised—Change of Doctrine as well as Practice—Reconciliation or Absolution still precatory, not indicative, and so up to end of twelfth Century—This is a Matter of Ecclesiastical Arrangement, not of Scriptural Obligation—Hence we must see what is the Practice and Teaching of our own Church.

Attempt to distinguish occasional from habitual Confession—Flaws in the Argument.

Mediæval Confession resulted from the public discipline.

IT is nevertheless an undoubted fact that private Confession, as it existed in Mediæval times, was the offspring, or rather the result, of the old penitential discipline, the place of which, as it passed away, was usurped by its counterfeit; this will be best explained by a brief sketch of the nature and decay of public discipline.

Primitive penitential discipline.

The case of the Corinthian furnishes us with the earliest example of the satisfaction demanded of a notorious sinner, with a view to his own spiritual benefit—by awakening him to repentance towards God—and to the general welfare of the Church, by the removing of the scandal, and neutralising the example, and by the restoration of the member, in whose loss all the members suffered loss. Of the Corinthian precedent I shall have occasion to say something presently: it sufficeth now to say, that here there is evidently no trace of private Confession or private absolution.

1. In the century immediately following the Apostolic administration, that which at first was only an occasional and extraordinary exercise of ecclesiastical power, assumed the shape of a systematic ordinance, which was day by day developed and worked out with more and more exactness and inflexibility. The lapsi, or apostates, furnished most of the cases for this discipline, on account as well of the notorious nature of the offence, as of the scandal and injury it brought upon the Church. Of course other sins of deeper die, if notorious and scandalous, were dealt with in the same way, as offences against the Church. But the sins of every-day frailty, as not causing any scandal to the Church and therefore not being regarded as sins against the Church, were not matters of ecclesiastical discipline or forgiveness, but were left to the ordinary remedies for sin against God, Confession to Him, and acceptance of His mercy through Christ, proffered to them by the Church or by God's Word; or possibly to the mutual prayers of those who disclosed their infirmities one to another. And sins of a more serious character, if unknown, were, of course, also left to treatment by individual consciences. (See page 69.)

At first.

We may suppose indeed that this was the case with by far the majority of sins, unless we suppose that the majority of the Church were at the same time under ecclesiastical discipline. However, there was no such thing as private confession and private absolution; the

No private Confession of private sins.

acknowledgment of the sin, and the reparation, were as public as the sin was notorious; in fact, the notoriety of the sin precluded private Confession; the confession required was not the disclosure of offence, but the sinner's acknowledging that he felt it to be a sin, that he repented of it, and promised to avoid it in future.

<small>Disclosure of secret sins of a heinous dye.</small>

2. One great characteristic of the sins subjected to public discipline being their heinousness, and the necessity of their being atoned for in public, it followed that secret sins of a heinous dye frequently presented themselves to awakened consciences as needing public expiation and reconciliation.[1] Men could not feel their consciences at ease without performing that public penance, which their sins, if notorious, would have demanded, as sins against the Church. They felt that the guilt which attached itself to their sin, as against the Church, was unforgiven. They did not like to avail themselves surreptitiously, as it were, of the Holy Communion or other Church privileges, from which they felt themselves virtually excluded. They therefore publicly accused themselves of the sin which was on their conscience, and accepted that penance at the conclusion of which public condonation would restore them to the rightful possession of the privileges of full Christian fellowship. And this voluntary accusation of themselves, so far from being viewed as an ordained point of religion, was regarded as a singular proof of tenderness of conscience, and a most meritorious act of repentance. Nor can it have any place except where public penitential discipline exists. Here, then, there was a disclosure indeed of secret sins, but not in private, nor yet followed by private absolution of a priest, but when necessary by the public absolution of the Church.

3. In course of time, as the energies of internal faith in God's promises of forgiveness waxed cold, and were

---

[1] See Usher, p. 86.

supplied by the artificial appliances of an external and ceremonial pardon, this public disclosure of secret sins, more and more recommended in certain cases, and even enjoined by the teachers in the Church,[1] became so prevalent, that the public attention was occupied by sins not of that heinous dye, which, if they had been notorious, would have required such solemn expiation; and, on the other hand, the public disclosure of certain secret sins might have been, and many times was found to be, scandalous and injurious to the Church. Thus it was considered advisable that no one should confess his secret sins publicly, before it had been ascertained, by some one competent to judge, that such sins were proper to be so confessed: and for this purpose those who were thus uneasy in their consciences were advised to open their souls to others; but it was a matter of Confidence, not of Confession in the Confessionalist sense of the word: not as in itself a healing or cleansing process, for then other remedies would not have been suggested—in the cases of sins of sufficient importance, public discipline and condonation—or in other cases, the ordinary means of making one's peace with God. It was not an act of discipline, but an act of prudence for the sake of its results: just as a man with a serious disease would have recourse to some one to tell him whether this or that remedy would be likely to work a cure, without expecting to receive any benefit from the mere act of seeking advice. And as such a one would most naturally and wisely go to some one who was acquainted with the nature of the remedies, so persons who were thus sick in their consciences were advised to go to some one who, not by virtue of his office, but by

Prevalence of this gratuitous Disclosure.

It was Confidence, not Confession.

---

[1] Greg. Nyssen. de Pæn. 'recommends, at once, public penance in order 'to gain the prayers of the people, and private disclosure to the priest that he 'may prescribe the fitting remedies, but the whole relates to public penitence.' Note on Tertullian, p. 385. The latter clause refers to the question whether the case was one for public penance or not. See also Note p. 381; and Usher, p. 86.

reason of his knowledge and skill, would be most likely to understand whether public discipline would be proper for the case. It was not that every priest *virtute officii*, as commissioned by God to receive such confessions, was to be consulted, but ' one who being tried had proved himself a skilful physician and a merciful;' nor yet, as far as we can gather from the writings of the times, is there any mention of its being necessarily a priest at all. Nor is the remedy private absolution, but 'if he should say ' anything or give thee any counsel, thou mightest follow 'it,'[1] evidently making the following it not an ordained act of duty, but a voluntary act of prudence, inasmuch as it resulted from a conviction of the person's prudence and skill. Here again, then, there is a private disclosure of sins but entirely differing in nature, theory, object, and result from modern Confession, approaching far nearer to Confidence—a disclosure for advice. Yet it is impossible not to see herein the fact, full of warning, that to this humanly devised method of dealing with sin may be traced the seed of the evil which afterwards overcast the Church and even Christianity itself,[2] more and more as it was developed into its full growth of Auricular Confession, Sacramental Confession, Penitence, Penance, and Direction.

Remedy not absolution but counsel.

Cases of this sort multiplied so much as persons sought more and more to substitute external and formal penance

---

[1] Origen, on Psalm xxxvii. See Usher, p. 83, note 33.

[2] The first author in whom we find any definite exhortation to confidence is Origen (230), but neither he nor Basil (370) makes any mention of a priest being the person to be applied to, but simply some one skilled in such matters. The spurious epistle of Clement to St. James recommends the president (or priest) as the person to whom such confidential disclosures are to be made. The remedy to be applied, however, was not absolution, but the word of God with wholesome counsel, 'ut ab ipso per verbum Dei et salubre consilium curetur' (see Bingham, vi. 484, note e; Usher, p. 84, note 36). It was, in fact, the confidence which is recognised in the exhortation to the Holy Communion (see p. 103). We shall soon see how this too was merged in the so-called sacramental confession.

for internal repentance, that about the year 300 it was judged expedient to take the matter out of private hands, and to appoint for this special purpose a priest or presbyter, who was called *Pœnitentiarius*,¹ to whom such questions were submitted: so that, during the eighty years for which this office lasted, the cases which had formerly been decided by private judgment were referred to the officer thus commissioned to decide upon them with authority. The tendency of this was, of course, to give a colour and authority and system to private Confession, which it had not before, especially as under its auspices the custom grew up of allowing the reparation to the Church to be made in private instead of public. And this is the nearest approach to the Mediæval system which our Confessionalists assert to be primitive, though the practice itself was not of really primitive, but rather of after growth. But the distinction between the two is marked and clear enough. The former was not viewed as an act of necessary religious discipline, beneficial in itself by God's appointment, but as a preliminary to an ecclesiastical reparation, if the sins were of sufficient importance in their relation to the Church, to justify permission being given to the applicant to avail himself of it. This Official was not to hear confessions as conditions of sins being forgiven, but he acted as a judge—what the French call a 'juge d'instruction'—to see if the case was one to require public discipline.² Nor was the confession made with a view to receive formal absolution from the Pænitentiarius; this officer did not go farther than to recommend public discipline if it was fit matter for it.³ If this was the case, his office towards the applicant ceased; except possibly so

Appointment of Pænitentiarius.

---

¹ Bingham, vi. 490; Sozomen, lib. vii. c. xvi.; Bingham, vi. 492, note q.; Note on Tertullian, p. 380; Socrat., lib. v. c. 19. See Usher, p. 87.
² Note on Tertullian, p. 381; Origen, on Psalm xxxvii. See Usher, p. 86.
³ August, 'Lib. de Pœn.' See Usher, p. 84.

far as to give him instructions as to the proper way of performing that public penance to which he was desirous to submit himself.[1] Where the sin was not of this character he left him, as before, to the ordinary remedies contained in God's word, or at the most he recommended some private penance,[2] which might relieve a weak conscience from the feeling of having deserved canonical discipline without having undergone it: and therefore I think my readers will see that the private disclosure to the Pænitentiarius, being in reality only an act of Confidence, differed essentially from that which it is now sought to introduce among us on the plea of its being primitive. I think, however, there can be very little doubt that in this working of the Pæniteutiarian system we can detect a further advance towards the substitution of the modern private sacramental confession in place of the former primitive public discipline. This, of course, is more clearly seen in those cases in which the sins disclosed were of so scandalous a nature, that the bringing the offender and the offence to public cognisance would have been to the serious detriment of the Church. In these cases, it was permitted to the Pænitentiarius to assign in private a penance, proportionate to the sin, which carried with it the same benefit which would have resulted from public and formal remission by the imposition of hands, viz. restoration to Church privileges; but still it must be remembered that this remission was of the sin as committed against the Church, and in lieu of that public penance which, according to the strict primitive rules of the Church, could only have been attained by a long course of public humiliation. And even this slight approach to, this shadow of, the Confessional produced so great scandal and injury to the Church that, after it had

Disclosure to him not Confession but Confidence.

---

[1] 'Apocryphal Epistle of Clement I.' See Usher, p. 84.
[2] Sozomen, lib. vii. c. xvi. See Bingham, vi. 492.

lasted about eighty years, it was by common consent, as well as by public authority, abolished; and from that time the penitential discipline of the Church gradually lapsed into that Confessional discipline, which was fully developed under the auspices of Mediæval Rome. It is curious to mark that no sooner had public discipline admitted, as its handmaid, private confession to a priest, than it began to wither, and, as we shall see presently, soon fell. Of course, nothing like this preliminary disclosure, with a view to public discipline, can find place where public discipline has been abrogated in the Church, by virtue of its power to arrange such matters; so that the disclosure to the Pænitentiarius can furnish no warrant for the Confession of these days, even if the differences between them were less marked than we have seen them to be. In fact, the appointment of such an officer as the Pænitentiarius tells against the Confessionalist notion, that confession of some sort, either private or public, was required as a duty from every member of the Church; for if it had been the former, so that each person had his father confessor, that confessor would have been able to decide the question with authority, and thus there would have been no necessity for the office of Pænitentiarius; and if public confession had been required of all, there would have been no question for this officer to decide.

_{Abolition of Pænitentiarius.}

_{Office of Pænitentiarius no warrant for Confession;}

_{Rather against it.}

Side by side with this public ecclesiastical discipline, on which, as we have shown, private disclosure of sins to man accidentally and gradually fastened itself, there existed a private personal discipline, from which confession to man was wholly excluded, consisting of private examination, private repentance, private confession and prayer to God, with reparation of sins against others, consummated by approaching the Holy Table on the private witness of each man's personal conscience;[1] in short,

_{Private personal Discipline.}

---

[1] Note on Tertullian, p. 399 sqq. (See also above, page 69, note 1.) In

exactly the same as is set forth in the exhortation to the Holy Communion, as the way and means to being received as worthy partakers of that Holy Table. As the public discipline has wholly ceased, the only one that has been handed down to us from the really primitive Church is this private and personal one: for the Prayer Book contains no directions or recognition of any other discipline whatsoever, though, as we have before shown, it does recognise confidential communications between a clergyman and individual members of the Church: not, however, as a discipline or an ordinance; exactly following herein the practice of the really primitive Church. For by the side of this enforced public acknowledgment of and reparation to, the Church for scandalous offences, and these disclosures of private sins with a view to a voluntary public acknowledgment, which have, in the nature of things passed away, there existed, of course, that spontaneous, almost instinctive unburdening of consciences for the purposes of relief and spiritual counsel, to learn how some doubt might be solved, or some temptation met, or some evil conquered. But it was not an act of confession for its own sake, nor yet for absolution, nor yet as a discipline, and therefore it differed in kind from that into which it in course of time merged, when private confession had usurped the place of public discipline, and private absolution that of public reconciliation. In the Church, then, up to the year 350, there existed 1. Public discipline. 2. Disclosure of sins with a view to public discipline. 3. Private personal discipline—Confession to God. 4. Con-

As in the English Prayer Book.

Which follows the primitive system.

Confidence in Early Church.

---

some of these passages Chrysostom uses the word *compel*, 'God does not compel us to speak out our transgressions before men.' From this the writer argues that he rather implies voluntary private confession: but it is evident that he is not contrasting compulsory private confession and voluntary private confession, but is speaking of compulsory public confession before witnesses, which though compulsory in the eyes of the Church, was not compulsory in God's sight, inasmuch as confession to God alone procured the remission of sin as against God.

fidential communications. The two first have passed away; the two last are retained in our Church.

After the abrogation of the office of Pænitentiarius, private confession became more a recognised form of the Church discipline in lieu of public penance. The scandal which frequently attended the public disclosure furnished a reason for sins which should have been disclosed as a matter of public discipline, not being made public. To this was added the fear that if publicity was enjoined on every private disclosure, men would be deterred from submitting to it, and thus sin would evade the penalties which the Church demanded, as a security against similar offences in future, and, as far as these penalties were known, a means of deterring others from sinning;[1] and the public disclosure of sins thus being dropped, the principle and the aspect of private confession was changed. The confession, which had been made to the Pænitentiarius, with a view to the question whether public discipline was desirable or admissible, assumed a substantive and independent phase; and becoming in itself an act of satisfaction, insensibly took the place of public penance: and this not only with respect to secret, but also notorious offenders. Of course the notion of public satisfaction to the Church for personal sins, whether notorious or otherwise, became weaker and weaker as excommunication became more and more sparingly exercised in such matters, and became more and more applied to offences against the supremacy of the clergy, or used as an instrument of attack or defence in polemical disputes among rival parties or rival bishops, or even rival sovereigns whom rival bishops favoured. As this public satisfaction to the Church was dropped, it naturally happened that the notion of sin as an offence against the Church was lost sight of, and penance and reconciliation, which at first were conditions of the Church's

Decay of public Confession.

Change in private Confession.

Change in public censures.

Public reconciliation superseded by private.

[1] Usher, p. 89, note 50.

forgiveness of sin as against the Church, began to be viewed as conditions of forgiveness from God of sins against Himself; and the sin to be forgiven being thus viewed as against God, the public act or sentence of the bishop or priest, which formerly was pronounced by him as representing the Church, and carrying with it the remission of sin as against the Church, gradually came to be regarded, when this public discipline was thus all but gone, as the act and sentence of the representative of God, carrying with it God's forgiveness of sins, as against Himself—a most portentous change, and one that brought the most fatal evils upon Christendom. It would even seem as if Nectarius, when he abolished the Pænitentiarius,[1] contemplated the permitting everyone to partake of the Holy Mysteries on the witness of his own conscience: a near approach to the system of our own Church, which would have got rid of the evils and scandals of public discipline, without bringing still greater evils and scandals upon Christendom. But this was not to be—for the great blow to the ancient public discipline seems to have been struck about the year 440, when by Leo I.[2] private confession was distinctly authorised in lieu of public

Personal discipline possibly contemplated by Nectarius.

---

[1] I do not think that there is any historical evidence that this was formally done. Socrates (Lib. v. c. xix.; see Bingham, vi. 490) says that a certain Presbyter, named Eudæmon, recommended it to Nectarius: but he does not record its being actually done. Chrysostom, however, writing about this time, recognises it. 'Let each one examine himself, and then approach.' Homil. xxviii. on 1 Cor. xi. And again, 'Within thy conscience none present but God —search out thy sins . . . and then with a pure conscience approach the holy table, partake of the hallowed sacrifice.' See Usher, p. 88, notes 46 and 47.

[2] Usher, p. 89. Leo Ep. 136 (or 80); see Note on Tertullian, p. 390. The whole of this Letter of Leo discloses a departure from primitive antiquity, not only in the practice, but in the nature and principle of the remission of sins, as well as the confusion which waits on a state of transition. Two sorts of confession are spoken of: confession to a priest, as sufficient up to a certain point, probably as standing in place of public confession and penance, and so procuring condonation for sins against the Church; but three lines lower down confession to God is spoken of as taking precedence of confession to the priest, probably as procuring remission of sins from God.

discipline, and as the condition of obtaining forgiveness of sin from God.¹ Of course the confidential communications, which I have spoken of above, rapidly fell into the same groove, and the man who disclosed his sins to the priest was at first counselled, and then directed, to undergo some private penance, as a satisfaction to God thereof, and was then reconciled. A practice, however, which in this phase did not begin till the year 440 can hardly be called a primitive one, or be alleged as any evidence that modern Confession, in the technical sense of the word, has the sanction of that previous practice of primitive antiquity from which, though it was its source, it differs in object, in nature, in result. Mr. Carter admits that there was a change of doctrine, as well as practice, in this new organisation of private confession in lieu of public discipline, not seeing that this cuts from under his feet his assumed ground of primitive precedent. *[Private Confession and penance recognised by Leo I. Not a primitive practice.]*

But even in this new organisation of private confession we find an element which entirely distinguishes it from the modern system. The priest was not to pronounce any formal absolution carrying with it or implying forgiveness of sins from God, but to approach God in prayer for the penitent.² This prayer for the forgiveness of God replaced the formal forgiveness of the Church by imposition of hands, and this was the form whereby the benefit of absolution was conveyed up to the twelfth century, when the former prayer, 'May God give thee remission and absolution,' was changed into 'I absolve thee;'³ and this preca- *[Distinguished from modern Confession by absence of absolution.]*

---

¹ Leo *ut supra* and Ep. 108 (or 91); see Note on Tertullian, p. 391. 'The succour of the divine goodness being so ordered that the forgiveness of God cannot be obtained but through the supplication of the priest,' to this he immediately joins private confession, and identifies private restoration of the penitent with the former public act of reconciliation.

² See Note on Tertullian, p. 391. Usher, p. 89.

³ This form is still used in public absolution in the Roman Mass. (See page 35, note 1.)

tory—or rather optative or invocative form, for it partakes rather of the character of a solemn wish or invocation than of a direct prayer—has been retained in our own Church in the absolution in the Communion Service.

Plea for auricular confession on the score of only being voluntary.

I think it will be seen that this failure of Scriptural and primitive warrant is a most serious breakdown in the Confessionalists' case, especially when it has been adduced in its favour by its supporters; in fact, it would furnish to most thinking men a reason for rejecting the system altogether. Nor is the difficulty met by saying that it is not pretended that habitual or enforced confession is enjoined in Scripture, or sanctioned by primitive antiquity: that what they advocate is only occasional and voluntary, not habitual and enforced. They forget, first of all, that the evidence of antiquity goes, as we have seen, against any auricular Confession, whether occasional or habitual, optional or enforced—there was no such thing; and next, that a Church has no more right to set forth an occasional and voluntary practice as a divine ordinance without divine warrant, than one habitual and enforced; and again, that if it were a divine ordinance at all for the remission of sins after Baptism, it must be of universal application on all who sin—obligatory and not voluntary.

CHAPTER VIII.

This a Matter of Canonical Arrangement—Argument from this—Pleas, that this accounts for the Absence of Primitive Sanction, and that our Church has a Right to enjoin the Practice—Logical Effect of these Pleas—If so, it cannot be a Sacramental Ordinance of Divine Appointment—Plea, that Language of the Church may indicate a Recognition of its Scriptural Obligation, or makes it binding on us, answered—Effect of such a Plea—Necessity for examining our Church's Language—Positive Assertions of Confessionalists on this Point—Mistaken Proofs they adduce—What it is they assert to be taught by our Church—Visitation Office—Method prescribed—Inquiry into the Fact of the sick Man's Repentance, not any Detail of his Sins—Special Confession—Not necessarily private—Absolution to be reluctantly applied—Pardon not given—But prayed for after the Absolution—This Prayer the Relic of the old precatory Form—Argument of Confessionalists about this Prayer answered—Why it is untenable—Precatory Form up to twelfth Century shows that Forgiveness was held to be a Matter of Petition, not as a "fait accompli"—Change to "ego te absolvo"—Caution of our Church in this Matter—Instances of the Nature of Absolution in other Passages of our Prayer Book—Morning and Evening Prayer—Must be essentially the same in Visitation Office, differently applied—Not Forgiveness, but God's Promise and Offer to forgive—Difference between Absolution and Pardon—Instances of this in the Prayer Book—In the Visitation Formula—The Special Confession comes nearer to Confidence—But at all Events it would furnish no Precedent for Cases essentially different—Certainly not for Confession in the only Case in which even Confidence is recommended by our Church.

THE changes thus made by the Church, in even public confession of sins, mark, as Usher observes, that this was held to be a canonical matter, appertaining to the external discipline of the Church, which might be changed on just occasion; it therefore was not of dogmatic or Scriptural obligation, as in that case it could not have been in the power of the Church to change it. For instance, if public discipline had been a definite part of our Lord's will for His Church, then the Church in abrogating it failed of our Lord's mind for His Kingdom; but as it was only an

These were matters of canonical arrangement.

Therefore not of Divine obligation.

ecclesiastical institution, it was liable to change and abrogation.

This results also from other pleas on the subject,

This, however, may give occasion for the Confessionalists to say, that the absence of their private confession from the primitive system may have been a matter of such ecclesiastical arrangement, and, therefore, does not furnish any proof that either Scripture or apostolic practice was against it. But first, this reason for the omission, inadmissible though it be, admits the fact: and further, though it evades the difficulty which arises from the absence of primitive warrant, yet, at the same time, it lays the axe to that which they hold to be the great characteristic of their system, namely, that it is the divinely ordained ordinance for the remission of sins; it negatives that sacramental character which is assigned to it; for the foundation of that position is, that it is of divine obligation and not of Church appointment.

and from claiming for our own Church an optional right to establish it.

The fact, however, of the early Church thinking itself at liberty to make what arrangements it pleased upon the subject furnishes, of course, to our Confessionalists fresh standing-ground. If it is a matter of ecclesiastical arrangement with which we have to deal, then, of course, our Church has a right to make for its own members what arrangements it pleases. But this plea, again, is an abandonment of its sacramental character, and leads them into fresh difficulties. The principle, indeed, is true in itself, and is logically sound as an answer to objections against non-essentials, drawn from the silence of Scripture and the absence of primitive sanction; but if it is attempted on the strength of the right thus inherent in the Church to establish a practice as of divine obligation, and therefore essential, then it is clear that one claim negatives the other. The logical result of pleading the authority of the Church for a practice claiming, both in its origin and results, to be divine, is that the claim is abandoned—

a see-saw argument, alternating between ecclesiastical arrangement and divine obligation, is fatal to both. If it owes its existence to mere ecclesiastical arrangement, it cannot be recognised as a matter of divine appointment: if it is a matter of divine obligation, it cannot fall within the province of mere canonical arrangement: and therefore, it is of no gain to their cause to make out, either that the early Church had a right to omit it, or that our own Church has a right to enjoin it; for, in either case, there is a clear admission of the fact that it is human and not divine, which deprives it of the place which they would give it in God's scheme of salvation.

There are, however, two other points of view in which the language of the Church may seem to bear upon the question; it may be taken as indicating the mind of our Church as to its being a divine ordinance for the remission of human sin. This could only hold good if our Church recognised it as of universal obligation, which is confessedly not the case. Or it might make the practice binding upon us as members of the Church, but this would prove nothing as to its possessing any of those supernatural properties and effects which the Confessionalists attach to it. *[margin: Two points on which our Church may be supposed to have spoken.]*

I am not sure whether the question might not be held to be settled by these abstract considerations, but the case of the Confessionalists depends so much on the assumption that the practice which they advocate is the law of the Church, and their chance of success depends so much on the recognition of this assumption, that it is necessary to examine it in detail. *[margin: Necessity of examining this in detail.]*

And the way in which the matter is often handled makes this all the more necessary. The use of language which unreservedly invests it with divine powers, and presses it on our acceptance as an ordinance of God, is mostly confined to those Ultraists who think to carry their point by uncompromising opinions and unflinching language.

Confession at first represented as an ordinance of our Church.

Men of more caution and less candour, and we may say of more feeble logic, generally keep Ultraisms in the background, until they have got their proselytes under the influence of their fascination by putting it before them in the modified form, as an ordinance of their Church; and then, when they have secured them, they gradually open it out little by little, until the advisable, desirable, compassionate, comfortable provision of tender Mother Church, of which those who want it have a right to avail themselves, passes into the divine ordinance for the remission of sins, which no man can neglect without peril to his soul. At first, however, the language of our Church is put in the front, or rather the injunctions which they assume to be contained therein: and therefore to this point I must now address myself.

And here, on the very point on which the Confessionalists are positive even to arrogance—viz. that the practice they advocate is the law of our Church—it will, I think, on examination appear they are utterly mistaken;

Mistake herein.

it will appear that the Auricular Confession they advocate is not only not recognised as of universal or general, or even occasional obligation, but that it is not recognised at all, any more than it was in really primitive antiquity; that it is among the Mediæval corruptions which were excluded at the Reformation; so that any clergyman, who endeavours to restore it to our reformed system, is not acting in harmony with the injunctions and directions and mind of the Church, but disregarding and violating them both in the letter and the spirit.

The five points adduced by Confessionalists.

The Confessionalists adduce, as expressing the will of the Church in favour of their Sacramental ordinance, the Office for the Visitation of the Sick—the last paragraph in the first exhortation to the Holy Communion—a Canon which provides for certain cases in which secret and hidden sins have been confessed to a minister—a passage in a homily—and the form used in the ordination of priests. These are the points to be considered.

Let us again lay down clearly what we are talking about. I think I am not misrepresenting the Confessionalists' view of our Church's teaching on the subject, when I say that they hold that our Prayer Book recognises a power given to our priests of privately and personally forgiving sins by a form of words; that this is the ordinary and most sure means of pardon, which no man can safely or wisely neglect; and that private confession is so closely connected with it as a necessary condition, that it partakes of its character as a necessary means of pardon. Here we have two points which the Confessionalists assume as determined by the Church in their favour. First, the superior efficacy, if not the absolute necessity, of the private forgiveness of sins against God, by the judicial sentence privately pronounced by a priest, carrying along with it God's actual forgiveness of the sins in question, or declaring that forgiveness as a *fait accompli*; secondly, the necessity of private confession to the priest as an antecedent and a condition thereof—an essential part of the supernatural ordinance, an ingredient in the pardoning and cleansing process. What we have to consider is, whether these two points are recognised by our Church, first remarking that the absence of such an ordinance in the early Church creates an *à priori* probability against its being recognised by our own.

<small>Auricular Confession as asserted by the Confessionalists.</small>

When we turn to the Office for the Visitation of the Sick, we find that confession of sins and absolution form no part of the method ordinarily prescribed to the minister in dealing with the sick man: he is not, in the first instance, to hear the sick man confess his sins, but to examine him whether he has truly repented of them. He exhorts him to repentance—to examine himself as to his state toward God and man, to condemn and accuse himself

<small>Visitation Office.</small>

toward God, and if necessary towards man, both being parts of necessary repentance. That this examination is not an exhortation to disclose his sins, we learn from the last rubric, where in a certain case the man is to be moved to make a 'special confession' of his sins, in case his conscience is troubled with any weighty matter; but even then this confession need not be that contended for by the Confessionalists—part of the supernatural ordinance for pardon of sins made up of confession and absolution: for it need not be followed by absolution: nor yet need it be, *vi terminorum*, secret, for others may be present; indeed, the prayers rather suppose the presence of others to pray with the priest and the sick man. But even here the priest is not to urge him to seek and accept the remission of sins at his hand and voice: but he is to give the sick man absolution only when he humbly and earnestly desires it. These expressions, surely, mark a reluctance and holding back as contemplated by the Church, rather than any encouragement to it, far less any suggestion of it, or any notion of its special benefit, far less of its absolute necessity.

<small>The Confession there spoken of, not that of the Confessionalists shown by the</small>

Further, the formula pronounced by the priest is not conceived of as conveying forgiveness of sins, for in its first clause this is specially prayed for by the priest as a gift from Christ. He does not regard it as appertaining to his authority, though he does so view absolution. Nor can the Church be supposed to view it as having taken place on the pronouncing of the formula, for in the very next prayer which the priest is directed to use, is a petition that God will not impute unto the sick man his former sins; and it is worth noting that in this prayer the man's repentance is assumed, yet forgiveness is prayed for, as something yet unfulfilled; this clearly marks that pardon or forgiveness which the Confessionalists hold to be consummated, or implied as consummated,

<small>Formula of absolution;

by the prayer following the absolution if pronounced.</small>

in the utterance of the priest, has not yet been absolutely given. The old precatory form (see page 66) is retained as far as the forgiveness of sin goes;[1] while as far as absolution goes, an absolute form is used. And indeed we may observe *en passant* that if the Church did believe that our priests had this power of thus forgiving sin, it is incredible that the seeking for and exercise thereof should not be enjoined, as it is in the Romish Church, as indispensable, generally speaking, for all death-beds, instead of being permitted only in special cases, and not in all of these.

I have lately seen it advanced that this petition does not affect the supposition that forgiveness has actually been

<small>Confessionalist notion that</small>

---

[1] 'The prayer which immediately follows the prescribed form is, in fact, the primitive prayer on which was founded the precatory form which has been given to dying penitents for more than thirteen hundred years in the Western Churches. This ancient absolution or reconciliation of a penitent near death is not only found in the old formularies of the English Church, where it was used long before the preceding indicative form was introduced, but in the Sacramentary of Gelasius, A.D. 494; and for many centuries was commonly used in the Churches of the West.'—Palmer, Or. Lit. ii. 226.

If anyone compares our form with that of the Sarum Missal given in Palmer, he will see that the sentence in the Latin form, '*the remission of sins having been received*,' is omitted, and the conclusion of the prayer, '*admit him to the sacrament of reconciliation*,' is replaced by '*impute not unto him his former sins*:' this also practically occurs in the present Romish form (as given in Guillois, 'Catechism,' iii. 342), which probably is an interpolated relic of the old prayer, adopted at the change of private reconciliation to the Church instead of public, after the abolition of the Pænitentiarius. If we compare our form with the Romish form we find that in our prayer, 'putting his full trust in His mercy,' spoken of as the ground of the petition for the forgiveness of sins, evidently referring to the assumed effect of the formula of absolution, does not occur in the Romish prayer.

The Romanists (see Guillois, 'Explication du Catechism,' vol. iii. p. 342), retain this prayer somewhat modified in the same conjunction with the indicative absolution, '*I absolve thee*,' and therefore it might be urged that as the Romish Church uses this prayer, and at the same time recognises absolute forgiveness of sins in absolution, so our Church may do the same. The answer to this is, that the formal and direct teaching of the Romish Church on this point prevents this prayer having any bearing upon the point; they use it without being conscious that it furnishes a direct contradiction to their teaching on absolution; while, as in our own Church there is no such teaching, the prayer, of course, has its natural and logical bearing on the preceding formula.

granted in the absolving formula; inasmuch as it is only a prayer that God would ratify what the priest has done.

<small>the prayer is otiose, answered by other passages in the Prayer Book.</small>

But when we compare the language of our Church, in cases where certain effects are held to attend on, or rather to be realised in, certain acts or forms, we find that no such prayer for divine ratification is attached, but thanks given to God for the benefit received; so in the Baptismal Service we find 'seeing that this child is regenerate' (whatever that may mean), 'let us give thanks,' and then, in the following prayer, the regeneration is assumed as a *fait accompli*. So in the marriage ceremony there is no prayer for the ratification of the act of the minister; nor yet in the ordination of deacons or priests or the consecration of bishops. And in the Holy Communion, before the administration, there is a prayer that we may eat His Flesh and drink His Blood; then in one of the prayers of the post-Communion we thank God that this has been done.

<small>On other grounds.</small>

The position is untenable on more grounds than one: Either the forgiveness pronounced by the priest is perfect and complete—is *ipso facto* ratified in heaven, as indeed the terms of the promise taken in the Confessionalist sense imply, and then the prayer that God would do that which has already been done, is mere surplusage; or it must have been incomplete, and then it would not have been actual forgiveness, but only possible forgiveness: then the literal sense of our Lord's words, for which the Confessionalists so stoutly contend, is negatived, for in these, taken literally, the pronouncing and the ratification are coincident. Again, if it is necessary that such ratification should be prayed for, forgiveness is not absolutely given, but only contingently; and contingent forgiveness is, in reality, only that declaration of God's will[1] and purpose

---

[1] Cyprian de Lapsis, p. 130, 'adeo non omne quod petitur in præjudicio petentis est, sed in arbitrio dantis.'

set forth in the Gospel, which I have maintained to be the essence of absolution. Nor could the ancient invocative, or the still more ancient precatory, form be viewed as a prayer for the ratification of any sacerdotal formula, inasmuch as no such sacerdotal formula existed. In fact, the ancient forms seem to settle beyond a doubt that any absolution pronounced by a priest from sins as against God, did not imply or convey the actual forgiveness thereof. It was nothing more than the setting before the sinner, in an impressive and direct form, the ambassadorial message of the possibility, or rather certainty, of being pardoned on repentance—the setting forth God's unlimited mercy as attainable by those for whom he was praying. And we may observe (though this rather belongs to another part of my subject), that as the invocative form of absolution from private sins was, from the date of its introduction into the Church up to the twelfth century, exclusively used, it exactly defines the nature and extent of the ministry which the Church practically believed to be committed to the priesthood in dealing with sin as against God. If the commission given by our Lord had been, in the early Church, conceived to convey actual forgiveness of such sins, it is clear that the formula would have been shaped to express forgiveness as a *fait accompli,* and not as a possibility or a promise wished for or invoked; in fact, when the modern notion of the judicial office of each individual priest had been developed and established, the formula was so shaped, and '*tribuat tibi Deus remissionem et absolutionem*' was changed into '*Ego te absolvo.*' Our Church, retaining (perhaps unfortunately) this indicative form in the visitation to the sick, has guarded, as we shall see presently, against the danger of being supposed to favour the erroneous doctrine, by putting into the mouth of the priest in the morning service a formula of absolution simply declaratory of God's general mercy, as well as by

[margin: Ancient forms. Indicates ancient notions of the power of the keys.]

retaining in the Communion Service the invocative form, and by the prayer after the absolution in the Visitation Service.

<small>What are the results of 'I absolve thee.'</small>

If, then, 'I absolve thee from thy sins' does not convey forgiveness or non-imputation of sins, what does it? This turns on the meaning and force of the word 'absolve.' To ascertain this we cannot do better than refer to some instance of the actual exercise of, and the results supposed to follow on, the power implied in this word. This we find in the absolution which follows the general confession in our morning and evening services—a full consideration of the nature of which I must defer to its proper place, when I consider more particularly the powers exercised in absolution (page 176); suffice now to remind my readers that this power is there exercised by an authoritative declaration of God's unlimited mercy as being within the reach of all who repent and believe. So far from the forgiveness of sins being viewed as having actually taken place by virtue of the priest's words, there follows a petition that God 'will grant us true repentance,' without which forgiveness does not take place. So here in the words 'I absolve thee' there must be an exercise of the same power in the same way, *mutatis mutandis*, that is, it must be a declaration of God's unlimited mercy, His promises of actual pardon, not actual pardon itself; with a special application of that promise to a man whose conscience is burdened with a sin so weighty that he fears that it is too heinous for God's mercy.[1] The result must be essentially the same; the conscience

---

[1] There seems to be an inherent flaw in absolution if taken as equivalent to forgiveness of sins. Why cannot a repentant sinner draw comfort from God's own promise? Is it not because his sins prevent him from believing in God's mercy? If so, how can absolution profit him without faith? What the repentant man wants, and what the priest has to create in him, is faith in Christ's promises; what the Confessionalists create is faith in the power of the priest. But faith in the priest's power cannot compensate for want of faith in Christ's promises.

is relieved by the declaration of God's ambassador that his sins are not what he fears they are, and he is set free from the bonds wherein his sin is keeping him back from God's promises; but the thing promised—the forgiveness or non-imputation of sins—is made the subject of a special prayer, as for something not yet accomplished. Thus, the absolution which sometimes follows this special Confession not reaching to the actual forgiveness of sin, the Confession itself is not part of any such ordinance as the Confessionalists pretend. The Confession, which they teach, is not recognised even in the place in which they are most confident of its recognition.

This leads us immediately to the distinction between pardon and absolution: between remission of sins by God and remission of sins by man. These are not identical, though in a particular combination so closely united that in other combinations the distinction has been lost sight of. The former is the remission of the guilt and punishment of the sin by God—its penal consequences. The latter, absolution, is the[1] loosing and unbinding, by the Gospel message of remission, the conscience from the fear and despair with which the notion of a sin being unpardonable weighs down the soul, and keeps it back from God and from amendment of life—the moral consequences of sin. When God is spoken of, pardon and absolution—pardon and peace—go together; as 'He pardoneth and absolveth all them that truly repent,' &c.; that 'they, whose consciences by sin are accused, by Thy merciful pardon may be absolved;' 'Grant unto thy faithful people pardon and peace,' and other expressions of the same sort. So the old invocative form runs, 'May God

Distinction between pardon and absolution.

---

[1] Augustin, Homil. 352, De Util. Pæn. 'Absolution freeing him from the bonds of the sins which he has committed.' Note on Tertullian, p. 394. St. Ambrose de Pænit, ii. 6. 'Confession (to God) looses the bonds of sins.' Note on Tertullian, p. 384.

give you remission and absolution.' Absolution comes from, or in, pardon: but that is a totally different proposition from the assertion that pardon comes by absolution, which is implied in the theory that when a priest absolves he pardons. The difference is recognised in the Visitation of the Sick, where absolution is spoken of as a power committed to the Church, but the forgiveness of sins as the prerogative of Jesus Christ: as well as in that prayer in the Visitation office, which, after absolution, speaks of all former sins as yet to be pardoned,[1] and we shall presently see that the forgiveness of sins is not recognised as identical with, or even an absolute result of, the other forms of absolution, which are by our Church put into the mouths of the priest.

We may further remark, that if absolution is restricted to the technical proclamation or declaration couched in a form of words used by a minister commissioned to use them, then the man to whom this form of words is used would be said to receive absolution (not forgiveness); and where no such form of words is used, but some one of the other methods applied, then the man would be said to receive, not absolution, but the benefit of absolution: that is, that realisation of God's mercy as applicable to his sins, which sets his soul free from the fears which are keeping him from God.

Conclusion as to the Visitation Office.

If, then, we review all that I have said on the form in the Visitation of the Sick, the conclusion we shall come to will be, that it lends no sanction to the theory of sacramental Confession as set out above (pages 19 and 91), for the Church evidently views the confession it speaks of as not necessarily private, or made with a view to absolution, and does not view absolution as conveying pardon.

---

[1] This is the view of Thomas Aquinas on this point—'it is not sufficient to say "may God give you remission or absolution"' (he is speaking of the old form), 'because by these words the priest does not signify that absolution' (he means forgiveness of sins) 'has taken place, but asks that it may take place.' See Usher, p. 115, note 97.

SPECIAL CASES NO PRECEDENT.

For, if pardon is not held to be conveyed, it follows as a matter of course that there is therein no recognition of sacramental Confession, that is, of Confession as part of a sacrament, wherein and whereby forgiveness of sins is *ipso facto*, or *ipso verbo*, conveyed to the soul. In fact the Confession here spoken of does not, as a general rule (that is except where absolution follows) exceed that natural method of relieving the conscience which I have termed Confidence, in order to distinguish it from Confession with a view to absolution; it need not be followed by absolution at all, if this method of relieving the conscience satisfies the patient: but where it does not so satisfy him, then what is technically called absolution is to be given: but this, as I have shown before, is not forgiveness of sins, and therefore there is herein no sacramental or auricular Confession, as the Confessionalists set it forth.

Before I proceed with this subject I wish to ask my readers to keep these essential differences in mind as bearing on the popular mistake of the Confessionalist theory being recognised in some cases, though not in all; in other words, the difference which is so commonly drawn, and that even by high authorities, between habitual and occasional Confession—admitting the one, while denying the other.

And even if it could be made out that the Church did enjoin the special Confession with a definite view to that absolution—which, as we have shown above, is not the case—and if the absolution thus pronounced was an absolute sentence of the sins being pardoned coincidently with the words being pronounced—which also, we have seen above, it is not—yet supposing such a case of sacramental Confession to be established, it would not furnish the least analogy for other cases in which all the essential particulars are different: that is, the cases, for which the

[Marginal notes: The Confession therein need not be more than confide. Bearing of these on the popular view. Furnish no precedent or analogy for Confession in]

every-day life. Confessionalists think, or pretend to think, they can find in it a sanction and a precedent. I need hardly point out the difference between the sick man lying *in extremis*, with some heavy sin on his conscience, with but little time, and possibly but little power, to realise mentally the promises contained in God's word, to which he has perhaps, for many years of his life closed his eyes and ears, and the young pious girl or boy in health and strength; or even a conscience-stricken sinner, with, humanly speaking, abundance of time, and abundance of power, to realise God's promises set forth in God's word, or proclaimed to him by the Church in our daily services and formal teaching. The circumstances which justify the use of the personal formula of absolution in the one do not exist in the other. And of course the precedent and the analogy for sacramental Confession in every-day life fail still more utterly, when the confession and absolution, permitted in the Visitation office, are viewed as being nothing more than we have shown them to be. The suggestion to a dying man that if his conscience is burdened, he should relieve his soul by confiding its secret to his spiritual pastor, or if he cannot thus find relief, that he may receive a personal and authoritative assurance from God's minister that his sins do not bind him as he

Differences between them. fears—is a totally different thing from telling, as these Confessionalists tell young girls and boys that their sins *may* be beyond the ordinary methods of God's mercy, that the only, or the best, and the surest way of finding pardon and being sure of it—the only safe preparation for the Holy Communion—is a disclosure to a priest of every sin they have ever committed—or fancy they may have committed—as an essential part and condition of a solemn sacramental conveyance of actual pardon, through words spoken by the priest, standing in the person of God and forgiving sins, with the same power as God Himself would exercise, if He were again to descend upon earth. It shows great trust in the slovenly acquiescence of the popular mind when one is urged as a precedent for, or as the same in kind with, the other.

Even if these points of difference did not forbid the arguing from the one to the other, no one would be justified in suggesting this special Confession, and applying absolution to the relief of the conscience in ordinary cases: for in the other case in which the Church recommends the having recourse to a spiritual person, a perfectly different method is prescribed; and this brings me to the consideration of the well-known paragraph at the end of the first exhortation to the Holy Communion, which has been a stronghold of the Confessionalist position, ever since the revival of the practice; not only as seemingly giving them a *locus standi*, but as perplexing those who would otherwise have opposed the system unreservedly.

<small>A different method prescribed in the exhortation to the Holy Communion.</small>

CHAPTER IX.

Exhortation to Holy Communion—Wrongly claimed by Confessionalists as decisive in their Favour—The best and indispensable Preparation set forth in the preceding Paragraphs—Case in which *Confidence* is recommended—State of the Man's Mind—What he is directed to do—The Remedy not Absolution, but the Ministry of God's Word conveying the *Benefit of Absolution*—Directions clear and precise, to the utter Exclusion of any Sacerdotal Action—Why and how different Interpretation has been admitted—Counterbalanced by the Fact of the Interpretation put upon it by general Usage.
Key of the Confessionalist Position—*Benefit* supposed to be meaningless—Absolution supposed to denote the Exercise of the Power of Forgiveness.
Exhortation may be read by a Minister—Confessionalist Argument on the use of this Term—Changes in the Terms in this Sentence—Other Alterations—Prayer Books of 1549 (1552), 1559—As revised in 1662—All these Alterations, Additions, Omissions, Point the same Way—Why '*Absolution*' was changed into 'Benefit of Absolution'—Attempt of Laud to introduce a Formula of Absolution—Meaning of the Term '*Ministry of Word*'—Language of Homily—Passage tells against the Confessionalists, and not for them—No Clergyman is here authorised to pronounce any Form of Absolution—Canon of 1603—Language of Homily.

This wrongly claimed by the Confessionalists.

IT is perfectly incredible that the Mediævalists should have been allowed, unchallenged, to claim this passage as sanctioning, and even enjoining, Sacramental Confession and Absolution. It is astonishing that so many sound men should have accepted their ruling, and felt themselves thereby precluded from opposing them in this point as decidedly and fully as they wished. Many, probably, will be, at first, startled by the position which I have taken up, and yet I have no doubt that it is the sound one: and I must request the patient attention of my readers while I lay before them the grounds on which I ask them to discard as untenable that which hitherto they may have received as undoubted. I am encouraged in this, by many persons having received with ready, and even grateful, acceptance a solution on which at first they looked with suspicion.

I must first again ask my readers' attention to the fact that, whatever be the method prescribed in the concluding paragraph, it is not represented as the best, or recommended as the one to be usually practised. *{Method the recommended not the first or best.}*

It must be observed, that in the exhortation to the Holy Communion, the clearest directions are given as to the method of preparation to be pursued in ordinary cases, where, if ever, it might be expected, auricular confession, if it were a general or the best rule, would have been prescribed or recommended. Nor is there any case in which this method is not enjoined. The way and means thereto is—self-examination—not examination by a priest: to examine our own lives and conversations by the rule of God's commandments—not by the questions put to us by a priest: to humbly confess ourselves to God—not to the priest: to resolve within ourselves to amend our lives—not to have our amendment dictated to us by a priest: penance finding no place at all, except so far as our offences are not only against God, but also against our neighbour:[1] then, we are to reconcile ourselves to him, and to make such reparation as is in our power. It is quite clear that there is not here one word of confession to man, except in the sense and on the occasion, which I contend is the reasonable interpretation of the passage in St. James. *{Exhortation to the Holy Communion only recognises personal discipline as the ordinary method.}*

Now, the man who thus contents himself with the method prescribed by his Church, is, according to the Confessionalists, utterly in the wrong; he ignores the *{Language of Confessionalists on this.}*

---

[1] The distinction between sins as against God and sins as against man (see p. 65), is clearly recognised here.

plain directions of his Church, the plain commands of the Bible, sets at naught Christ's commission to His clergy, Christ's provision for man's forgiveness, and is unable to feel that sure trust in God's mercy which is the result of the consciousness of true repentance combined with a lively faith.

Case in which it is recommended. But in some cases, a man of weak faith and timid conscience, though thus prepared—though these ordinary and necessary means have been all gone through—is unable to have that full trust in God's mercy, without which it is requisite that no man should come to the Holy Communion; and without which repentance, however sincere and fruitful, will not relieve a conscience from the chains in which his sin has bound it, inasmuch as, lacking faith, it does not bring with it any assurance of pardon: and this it is which troubles his mind; he cannot bring himself to believe that his sins can be pardoned, though he has repented of them; that God's mercy is greater than his provocation. In consequence of this inadequate view of God's mercy, he has not that full trust in it, without which his preparation, however complete in all its other parts, does not make him fit to approach the Lord's table. This is his grief. And what is he to do? To whom is

Directions in the exhortation. he to go? To a priest in the Confessionalist sense of the word, that is, a clergyman looked at in a sacerdotal character, and as invested with a sacerdotal power of forgiving sins—being as God on earth? No, but to a clergyman looked at as a 'minister of God's word.' And what is he to do when he comes to this minister? Is he to confess all his secret sins, small and great, or any particular sin, kneeling at his feet as an act of discipline and penitence, an act of religion, the same in kind as confession of sins to God? No—but to open his particular grief, namely, that though he has repented and confessed his sins to God, he is unable to have a full trust in God's mercy. And what is the minister to do? To suggest a special Confession? there is no such direction. To question him as to all the details and particulars of the sin, or of his life, or as to his having committed any of the sins which, through the weakness and wickedness of human nature, may possibly enter into human imagination? I think not—this would be to burden and defile a conscience, not relieve and cleanse it; to increase the distrust in God's promises, to aggravate the morbid state which makes the ordinary method of preparation incomplete for him. Such a practice seems to me to be founded on a misconception of our Lord's message to sinners, and the office of the messengers of that message. Or is the minister to pronounce a form of absolution, whereby the man, trusting in the priest's power, instead of Christ's invitation and the words of the Spirit, may be reassured? I think not—for then he would, as Cyprian says in reference to this very matter, fall under the sentence, 'Cursed be he that puts his trust in man.' Nor is it so directed. No—the minister is to use the ministry of God's word, the 'comfortable salve of God's word,' as the Homily calls it. He is to bring before him as applicable to his case, suitable passages of Scripture, such as the parable of the prodigal son, or the four sentences after the invocative absolution in the Communion service or the like declarations or illustrations of God's unlimited mercy in Christ. And what does the man receive at the minister's hands? Not a formal absolution —for there is not, as in all other cases of such absolution, a formula put into the priest's mouth—but the *benefit* of absolution: that benefit which, under the modern Mediæval system, absolution, in the technical sense of a declaratory, prescribed formula, professes to give: in one word, comfort; and the minister is to give him, if he needs it, ghostly counsel and advice, to the quieting of his conscience and the avoiding of that scruple and doubtfulness which, arising from a conscience disquieted by heinous sin, made him fear that he was out of the pale of God's mercy: this being, as I said before, the grief from which relief is sought. Not a word about the forgiveness of sins, or penance, or direction, in the technical sense of the word. Nothing can be clearer or more precise.

Nothing can be clearer or more precise—every word and every notion point the same way. The particular grief to be opened—the status of the person to be applied to—what is to be sought from him—how it is to be administered—all point the same way, to the utter exclusion of any sacerdotal action, any formula of absolution: clearly laying down the ministry of God's Holy Word to the repentant man, as the source whence he is to receive comfort.

How different interpretation has been admitted. But anyone may very reasonably ask, How is it that this passage has, especially of late, received a different interpretation? The answer is, that the word 'absolution' was taken as the emphatic word of the sentence, and allowed to give the clue to its meaning; thus at first sight it seems to imply that which the Confessionalists and Sacerdotalists contend for. In fact, for very many years the whole thing was so obsolete that few, unless writing professedly upon it, troubled themselves much about it; and even those who noticed it in their writings, rather as a matter of traditional polemics against the Romanists on one side, or the Puritans on the other, did not attach any very clear or definite meaning to it. The notion of sacramental or auricular Confession was so contrary to the theory and the practice even of men who thought most about religion, that they were content to let the passage pass with a very cursory and vague notice; not caring formally to guard or protest against a meaning being put upon it, contrary to what it received from general opinion and usage. Thus, when the Confessionalists were seeking about how to revive the ante- —as well as anti- — Reformation practice of auricular Confession, they were able by a dexterous and bold stroke to seize on this passage, and, appropriating it to themselves by the weight of their assumptions, to give it a force which the words, read carelessly, seem to convey, but which we have seen that every word really refutes and excludes.

But even if the fact of the acquiescence of the present generation in the Ritualistic interpretation is in its favour, then the fact of so many former generations having never regarded it in this light, or recognised absolution as an element in the preparation of the Holy Communion, is still, at the least, as strongly against it. Up to within the last few years, and previously to the modern Confessionalist revival, it has not, at least in the sense in which the Ritualists understand it, been generally acted upon as a practical part in the preparation for the Lord's Supper;[1] nor in the books of preparation was it usually mentioned or recommended. Self-examination is constantly insisted upon, recourse to a clergyman in exceptional cases occasionally, formal absolution very seldom, if ever. *Counterbalanced by general disuse.*

The key of the Confessionalists' position in this passage is, as I said above, the word 'absolution' (the word '*benefit*' being supposed to be simply otiose), denoting the employment of some formula or other as an exercise of a priestly power of privately forgiving sins, supposed to be conferred at ordination. *Assumed force of the word 'Absolution' true.*

Now, without stopping to enquire, or even to express an opinion, whether this power is so conferred or not, it is placed beyond a doubt that it is not supposed to be exercised in this passage by the fact that it is expressly stated that the ministration, whatever it is, *may* be exercised by *Exhortation need not be read by a priest.*

---

[1] For the Primitive Preparation for Holy Communion, see Note on Tertullian, p. 403.

the third order of the clergy to whom the priestly power (whatever it is) is not committed in ordination: for the exhortation may be read by a minister. Of course it is easy to say that the word minister here signifies priest. One Confessionalist writer, whether instinctively or dishonestly, uses, in explaining the passage, the word 'priest' instead of 'minister;' it shows that he felt the word priest was essential to his point, and so it is: in all other cases of absolution being pronounced the word 'priest' is used, even when 'minister' is used on both sides of it. It is true that a priest is a minister: but it is laid down and accepted by Confessionalists, if it suits their purpose, that when the exercise of sacerdotal powers conferred on the second order of the clergy is supposed to be meant, the word priest is always used.[1] I will not stop to enquire whether this is so or not, contenting myself with remarking, *en passant*, that assuming it to be true, it settles nothing as to what these conferred powers are, which is the real point to be presently considered. At present, I am willing to accept what they say about the word, as at the very least binding on those who propound it; and I will call my readers' attention to the decisive fact that the word 'priest' originally stood in the rubric in the first Book of King Edward VI. In 1559 'curate' is substituted for priest in the rubric prefixed to this exhortation—curate of course being either deacon or priest, as in the prayer for all bishops and curates, 'priest' still stand-

'Priest' changed to 'Minister.'

---

[1] My readers will detect the usual Confessionalist fallacy in their reasoning on this point. Instead of proving the point necessary to their position, they prove another, and then assume the other as proved. The point to be proved is that the Church regards the second order of ministers as invested with sacerdotal powers; and this might be done either by proving that the second order of ministers are so regarded, or that the functions entrusted to them are sacerdotal; instead of which they prove that certain powers are confined to the second order of the clergy, and draw from this first one conclusion, then the other; arguing in a sort of double circle that the functions are sacerdotal, because committed to priests, and that our own is a sacerdotal priesthood, because these sacerdotal functions are assigned to them.

ing in the rubric before the exhortation in the service. In 1662 the 'curate' was struck out, and the word 'minister' substituted, and not 'priest' restored, as might have been reasonably expected, out of the second rubric; while at the same revision, in the rubric for the absolution at morning and evening prayer, the word 'minister' was struck out, and the word 'priest' substituted. It is scarcely possible to have a more decisive proof of the force of the word 'minister' in this exhortation than the combined light thrown on it by these two alterations.

But we have not yet done with alterations. There were several such made in the passage mostly in (1552) 1559, probably to guard against the very practice which the Confessionalists try to fasten on it. Every expression in favour of the Mediævalist system of confession, which clung like ivy to a tree after its roots had been cut, was struck out. I give the passage as it stood, in the Prayer Book of 1549: 'And if there be any of you whose conscience is troubled and grieved in anything, lacking comfort or counsel, let him come to me, or to some other discreet or learned priest, taught in the law of God, and confess and open his sin and grief secretly, that he may receive such ghostly counsel, advice, and comfort, that his conscience may be relieved, and that of us (as of the ministers of God and of the Church), he may receive comfort and absolution, to the satisfaction of his mind, and avoiding of all scruple and doubtfulness. Requiring such as shall be satisfied with a general Confession not to be offended with them, that do use to their further satisfying, the auricular and secret confession to the priest: nor those also which think it needful and convenient for the quiet of their own consciences particularly to open

Other changes.

their sins to the priest, to be offended with them that are satisfied with their humble confession to God, and a general confession to the Church.'

Compare this with that of (1552) 1559: 'And because it is requisite that no man should come to the Holy Communion but with a full trust in God's mercy, and with a quiet conscience: therefore, if there be any of you, who by this means cannot quiet his own conscience herein, but requireth further comfort or counsel, let him come to me, or to some other discreet and learned minister of God's word, and open his grief; that by the ministry of God's holy word, he may receive comfort and the benefit of absolution, together with ghostly counsel and advice, to the quieting of his conscience, and avoiding of all scruple and doubtfulness.'

Comparison of the two forms. When we compare the old form with the later one, we find alterations—omissions—additions; all pointing the same way. It will be seen at a glance that in the old one, the grief is not specified; it is any grief, any trouble of conscience; in the present form it is the definite grief of not having a full trust in God's mercy, and the disturbance of conscience consequent thereon. In the old form the person to be applied to is a **priest**, now it is a **minister of God's Word**; there he is to confess his sins; here to open a particular grief above defined; there he is to do it **secretly**, here this injunction is omitted—there he is to seek the relief by the formal sentence of the minister of God and the Church, as given in the rubric in the Visitation service in Edward VI.'s first book, '*and the same form of absolution shall be used in all private Confession;*' here from the minister of God's Word, by the **ministry of that Word**; there he is to receive absolution, here the benefit of absolution. There we find added a direct recognition of auricular confession, and an exhortation not to speak against it; here this is omitted; in short the only point in which the old form, which has been thus altered, differs from the revived Mediævalistic theory, is that Confession is not definitely spoken of as a discipline as in the modern school. It need not be said that the fact of these alterations has a direct bearing on the meaning of the passage, and would make the interpretation I have suggested almost unavoidable, even were the terms of the change in themselves less express and definite.

Turning now to the revision of 1662—the word 'curate' in the rubric, 1559 (formerly, 1549, 'priest'), is altered to 'minister,' and the word 'comfort' before 'the benefit of absolution is' struck out, for the simple reason, that the benefit of absolution being comfort, it is tautology to keep both words, unless by the 'benefit of absolution' was meant technical absolution, and not the results held to follow on it; so that the striking out of 'comfort and' indirectly throws light on the meaning of 'benefit of absolution.'

I do not think that anyone who really looks into the subject will be inclined to accept the suggestion that the phrase 'benefit of absolution' is simply a periphrasis for 'absolution;' if so, why was it altered? One can understand a person writing originally, 'benefit of absolution' and then shortening it into 'absolution,' but we cannot understand a person altering 'absolution' into 'benefit of absolution' without some definite reason. Why—contrary to the rule discernible in the other alterations—is the longer form preferred to the shorter? The clue to the change is, I think, found in the fact that in every alteration some element of auricular confession and sacramental absolution is excluded. The reason for the

'Benefit of absolution.'

Why 'absolution' was altered into 'the benefit of absolution.'

alteration of 'absolution' into 'the benefit of absolution' is clear enough, when we consider that the new method prescribed—the ministry of God's Word, not the ministry of absolution—actually and definitely excludes absolution in its technical sense—especially when contrasted with the formal act of priestly power, prescribed by the Visitation Office rubric of 1549. When this formula was abrogated, the alteration became absolutely necessary; while it was no less necessary to mark that the result of this ministry of God's Word was the same as that supposed formerly to result from absolution; that they who were comforted by the ministry of God's Word receive the benefit which absolution had been supposed to bring. The method is clearly marked out—is it absolution? No. The result is clearly marked out—is it the same? Yes.[1] I would ask, in what other words or phrase could this difference of method and identity of result have been equally well expressed?[2] Besides which it is remarkable

---

[1] The following anecdote illustrates the benefit received by the ministry of God's Word, as identical with that held to be given by absolution. When Bishop Butler was on his death-bed he called for his chaplain and said, 'Though I have endeavoured to avoid sin, and to please God to the uttermost of my power, yet, from the consciousness of perpetual infirmities, I am afraid to die.' 'My lord,' said the chaplain, 'you have forgotten that Jesus Christ is a Saviour.' 'True,' was the answer, 'but how shall I know that He is a Saviour to me?' 'My lord, it is written, "him that cometh to me will I in no wise cast out."' 'True,' said the Bishop; 'and I am surprised that though I have read that Scripture a thousand times, I never felt its virtue till this moment, and now I die happy.'

[2] The *non-otiose* use of the term benefit to express, not the thing itself viewed in its beneficial aspect, but the beneficial effects attached to the thing, is illustrated by the obsolete legal term, *benefit of clergy*; that is, the benefit enjoyed by being clerks; and we find it also in a passage in 'Macbeth,' act v. sc. 1: *A great perturbation of nature, to receive at once the benefit of sleep and do the effects of watching.* And Wheatley, ch. xi. 5, p. 437, recognises this interpretation of the passage, though I was not aware of this till it has impressed itself on my own mind as the only one consistent with the change of 'absolution' into 'benefit of absolution' taken in connection with the other coincident changes to which I have called the reader's attention. Usher also, p. 110, says: 'That the Church might pray for them, and impart the benefit of absolution unto them.' The Confessionalists pretend that the phrase is taken from an obscure Council in Spain, whence Bonner introduced it into his writings;

that Laud, conscious of the bearing of this passage against the Mediævalism which he was trying to re-introduce, proposed to get rid of it by adding after 'absolution' 'according to the form prescribed in the Visitation service;' an attempt in which it need hardly be added he failed. He evidently wished to restore the formula prescribed in Edward VI.'s first book to be used in all cases of private confession. The Confessionalists have to explain why this was omitted, if, as they say, the practice was intended to continue.

The Confessionalists sometimes try to interpret 'the ministry of the Word' as meaning the ministry mentioned in the Word; that is, the priestly office.[1] It may

but my readers will judge whether the Reformers were likely to adopt a phrase from Bonner, except to use it in a sense different from that in which he used it. He probably meant to call attention to the notion that there was a definite benefit attributed in the Romish system to absolution—they may have taken the words from him to indicate that the same benefit resulted from the ministry of God's Word as from formal absolution.

[1] The terms in which this expression is treated of by the Confessionalists, is a remarkable instance of the way in which they try to throw dust into their readers' eyes. '*It may be useful to observe that the Ministry of God's Word does not mean the reading of exhortations from Scripture, but the exercise of the Ministerial Office, which, among other designations, is termed the Ministry of the Word.*' Acts vi. 4. (Gray's Confession.) 'May be useful'!! as if it were a trifle scarcely worth notice. It would have been a good deal more true if it had been said, '*It is absolutely necessary to our interpretation, that the words Ministry of God's Word shall not be taken to mean, &c.*' Of course 'the ministry of the word' in the Acts cannot mean the reading of the New Testament Scriptures—any more than it can mean the ministerial office mentioned therein—for these Scriptures were not then in existence; but it may, or rather does, mean the Ministry of the Word which God spake through Christ, which was preached by the Apostles, and afterwards embodied in the New Testament. From the Confessionalist interpretation it would follow that prayer was no part of the Apostolic Office. Another writer boldly asserts it is a technical term used in Scripture to express the ministerial office. He must have been hard put to it to get rid of its natural and obvious sense, when he assumes that a term used only once can be a technical term. A technical term is a word in common use in some particular art or science. But even if it were what they say it is, there would be no proof that this Ministerial Office was the sacerdotal power claimed by this school. Why should it not be used to denote the ministration of the word and sacraments (see page 171)? It is observable that in the document lately put forth in the 'Times' the 'ministry' of the Sacraments is spoken of. Again, the clergyman is to be consulted as the

be true that when the word is used absolutely, or in connection with words implying persons or institutions, it signifies an office, performed in the service of those persons or institutions, as when St. Paul speaks of himself as put into the ministry; or of the ministry of the saints. But in conjunction with other words—and I think it is not too much to say that this is the case with all words which are capable of such an interpretation—it means the ministering that which is signified by the words joined to it, as where the Apostles gave themselves to the ministry of the Word and to prayer; so here it means that particular part of that clerical office. If the meaning contended for by the Ritualists was the one intended by the framers of the passage, there can be no reason why the words 'of us as the ministers of God and the Church' should have been struck out, only to substitute the phrase 'ministry of God's Word,' used in a very unusual sense. The Homily of Repentance, Part II., indicates, I think, the sense in which our Church intends it to be used, '*I do not say but that if any do feel themselves troubled in conscience they may repair to their learned curate or pastor, or to some other godly man, and show the trouble and doubt of their conscience to him, that they may receive at their hands the comfortable salve of God's Word.*' [1]

Meaning of 'Ministry of God's Word.'

The ministering God's Word or Gospel.

Results of the analysis of this passage in the Exhortation.

I am inclined to hope and to think, that anyone who has followed me through my analysis and examination of this passage, so triumphantly pressed by the Confessionalists as setting the matter beyond doubt, will see that it does indeed set it beyond doubt, but exactly in a different way to what has been assumed. I do not, indeed, suppose that the Confessionalist school will admit that I am right. It is seldom that those who have taken a decided view of

Minister of God's Word, and not as priest: and if the 'Minister of God's Word' is merely a periphrasis for 'priest,' why is the long phrase substituted for the single word?

[1] Homilies, p. 489.

any subject from an offhand superficial glance, without condescending either to test it or support it by analysis and argument, will listen to anything advanced on the other side; but my object is to show those whom the Confessionalists dazzle by flourishing this weapon in their face, that they may easily wrest it out of their hand, and inflict a deadly blow on their assailants. In other words, this passage, so far from obliging them to bow their heads in submission to the sacerdotal yoke, in reality frees them from it. So far is the Church of England from prescribing, or even recommending, in this passage sacramental Confession to those who stand in need of comfort, that a different method, simply excluding it, is the one suggested; or, if they like it, prescribed.[1]

It excludes Sacramental Confession.

Further, it will be remembered that since the Confessionalists urge this passage, interpreted in their sense, as decisive in prescribing a positive rule for dealing with certain cases, it may fairly be urged against them that they cannot in common honesty, logical or moral, refuse to accept the contrary conclusion as a positive rule, unless they can dispute or disprove what has been said above. They cannot say, 'All this may be very true, but what we advocate may be proved in another way;' they must abide by the force which they themselves have given to the passage; if it is not for them, it is directly and conclusively against them. So that if there be any reality in the point urged so warmly by the Confessionalists, that with this passage so directly, as they say, sanctioning

If so, no clergyman can teach such Confession as a

---

[1] This formal direction for the ministry of God's word, as the method to be used in cases of despair of God's mercy, seems to have been foreshadowed in Edward VI.'s injunctions, '*That the damnable vice of despair may be clearly taken away, and firm belief and steadfast hope surely conceived of all their parishioners, being in any danger, they (the curates) shall learn and have always in readiness such comfortable places and sentences of scripture as do set forth the mercy, benefits, and goodness of Almighty God, towards all penitent and believing persons.*' See Cardwell's Doc. Ann. i. 219.

preparation for the Holy Communion.

private confession and absolution, no clergyman can consistently with his duty to the Church and his ordination vows, refuse to practise their system, or decline to pronounce a form of absolution; they must, unless they wish to stultify themselves, admit that if a directly different method, excluding absolution, is enjoined in this paragraph, they cannot teach, or offer, or use their system consistently with their duty as ministers of the Church of England. The rule that they have framed to guide public opinion in its judgment of the anti-Confessionalists, must be applied by public opinion in its judgment on themselves, so far as it accepts the view of the paragraph, which I have put forth, as resting on the strongest foundations of logic and common sense. And further,

Nor in any analogous case.

it may suggest in the way of analogy, confirmed by the abrogation of the formerly ordained formula for any cases of private confession, that, in any analogous case which may occasionally arise of a troubled mind disclosing its difficulties to a pastor, the pastor must minister comfort, not by any formal exercise of sacerdotal power, but by the ministry of God's word. In saying this, however, we must not lose sight of the fact, that this is the only case in which the Church suggests to persons in health that they should have recourse even to confidential communications with a clergyman. These may be natural, and in themselves occasionally useful, but there is no rule prescribed, nor even advice given by our Church in their favour, unless it be by implication in the Canon to which I now turn—I say by implication, because the case contemplated by the Canon may be nothing more than what is suggested in the passage of the Exhortation, or in the Visitation of the Sick, when the special confession is not followed by absolution, and therefore is not technical Confession.

This allegation in favour of Confession is found by

them in one (113) of the Canons of 1603,[1] '*If any man confess his secret and hidden sins to the minister for the unburdening of his conscience, and to receive spiritual consolation and ease of mind from him, we do not in any way bind,*' &c. &c. On this, it may be observed, the Canons furnish but a very doubtful authority for establishing the actual consent of the Church to the revival of anything which has become practically obsolete; in the 72nd Canon, for instance, ministers are not allowed *without licence to attempt, upon any pretence whatsoever, either of possession or obsession, by fasting and prayer, to cast out any devil or devils.* Can it be argued from this, that if anyone attempted to revive this truly Mediæval practice, the above Canon would justify him in applying for a licence for it, and maintaining that he was only doing what the Church of England sanctioned? {Alleged canon of 1603.}

Further, it is to be remarked that the Confession spoken of is not necessarily, nor by the terms used, Confession in the technical sense of the word, but the reverse; for the confession is spoken of as being made for the unburdening of the conscience, that is, Confidence; which is distinguished from Confession, which is with a view to forgiveness of sins by absolution. And it is to be made to a minister, and not to a priest. If the Confession of the Confessionalists was intended, why was it not spoken of as made to a 'priest, to receive absolution from him?' And the force of this observation is much increased when we remember that at the time these Canons were composed, Mediæval confession had all but, if not wholly, passed away, and therefore the Canon must be taken as indicating the practice of recourse to a priest, not for absolution but for counsel. {Not to the point.}

[1] I give the date of the Canons, because the Mediævalists are fond of quoting the Canons of 1640, under the term of Canons, as if they were binding on the Church; they were simply a manœuvre of Laud's, in which he was checkmated by the refusal of Parliament to allow them.

Another point advanced is a passage in the Homilies,[1] which is thus quoted by the Confessionalists. '*Absolution hath the promise of forgiveness of sin.*' But the passage reads very differently with the context; instead of the unconditional proposition, 'Absolution hath the promise,' &c., my readers will see it is '*Although* absolution hath the promise;' so that the categorical form becomes a conditional one, and the word 'hath' is used in a subjunctive force. It is clear that the writer is looking at absolution as it existed in the mediæval reconciliation by the imposition of hands, which is retained in the Romish system by the holding the hand over the penitent; and he means to say that even supposing the rite to have one of the requisites of a sacrament—the spiritual grace conveyed—it lacks the other, a visible ordained sign: the imposition of hands was not ordained. This is no straining of the passage to escape its legitimate meaning, but is forced upon us by what is said ten lines lower down, where it is distinctly asserted that the promise of remission of sin is given to no other ordinance save Holy Baptism and the Supper of the Lord. And in the end of the passage, Visitation of the Sick, of course including the absolution contained therein, is classed among those ordinances which make not for the forgiveness of sins—but for the instruction, comfort, and edification of the whole Church; nor must we lose sight of the passages in the second homily on Repentance,[2] in which two sorts of Confession are mentioned; one, Confession to God, another, the acknowledgment of offences against a brother Christian; while shortly afterwards auricular Confession is spoken of almost contemptuously.

---

[1] 'Homily on Common Prayer and Sacraments,' p. 324, Oxford edition, 1832.
[2] Page 487, Oxford edition, 1832.

CHAPTER X.

Ground of the Discussion shifted to private Absolution—Confessionalist Argument from Ordination Formula—Question at Issue—Relation between our Lord's Words in St. John, and the Ordination Formula—Analysis of the Formula—Relation of the third Paragraph to the second—Twofold Power conferred—These were held in Early Church to be exercised by the Dispensation of the Word and Sacraments, and in our own—Not by any Sacerdotal Power or Sentence—This Method exhausts our Lord's Commission as far as private Sins are concerned—No private Power of repelling from the Holy Communion contemplated in the Exhortation to the Holy Communion—Language of our Church on this Point—'Discipline of Church' in the Promise made by the Candidate for Ordination—How limited—These Limitations confine the Exercise of any Power to notorious Sins—Directions before the Communion Office—Summary of the Argument Practice of our Church—Does not recognise actual Forgiveness as the Result of the Power in any of the Places where it is exercised—Reason and reasonableness of this—Possible Translation of the Formula does not affect this View—What the Power is not—Not judicial—Not operative or effective—Not a Grant of Pardon—Not Supernatural—Not Sacramental—Private Confession to a Priest not necessary to the Exercise thereof—Special Confession in Visitation Office not necessarily Private—Not necessary as giving the Priest Information on the Case—Knowledge of a Man's Sins not recognised as necessary to the telling him he can be saved—Nor to determine the Amount of Penance or Penitence.

WE have hitherto been considering private Confession in its relation, indeed, to Absolution, and as part of an assumed sacramental ordinance, but still, rather in respect to the pleas and proofs which are adduced directly and independently in its favour. We must now rather shift our ground, and follow the Confessionalists in their attempts to prove the other part in the sacramental ordinance—the forgiveness of sins by private absolution. It is clear that if this part of the sacramental ordinance cannot be established, and there is no such sacramental ordinance, then, of course, all arguments in favour of private confession as part thereof, fall to the ground as baseless. From private confession, then, we turn to private absolution, as a grant of actual forgiveness of sin.

Argument from the ordination formula.

The argument on which the Confessionalists lay most stress—amounting sometimes to an arrogant defiance, which betrays to those who have really studied the question that these men know next to nothing about it—is this; that Christ gave to the Apostles this power of remitting sins, and that the clergy of the Church of England are invested with this power at their ordination: and that therefore those who speak against, or refuse, sacramental Confession, speak against the express words of the Bible, and refuse God's ordinance, while the clergy are guilty of the additional sin of ignoring their ordination vows if they deny and disown the powers which have been thus solemnly conferred on them. This proposition stated with an oracular confidence, which challenges denial as impossible, seems at first sight solid enough: and yet at the first touch of logic it shakes to its very foundations: for

Real issue. its whole force is derived from a misstatement of the question. It is not what they assume it to be, whether our Lord invested his Church with any power of remitting sins, nor yet whether our Church confers an especial authority on the second order of our clergy—the establishing of these points does not settle the matter in the off-hand way they think. The question is, whether the power conveyed by our Lord's words, and by our own Church in the form of ordination, is *the* power they contend for; or, to put it in other words, whether the mode in which they exercise their office is the way intended by our Lord when He spoke these words, or by the Church when these words are used in the formula of ordination. My readers will immediately see the fallacy on which their argument is constructed; it is technically called *ignoratio elenchi*, the

What they ought to proving one point when they ought to have proved another. They ought to have proved that the power intended by our Lord, and conferred by our Church, is the forgiveness of sins by means of a form of absolution privately pronounced by the priest, consequent on, and conditioned by, a private confession of sins to that priest. It does not serve their purpose to prove the existence of some power of remission of sins; they ought to have shown that their particular exercise hereof was recognised in the early Church, or contemplated by our own. have proved. The extent of what they do prove.

The two questions—the power conveyed in our Lord's words, and the authority intended to be conferred on our clergy by the Church—so overlap one another that a separate consideration of them is somewhat difficult: though at the same time it is necessary to separate them as far as practicable, especially as each throws light reciprocally on the other. If we have evidence of the true force of the original words, we may argue this to be the sense in which our Church uses them; or, if we find in our services proof of the sense in which our Church uses them, that is to us, at least so far as our Church is concerned, an argument as to the meaning of the original: for I suppose that the Confessionalists would be willing to accept the proposition, that our Church uses the words in the same sense and with the same results, as were intended when they were originally spoken: and that those clergy of the Church of England who are ordained to their office by this formula receive the same powers as those who were ordained in the early Church—with the exception, of course, of any miraculous gifts which might have been attached thereto in those ages: the same powers and no more: so that whatever powers were attached to the clerical office in later ages do not derive any validity or sanction from our Lord's commission, as expressed in the well-known words of St. John. We will first examine the force of the ordination formula, in itself, and as evidenced by the way in which our Church in our services contemplates the exercise of the power conveyed thereby. Our Lord's words and the ordination formula.

When we examine this closely we see that there are three distinct parts.

Three parts of the ordination formula.

First—the office is conferred by the gift of the Holy Spirit: 'Receive the Holy Ghost for the office and work of a priest in the Church of God, committed to thee by the imposition of our hands.'

Secondly—the power requisite for the execution of that office—the authority to exercise the ministry of the forgiveness of sins—is given in words nearly, though not exactly, equivalent to those in which our Lord originally gave that power, whatever it was, to his disciples: 'Whose sins thou dost forgive (remit) they are forgiven (remitted); whose sins thou dost retain they are retained.' I say *nearly* equivalent, because the notion of forgiveness is slightly different from that of remission, and the latter is the more accurate translation of the original term, especially in relation to the word 'retain;' and it is clear that our Church's words must be interpreted as nearly as possible in exact accordance with the original.

Thirdly—an exhortation to be faithful in the execution of that office, and exercise of that ministry; the particulars being specified in which the office is to be executed, and the powers exercised: 'Be thou a faithful dispenser of the word of God, and of His holy sacraments.'

Bearing of the third paragraph.

The view here taken, that the third paragraph does not confer the power of dispensing the Word and Sacraments, as something distinct from the power of remitting or retaining sins conferred in the second paragraph, is clear from the views, the language, the usages of the primitive Church as well as our own. In the commission of the keys, there are two separate parts and powers—one the remission of sins, the other the retention thereof.

Remitting power: how recognised in early

As to the first, the remission of sins by the Word and Sacraments was distinctly recognised by the Early Church among the ways (see page 166) in which the powers conveyed by our Lord's words were exercised;[1] this same power was also held to be exercised in the remission of ecclesiastical pains and penalties, signified by the imposition of hands—a method which cannot enter into the present question—and by intercessory prayer, which is founded on, and is the application of the general promises to prayer in God's word, and does not depend on any private sacerdotal power enjoyed by him who utters it, or any sentence pronounced by him. At all events, it is not the absolute granting of pardon, but the asking that pardon may be granted. So that, according to the view of the ancient Church, the dispensation of the Word and Sacraments exhausts the positive or remitting power conferred by the ordination formula, as far as it deals with sins other than those against the Church, or is not exercised by intercessory prayer. Church by dispensation of word and sacraments.

And those who admit or hold that our Church in such matters must, and does, follow the primitive Church, must also admit that no power of remitting sins is given in our ordination formula save the dispensation of the Word and Sacraments, whereby remission of sins is ministered—in the first by presenting to nations, or congregations, or individuals, being penitent, either publicly or privately, the promises of forgiveness—actual offers, and certain promises—to all who repent and believe. In the other by administering Baptism, whereby the promises of forgiveness are visibly signed and sealed to those who, professing their repentant belief in Christ, desire to be accepted into the faith and fellowship of Christ; or admitting to the Lord's Supper those who desire to be restored thereto; and this is manifestly a different thing from a priest's granting forgiveness of sins by a form of words expressive of an act of sacerdotal power. So in our own.

The same holds good, too, of the power of retaining; Retaining power.

---

[1] Usher, 109.

for this is exercised in no other way than by refusal of the sacraments to, or withholding the promises of God's mercy from, impenitent nations or individual sinners; and this faithful dispensation of the word and sacraments implies the withholding them from the impenitent, as well as administering them to the repentant. In the early Church this power of retaining sins was also exercised in public discipline by the formal exclusion of notorious offenders from the Holy Communion and Church fellowship; and in our own Church this faithful dispensation of the sacraments—this exclusion from the Holy Communion—the candidate for orders promises to administer as the Church, with the sanction of the State, shall direct. This gives no power of retaining sins privately, inasmuch as it is limited to certain cases of the open repulsion of notorious offenders until public satisfaction has been made, when they are to be admitted to the Holy Communion without any definite sentence of the priest (see page 127). Thus the dispensation of the word and sacraments exhausts the power both of retaining and remitting sins of individuals, otherwise than by intercessory prayer.

Also by faithful dispensation of word and sacraments.

We may observe, too, that in the exhortation to the Holy Communion the minister has no authority to repel, nor is he contemplated as repelling, the repentant or doubting person with whom he has to deal; his office is to explain and solve his grief; to relieve his conscience from the doubt of God's mercy, so that he may come to the Holy Table without any scruple or doubtfulness. He is not to repel him—that is, to exercise any power of retaining his sin by excluding him from the Holy Table—but to do his utmost to persuade him to come. So in the Visitation office, the priest has no power to refuse absolution by reason of any sins confessed, or for any cause save lack of earnestness (to exclude mere formalism), and humility (to exclude the notion of a man having a right to it).

When we now turn to the language of our own Church we shall find that in the other passages, in which the particulars of the priest's office are given, there is no mention of anything besides the administration of the word and sacraments, so that in all such passages according to the view of the Confessionalists, the most important and essential part of the priestly office and power is wholly omitted. {None other spoken of by our Church in other parts of the Prayer Book.}

Thus, in the passage immediately after the ordination formula, which we will call the second ordination formula, giving episcopal and ecclesiastical authority to do what is necessary for the due execution of the priestly office by the due exercise of the priestly power, we find '*take thou authority to preach the word of God, and to minister the holy sacraments.*' Why no mention of absolution in the sense which the Confessionalists put upon it, namely, the actual forgiveness of sins? The omission is accounted for, if we suppose our Church to mean by absolution that authoritative holding forth of God's promises, so as to free or loose the repentant conscience from the chains of sin, which falls under the dispensation of the Word. So again in the prayer for the Church Militant, 'that they may set forth Thy true and lively word, and duly administer Thy holy sacraments;' and in the Articles, preaching of the word of God, and the due ministration of the sacraments are alone mentioned, to the exclusion of any other method of exercising the priestly office as conferred in our Lord's original commission.

In answer to this last point, it may be said that in the questions put to the candidate previous to his ordination, he is called upon to promise that he will '*minister the doctrine and sacraments and discipline of Christ as the Lord hath commanded, and as this Church and realm hath received the same according to the commandments of God.*' But it must be observed, first, that the mention here of the discipline of Christ makes the omission of any definite {Mention of discipline of Church in preliminary promise.}

mention of it in the formula, as well as in the other passages in which the particulars of the clerical office are specified, still more remarkable. But not so, if we take it to signify, not what the Confessionalists contend for—the exercise of a power conferred on every individual priest of dealing out pardon to private sins in his personal and sacerdotal capacity, after the confession thereof privately to himself—but the administration in the congregation of an ecclesiastical system: answering somewhat to the public discipline of the primitive Church, by excluding offenders from Church privileges, especially from the Holy Communion: this would fall under the faithful dispensation of the sacraments; a system not to be regarded as a divine ordinance for the forgiveness of sins against God, but a Canonical enactment or arrangement, instituted in the Church, for the punishment of offenders against itself, and exercised with more or less publicity by those who *ex officio* held the chief place in the several congregations; and this is not what our Confessionalists contend for.

Analogous to ecclesiastical tenures.

Again, the term 'the discipline of Christ,' in the preliminary promise, cannot be reasonably supposed to represent the exercise of any separate power conferred in the second clause of the formula, other than the dispensation of the word and sacraments: for then it would have occupied the same place in the promise which, on the Confessionalist theory, it does in the formula. It would have run 'minister the discipline, and doctrine, and sacraments of Christ,' corresponding to the paramount importance which the Confessionalists attach to it: nor would it have been omitted in the other passages in which these particulars of the priestly ministrations are mentioned.

Express the retention of sins not the absolution.

Again, what the Confessionalists contend for is the power to forgive sins, while the words 'the discipline of Christ,' as far as they bear on the subject at all, express rather the retention of sins.

Again, the application of this discipline—this retention of sins, by exclusion from the ministrations of the Church—is not entrusted to the priest to be exercised privately after confession, as a punishment for secret sins; but he is bound by the express words of his promise before his ordination, and by the corresponding word 'faithful' in the ordination formula, to minister it as the Church has accepted and the national law has recognised it—'as this Church and realm have received the same.' And when we come to look into the cases in which the Church has accepted and allowed this discipline, we shall find that it is to be exercised, as it was exercised in the earliest days of the Church: not in private, but in public; not after private confession of secret sins, but on the notoriousness of certain sins or states of sin.[1] Thus, in the rubrical directions before the Communion, the first case is that of a notorious evil-doer who has scandalised the congregation: the curate having knowledge of this scandal is to advertise him not to come to the Holy Table; nor does his admission to the Communion depend on the private judgment of the curate, or on that full knowledge of the facts of the case which private confession might be supposed to give; he is not to be admitted to the Holy Table till he hath openly (not privately) declared himself to have repented to the satisfaction of the congregation. The other case, where the curate perceiveth malice and hatred to reign between two persons, puts the matter in exactly a similar point of view. There is no mention here of private confession as a ground of exclusion from the Communion: nor is he to require any private confession of sins before he administers the Holy Communion—he must ascertain either that they are reconciled or willing to be reconciled. And, again, in the Canons [2] the discipline of the Church requires that in certain cases—not to be ascer-

No private exercise of retaining power.

Directions before the Communion Office.

---

[1] Cardwell's 'Synod,' i. 221.   [2] Canon 27.

tained by private confession, but matters more or less of notoriety—the curate is not to administer the Holy Communion to the offenders: nor are they to be admitted until they shall first acknowledge their repentance to the minister, not by himself or by private confession, but before the churchwardens, and in writing, if they can write.

<small>No private absolution or Confession here.</small>

It is clear that in all these cases the ministry of discipline has nothing to do with the hearing of private confession or private absolution: so that if anyone should insist that the power contemplated in the second clause of the ordination formula is the ministration of the discipline spoken of in the preliminary promise, it is clear that he must be held to admit further, that private confession and private absolution is no part of that power; for the discipline sanctioned by the Church and realm, which they thus identify with this power, is to be exercised only in cases of sins notorious, not secret—perceived, not confessed. If there is no exclusion from Church privileges, except in cases where confession is not needed, the power conferred by the second clause of the ordination formula cannot, if identical with the discipline mentioned in the promise, be held to confer any power for cases of admission to Church privileges depending on private confession of the sin and private absolution.

<small>Argument deducible thence.</small>

<small>Summary of what has been said.</small>

We may sum up what has been said as follows:—Two powers are conferred in the ordination formula, viz.: '*Whosesoever sins thou dost forgive they are forgiven, and whosesoever sins thou dost retain they are retained.*' The former power is exercised by the ministration of the word and sacraments—the authoritative preaching of the remission of sins, and the authoritative administration of baptism for the remission of sins, and admission to the Holy Communion,[1] in which there is a remembrance of

---

[1] I confess that to my mind there is great doubt whether remission of sins is actually conveyed in the Lord's Supper; it may indeed be considered as a

that death and passion of Christ whereby our sins are remitted, and which is thus an act of faith in that remission, and therefore of acceptance of it—a renewal of our Baptism. The second power would be exercised by *faithfully* dispensing the word and sacraments—that is, the not setting before persons openly disbelievers, or impenitent, the promises of God's word, as applicable to their case; nor administering to such persons, at least until they are repentant, the sacraments of baptism and the Lord's Supper; and this refusal, as far at least as the notion of discipline is concerned, he who receives his ordination from our Church has promised to exercise only as the Church directs, and not according to his own fancies or theories—that is, only in cases which exclude private confession. It will be seen in a moment how foreign and fatal this is to the theory which the Confessionalists maintain, and to the practice they adopt.

And, when we come to look at the power which the Church practically believes to be exercised by virtue of the ordination formula, we find that in no case does our Church recognise the power of forgiving the sins of this or that person, in the sense of the word in which the Confession-

Practical exercise of the power conferred at ordination.

---

renewed act of profession of faith in Christ's death, and therefore may be said to convey remission of sins just as any other act of faith may: or the Presence of Christ in our souls may be taken as a proof that our sins are remitted; but still, in either case, this is distinct from the actual remission of sins itself. Remission of sins is not mentioned in the address to the communicants at the time of the Holy Communion, nor yet is it specified in the Articles or Catechism, while, both in the Articles and in the Services remission of sins is distinctly attached to Baptism on the authority of the Apostolic words of Scripture 'repent and be baptised for the remission of sins,' and in the prayer in the post-Communion Service there is a distinct petition for the remission of sins. This notion probably was attached to the Holy Communion, in consequence of the admission to this Holy Ordinance being the result, and in some sort the witness, of the condonation of sins against the Church. It is not attached in Scripture to the Holy Communion, which is stated to be the Communion of the Body and Blood of Christ, the remembrance of Him, and the showing forth the Lord's death till he come. I think the point deserves more accurate consideration than perhaps it has hitherto had.

alists use it: or conceive that the actual forgiveness of sins of this or that person depends on, or is effected by, the priest's pronouncing a form of absolution; or can be regarded as a *fait accompli* when such a form has been pronounced. It is not so in the absolution in Morning or Evening Service, for this is simply the declaration of God's general promise of mercy, without any application even to those who are present; it is not *to you who are there present*, but to *all;* and it is made to depend upon a repentance which is yet in the future, and prayed for as being such. In the exhortation to the Holy Communion we have seen that there is no formula given, but that a rubric which prescribed such a formula has been abrogated, and a totally different method—the ministry of God's word—prescribed in place of the exercise of a priestly power of formal absolution. In the Holy Communion the earlier invocative form has been retained. And in the Visitation of the Sick the forgiveness of sins is still only invocative, '*Our Lord Jesus Christ—of his great mercy forgive thee thine offences;*' and the form of absolution pronounced by the priest does not extend, as we have before shown (page 92), to the actual forgiveness of sins.

The reason, and the reasonableness, of this are clear from the nature of the matter. Supposing an absolute sentence of forgiveness thus pronounced, it may be false, and cannot be pronounced beyond doubt to be true; for the sins may not be forgiven, in consequence of the repentance not being real; it is impossible for anyone, unless he can look into the human heart, to say absolutely and judicially that any man's sins are actually forgiven him. That they may be forgiven him—that they are not beyond God's mercy—that God's mercy is certain if he repents—is absolutely true, even though he does not repent; but to say the same thing of absolution, taken as absolute forgiveness of sins—to say that the sentence of this or that priest as to the forgiveness of the sins of this or that man holds good, if he repents, is merely to say his sins are forgiven if they are forgiven. The proposition 'If he repent [1] his sins are forgiven,' does not admit of any conclusion being drawn unless the antecedent is assumed— unless the repentance is certain, it states nothing as certain. But to say that the sins of these men (or of that man) may be forgiven if repented of, holds perfectly good even though they are never repented of.

[1] Logically we might state it thus:—'*If this man repents his sins are forgiven*,' is a perfectly pure conditional premiss; but no conclusion can be drawn unless the antecedent, viz., the repentance, can be affirmed, which it cannot; a defect which is not cured by any sentence of the priest. And even if the universal be substituted for the particular, '*if men repent they are forgiven*,' still no conclusion can be drawn, nor can the premiss be stated categorically without too an undue assumption of the repentance. To say absolutely '*all these persons are pardoned*' would be to assume their repentance. But '*if men truly repent they will be forgiven*,' is not really a conditional premiss, but only a form of stating the universal, '*The sins of all repentant sinners are forgiven*,' and this, as we have said in the text, holds true, whether the repentance is or is not a reality.

This view of the Commission conferred by Christ being a general declaration of the Gospel fiat for the remission of sins harmonises likewise with what is possibly the grammatical force of the original ἔσται λελυμένα *shall have been loosed*, ἔσται δεδεμένα, *shall have been bound*, ἀφίενται *they are already remitted*: κεκράτηνται *they are already retained*.

Two points would follow from this very decidedly.

1. That which is spoken of in Absolution already exists as a fact in heaven, and therefore Absolution is declaratory and not efficient.

2. That whatever is declared must be of such a nature that it can be declared infallibly by the fallible minister pronouncing it.

But after all there is not so much difference between the two cases as appears at first sight: for such a fiat as '*He pardoneth and absolveth*,' presented for a man's acceptance, is in its relation to man, a promise or offer; so that whether we admit the possible grammatical force of the original, or our no less possible translation (whereby the declaration is rather of a promise or offer than of a fiat), it still must be of such a nature as to be true in all cases, and under all conditions, so that it may be pronounced without any possibility of error; now this cannot be actual pardon, because this depends on the person accepting the offer in repentance and faith; but it may be the fiat of that remission of sins which is the Gospel—the remission of sins to all who repent and believe. It is equally true, whether addressed to a penitent or impenitent man, that God has immutably decreed to pardon all those who repent and believe; and I need not remind my readers that this is the shape in which absolution is usually presented to us in our Church.

It may serve to complete our notion of what it is, if we go a little further in defining what it is not. It is not judicial. First, because the absolution is not so in the Morning and Evening Services, for the minister is commanded to pronounce what has already been willed and settled and promised by God—God's will that men should be saved by turning from their sin—the promise, and the conditions of that promise, repentance and faith; he has no choice but to pronounce it; his office is merely that of a deputed minister empowered to declare, as by authority; he has not to decide as to the repentance of any one. It is not so in the Communion office, because it is merely invocative. For here of course he decides nothing. Nor is it so in the Visitation office; first, because it may, I think, be taken as a settled point that all absolutions, though differing in form, must be essentially the same; and next, because the priest has no power to withhold it from anyone who humbly and earnestly desires it. It is not operative or efficient of that which it declares; it would not be so even if it were an absolute declaration of pardon as a *fait accompli*; for this from the very terms of the formula is Christ's reserved prerogative; still less if we take it as a ministerial, official, declaration of God's mercy being open to the penitent; for God's mercy, as well as the purposes of that mercy exist, and must in the nature of things exist, prior to the ministerial declaration thereof. It is not a grant of pardon, or an assurance of pardon granted, except so far as God is pledged to the fulfilment of the message which He has entrusted to His Church. Nor, though resting on a supernatural commission, is it in itself either supernatural or sacramental; not supernatural, because the effect produced is natural, the same in kind as that produced by our Lord's miracles—it is not accepted by virtue of any supernatural action on the mind, but in obedience to the law of our rational and moral nature, the result of a message from God, delivered by one whose authority to deliver it is acknowledged—it is not sacramental; first, because it is not supernatural in its operation, and next, because there is no visible sign ordained by our Lord.

Before we leave this branch of the subject we must observe, that even had it been our Church's intention to convey in ordination the power of actually forgiving sins contended for by the Confessionalists, yet this would not imply or necessitate previous auricular confession to a priest; for not only is it perfectly possible to conceive such a power being exercised without any such confession, but the power, whatever it is, which is actually exercised in our Church by her ministers in pursuance of their ordination commission, is in two cases preceded by public confession to God only, namely, the absolution in the Morning Service, and that in the Communion Office; and even in the third case, the Visitation to the Sick, there is nothing to show that the special confession is not to be made in the presence of other persons besides the priest. Special confession is not the same with private confession: on the contrary, the Office implies the presence of others. *[Auricular confession not necessary to the exercise of the Priest's office, even as the Confessionalists conceive of it.]*

The Confessionalists, however, think to make out their case for Confession by representing it as necessary to give the priest a knowledge as to whether a man repents or not —whether he may pronounce him forgiven, or refuse to do so: but first, the priest is never authorised to represent forgiveness as unattainable by the sinner, or to exclude from the Holy Table, except for notorious sins in which private confession to the priest is out of the question, for it is known to him already as being notorious. And it is evident that at the very best it only gives an approximation to that knowledge, and this a very uncertain and deceitful one; at the best it cannot justify an absolute *[Confession not necessary as informing the priest,] or as enabling him to judge whether the sin is unpardonable.*

declaration of any sins being actually forgiven, nor yet any absolute declaration that they are not forgiven; and if so the alleged ground fails. Confession cannot enable anyone to say that a man's sins are not within God's mercy, by reason of the repentance not seeming to him as perfect, as he arbitrarily chooses to think it ought to be: the only sin that excludes from this mercy is the sin against the Holy Ghost; and as no man knows, or even guesses, what this sin is, it is impossible that any completeness, or any minuteness of the detail of sins can enable anyone to say that they constitute the sin against the Holy Ghost: for this being unknown it is impossible to compare the sins with it. All that can be said is, that as Christ has declared that if any man come unto Him, He will in nowise cast him out, so no man can have committed the sin which shuts him out from the hope of mercy so long as he comes, or wishes to come to Christ. And any clergyman who ventures to say on his own judgment that the sins of a man seeking forgiveness are not forgiven, seems to fall under the ancient Canon,[1] which says, that if any presbyter rejects a man who is turning from his sins, 'let him be deposed as grieving Christ.' Nor, indeed, do the Confessionalists profess to a man who applies to them that his sin is, or may be, unpardonable, but that they can point out a special way of procuring the pardon, which their very offer thus represents as pardonable.

The knowledge of each case not recognised as necessary in our Church.

Nor do I see in our own Church any recognition of the notion of a knowledge of each man's particular sins being necessary to the exercise of the clerical commission; nay, the language and directions of our Church seem to me to exclude it. Thus, the absolution in the Morning and Evening Services and in the Communion Service is pronounced without any such knowledge being required; here evidently it finds no place. In the occa-

[1] Bingham, vi. p. 432.

sional preparation for the Holy Communion in cases of morbid distrust of God's mercy, the point submitted to the minister is not the insufficiency of the repentance—this is assumed to be real and sincere; the knowledge of the particular sin is not held necessary for the proper doing of that which the minister has to do. In the Visitation to the Sick the minister is supposed to be satisfied of the man's repentance, as to the fact, though not the details of which he has examined him, and the reality of which has been tested by any acts of reparation which may be necessary. The special confession of any particular sin is primarily intended only to relieve the conscience from the burden of unrevealed sin, or from the fear of which I have spoken above, or it may be sometimes as an act of reparation to society: it is not necessarily followed by absolution. It is evident that the special confession is not made to enable the priest to judge whether God's mercy is or is not applicable to the case; for that which would follow on such judgment being in the negative, viz., refusal to absolve, is not contemplated or permitted.

Still less is it recognised by our Church that the details of the sin or sins must be made known to the priest for the purpose of *penance*, that is to enable him to fix the proper amount of reparation and satisfaction due to God for the sin which has been forgiven, as they say, by the priestly absolution. The notion of penance, in the Confessionalist sense of the word, is utterly alien to the views of our Reformed Church, the language of our formularies. It is true that the word penance is once used in the Commination Service, but this is in the sense of repentance, or change of mind, as is seen by the original of which the words used are a quotation; but *penance*,[1] in the

---

[1] I recollect a Spanish priest with whom an acquaintance of mine had conversed on the sacrament of penance, saying on being told she was going to Christ, '*Eh donc! vous faites pénitence aussi.*'

ecclesiastical sense in which the Confessionalists use it —bodily acts of fruitless toil and self-inflicted pain, which under these auspices assume the garb, and thus discredit the name of genuine devotion and piety—weariness and heaviness—not the sighings of a contrite heart, known to none but God, but artificially created by external self-inflicted mortification as a reparation to God for sins committed against Himself—sometimes, alas! the saying prayers to God—is unknown to our own as it was to the early Church. For the penance then required—having in it more of pagan severity than Christian mercifulness, more of earth than heaven—belonged wholly to public discipline, in which it was attached to forgiveness of sins against the Church, by the will, and authority, and act, of the Church. No penance was exacted, or performed, for sins which did not touch the Church, even though they were of the gravest character before God—such as avarice, lustful feelings, luxury, and the like (see page 67)—though if penance were required by God for any sin it surely would be required for these. In the scheme, then, of forgiveness from God of sins as against Himself, penance finds no place: and this is the forgiveness with which our Church and our Clergy have to deal, except in one or two specified cases of the public condonation of grave offences by admission to the Holy Communion (see page 12), to which our Church has in no case attached privately imposed penance. But more than this, it is an absolute negation of the freeness of the pardon procured, of the sufficiency of the satisfaction offered, by Christ; it is an assertion of the inadequacy of the price paid as our ransom—it is, in fact, an act of disbelief in a vital point of revealed Christianity.

It might be thought that no greater despite could be done to Divine Mercy than thus to doubt what it had revealed of Itself; but I think the notion of *penitence* to which the Confessionalists sometimes shift their ground as a defence for confession, is still worse. The notion that the priests ought to know the exact details of the sin, in order to estimate the exact amount of the debt due to God—in order to arrange equitably the terms of payment on which God will forgive this or that sin, or sinner—to strike a balance between what the sinner is able and willing to pay in his own person, and what God can be expected to forgive him, or will forgive him—seems to me to betray a disregard for, or ignorance of, the Gospel scheme which borders on infidelity—a misrepresentation of God as He is revealed to us, which borders on blasphemy. There is not—we may thank God for it—the smallest trace of any such thing in our Church's teaching. The system, which adopts and embodies such notions as these, carries with it its own condemnation. If Confession is needed for these, then Confession is not of God.

CHAPTER XI.

Sense of our Lord's Words in St. John xx.—Bearing of this Point on our Church's View—Real Question at Issue—Points required to prove the Confessionalist case—Twofold Question—To whom were the Powers given—And what were the Powers—Powers given to those addressed—This assumed to be the eleven Apostles—Admitting this, the Power might have been confined to them—They had Faculties whereby they could pronounce absolute Forgiveness—Which Priests now have not. 'I am with you always' does not carry on this Power—Others addressed besides the Apostles—Others were with them—Power conferred on the Church—This Difference Important—What were the Powers given—Clearly the Power of remitting ecclesiastical Offences—But this not exhaustive—Comparison of Accounts of different Evangelists—St. Luke states the Commission to have been preaching Repentance and Remission of Sins—St. Matthew and St. Mark relate the giving this Commission to the Apostles on other Occasions—How the Accounts may be reconciled—Both embodied by our Church—How the Power was exercised in apostolic Age—Confessionalist Assertion—Negatived by Facts—No such Power exercised or claimed by Apostles—Simon Magus—Case of Corinthian Penitent—Tells against the Confessionalists, not for them, even on their own View of it—Literal Meaning of St. John's Words—Not taken by anyone—St. Matthew ix. 8—Practical Test of the Power claimed under this Passage—2 Cor. v. 18—'*As my Father sent Me, so send I you*'—How far the Mission of Church is identical with that of Christ—Confessionalist Position assumes that the Power they claim is the only Method of exercising our Lord's Commission—How answered—Flaw in the Position that this Way is one out of many—Practical Test of this Argument.

SUCH, then, are our Church's views on the functions conferred on the priest at ordination, as far as they can be gathered from the formula itself—the mode of exercise prescribed by the formula—and the actual exercise thereof in the services.

Meaning of our Lord's words in St. John

The next point is to ascertain the sense in which our Lord used the words when the original commission was given, in order farther to see whether the sense in which our Church thus seems (*prima facie*) to use them is in harmony with the sense so ascertained. For it is clear that our Lord's words must govern, or over-ride, the view or scheme of any particular Church; and therefore if our Lord's words contradict what has been said above, we must admit, either that the above view of our Church's meaning is not the true one, in spite of all the evidence and facts to the contrary, and that therefore the Confessionalists are right in insisting on and maintaining their view; or that our Church is wrong, and that therefore the Confessionalists are in some sort justified in trying, as they are trying, to re-introduce it among us; I say *in some sort*, because I think it more than doubtful, as a point of divine morality and of human honour, whether a person, holding his Church to be wrong in so essential a point, is justified in exercising his office and holding places of trust and profit, with the view and hope of altering it without any sanction from those to whom the government of the Church is entrusted, the doctrine and practice which he has promised to uphold. Our readers may be helped in forming a judgment on this point by supposing a Jacobite, 130 years ago, obtaining his commission in the army with a definite purpose of restoring the Stuarts; or the Irvingites having taken advantage of some legal quibble or technicality to retain the position of incumbent, in order to supersede the doctrine and ritual of our Church by their 'Catholic Apostolic' system.[1]

Bearing of these words on our Church's view.

At the very commencement, however, I must recall to my readers a point to which I have already more than once called their attention. The question is not whether our Lord intended by these words to create and convey some powers to the Church, but whether He intended

Question raised in our Lord's words.

---

[1] However mistaken we may think the Irvingites to be in their views of truth—as much mistaken, we will say, as the Ritualists—yet we must do them the justice to acknowledge the reality of their professed love of truth. They have not stultified themselves by alleging their love of truth as an apology for insincerity and evasion.

to convey to every ordained priest that particular power to which every Confessionalist priest pretends, as vested in him, and which he claims to exercise, personally and directly, *jure divino*. Unless it is certain that our Lord's words did convey this power when they were spoken, then the Confessionalists' case cannot be sustained by them.

The principal passage which is brought to support this momentous claim deserves the most careful consideration in all its parts; a more minute consideration than can have been given to it by those who allege it offhand, as decisive in favour of a view to which it is in reality opposed. I will take the points which are sufficient for my present purpose. To prove the Confessionalist case the passage must mean—

Points advanced by Confessionalists.

1. That when our Lord spoke the words in question a certain power was conveyed specially and personally to the Apostles; or to the Church, and delegated by the Church to the Apostles.

2. That this power was continued and perpetuated to priests in all succeeding generations by right of succession, or by successive delegation.

3. That this power is the private forgiveness of secret sins, on the condition of these having been privately confessed to themselves.

The failure of any one of these points will overthrow the Confessionalist position as to the special functions and powers which they claim as appertaining to the second order of the ministry at the present day, by virtue of a divine right inherent in ordained persons, or delegated by the Church to them as its ministers.

Points into which the question divides itself.

A double question then occurs at the outset—

a. To whom the powers were given.

b. What powers were given.

The first subdivides itself again into two questions—

Whether the powers were given to the Apostles, and

thence appertain, *jure sacerdotali*, to presbyters, as the successors of the Apostles, independently of the Church; or to the Church, and thence delegated to Apostles, as now to their successors the presbyters, as officials of the Church.

The second also subdivides itself into the questions whether the power conveyed was—

1. A particular special commission and power—actual forgiveness of sins,

2. Or a particular special commission and power of declaring private sins forgiven,

3. Or only a general ministry or dispensation (οἰκονομία) of reconciliation in the forgiveness of sins—a general commission to publish and administer the Gospel scheme of mercy, as by divine and not by human authority.

Now, so much, I think, must be admitted, that some great promise was given, and some great power was conferred on the persons addressed; and as there is no limitation implied or expressed, the words must be taken to have been addressed to all those who were then and there present on that occasion, as in the parallel, though not identical, occasion given in St. Matthew xviii. Here is the first flaw in the Confessionalists' position, or at least in the position of that portion of the school who maintain that the power of each priest proceeds directly from our Lord, and not mediately through the Church. It is assumed as a fact patent on the surface, which needs neither search to find nor proof to maintain, that the words were addressed to the eleven Apostles exclusively: though, first of all, it is beyond doubt clear that all the eleven Apostles were not present, St. Thomas being absent; and I think it will strike my readers that it is hardly likely that our Lord would have chosen this moment to give such a commission to the Apostles by breathing on them, when one of them at least could not have felt the

To whom were the words addressed?

Not to the Apostles alone.

divine influence of his breath, nor personally have been partaker of the gift.

But supposing they were so addressed,

We will, however, first allow it to be assumed that our Lord's words were addressed exclusively to the eleven Apostles; even were it so, we are not bound to concede the same sacerdotal prerogative to every priest now; for we can see good reason for supposing that the power of forgiving sins—supposing for a moment that it were quite certain on other grounds that such power could be exercised by men—might be thereby conveyed to them absolutely, without its being passed on from them to those who succeeded them: for they had that which is absolutely necessary for such absolute forgiveness, or for the declaration thereof to any given individual. For that which puts absolute forgiveness, or the power of declaring it, as an actuality, to any individual out of the power of any clergyman at the present day is the impossibility of his knowing whether the repentance is real: without this, the infallible declaration of actual forgiveness of this or that sinner is an absolute impossibility (see page 130); the man who pronounces it, does not know whether his sentence is, or is not true: for it is not surely maintained that the pronouncing the sentence cures the lack of repentance, or that a lack of repentance does not cancel the sentence. But the Apostles had no such difficulty: for the same miraculous power (probably that of discerning spirits) which enabled them to see that a man had sufficient faith to be healed, would enable them to see whether a man's repentance was real; so that taking our Lord's words as addressed to the eleven, or rather the ten exclusively, the commission may be understood in its literal sense, and in a way which gave them the power of declaring absolute forgiveness, while it does not give it to those who are not similarly endowed. It is quite clear that those to whom this formula is now

Why to be viewed as confined to them.

Apostles' power of discerning spirits.

addressed at ordination have not the gift of the discernment of spirits, or any other miraculous powers whatever; and therefore the commission cannot give to them the same power and authority as it might have done to the Apostles, inasmuch as in the very nature of the case they could never exercise it. And, as I have before said, it is clear that the meaning of any such passage must be modified by the admitted possibilities or facts of the case. And I think that no one, not even the most sturdy Confessionalist, who reflects on the subject, will deny that the validity of any priestly declaration of forgiveness must be modified by the known validity of the repentance; and if so, our Lord's words at the very utmost cannot go, as far as regards the clergy of the present day, farther than to convey a power of declaring the possibility of any sins being pardoned; in other words, the declaration of the unlimited extent of God's mercy on condition of repentance—exactly the phase in which, as I contend, our Church sets it forth in the morning and evening service.

But then the Confessionalists urge that the powers given to the Apostles were continued to their successors by the words, 'I am with you always unto the end of the world.'

<small>Our Lord's promise, 'I am with you always even unto the end of the world.'</small>

Now, allowing that these words have this force, it is sufficient to call my readers' attention to the fact that they were not uttered by our Lord at the time when He said, 'Whosoever sins ye remit,' &c., but at a later period, when he conferred on the eleven Apostles alone the commission of preaching and baptising. So that if these words are to modify or interpret our Lord's commission, and through them the ordination formula, then the powers attached to that formula must be those to which the words were originally attached, viz. preaching and baptising; and the Confessionalist deduction of an authority to forgive sins in any other way than these falls to the ground: or if they are, as is most natural, to be referred to those words in the context of which they occur, then the Confessionalists' application of them to our Lord's other words becomes clearly inadmissible; the former argument remains unanswered, that no inference can be drawn even from the admitted possession of these powers by the Apostles, the exercise of them by whom is conceivably possible, to the possession of them by those of whose exercise thereof there is no such conceivable possibility.

<small>But not spoken to the Apostles alone.</small>

But when we look into the matter a little more closely, and compare and harmonise the accounts, given by different evangelists of that memorable evening of the first day of the week, it seems perfectly certain that the ten Apostles were not alone when the Lord appeared to them, for the two disciples returning from Emmaus found '*The eleven gathered together and them that were with them,*'[1] and therefore it was not to the Apostles only that the words were addressed; and this is brought out still more strongly by the fact that when our Lord afterwards gave the eleven Apostles their personal authority to preach and baptize, it is expressly mentioned by the evangelists[2] that He was alone with them; so that our Lord's words were addressed and the powers committed to, not the Apostles personally, but the whole Church.

<small>Difference material.</small>

The Confessionalists say it makes no difference whether the words were spoken to the Apostles or to the Church. This is nothing more than a device usually exercised by them for evading a logical defeat by pretending, when arguments utterly fail them, that they entirely agree with a man with whom they have been arguing, calmly saying, 'We mean the same thing.' But if anyone uses this plea with the notion of its having any logical force, he means that the powers are the same, and

---

[1] St. Luke xxiv. 33.
[2] St. Matt. xxviii. 16; St. Mark xvi. 14.

can be exercised with the same force and result by those to whom the Church has delegated them, as they had been if conferred directly on the priesthood. But with due deference I would say, this hardly meets the question, and that the Confessionalist view is very greatly affected hereby. First of all, they can no longer pretend, as they have pretended, that the formula used by our Church in delegating these powers is to be interpreted by the existence of an essential right, vested directly by our Lord in a sacerdotal caste, and held directly from our Lord by those whom the Church at ordination admits to that caste. The words used by the bishop and presbyters must be interpreted according to the powers which the Church authorises them to confer, and by the powers which, according to the offices of the Church, they have power to exercise: and these we have seen above do not include the actual forgiveness of sins, but the proclamation and offer, in one form or another, of the unlimited mercy of God on repentance. *If given to the Church, then delegated according to the will of the Church*

Again, if the power be delegated by the Church it must be the same in kind as that possessed by the Church. The Church cannot delegate that which it does not itself possess: and this is only the power of absolution, not that of forgiveness, as expressly stated in the formula of the Visitation office. *No other than that given to the Church.*

Again, the exercise of such powers vested in the Church must primarily and essentially be public: and these public ministrations, to speak generally, exclude private absolution; and where, in the particular case of a dying man, the private application of these public ministrations is permitted, the former must be essentially the same in kind as the latter: and if privacy can enter in at all, it is only accidentally, in consequence of the exceptional nature of the circumstances, and not of anything essentially inherent in the power of the priest, as is the *The exercise of Church powers must be public.*

L

theory of the Confessionalists. In fact, such an exceptional exercise cannot govern the general nature of the power to which it is, accidentally and up to a certain point, in opposition; the private must be the same in kind as the public; and the public we have seen is nothing more nor less than an official declaration of God's mercy, and therefore the private must be the same, applied individually.

We now come to the second point, though, as I have before observed, the points so overlap one another that it is difficult to keep them entirely distinct. What were the powers given? It is evident that certain powers were granted, conferring upon the Church authority to carry on in some way or other His scheme of salvation as already revealed by Him, or to be revealed—either by His personal revelation or by the guidance of the Spirit of Truth—to those whom He had chosen to be His Apostles, and who in the Early Church were universally recognised as the exclusive channels of revealed truth, so that what they taught while they were alive, and after their death what they had left behind them in writing, was received by the Christian world as the sole rule of faith. In the undisputed formula, 'What is written we receive, what is not written we reject,' there is a distinct recognition both of the authenticity of the Scriptures, and of no other teaching or writing being accepted as inspired.

[margin: What are the powers given?]

If we consider, as I think we may, with all but certainty, that the commission of St. John was given primarily to the Church, and by the Church delegated to the ministers thereof, then its most obvious force would be to give authority for public discipline, and public Confession, and public reconciliation with the Church, as the body against whom the offence had been committed; but it would give no sanction to what the Confessionalists contend for, private discipline, private confession, and private forgiveness of

REMISSION OF ECCLESIASTICAL CENSURES.

sins, and private reconciliation to God by a priest. It is true that public reconciliation to the Church would according to the terms of the promise be followed by the forgiveness of the ecclesiastical guilt incurred by an offence against the Church: and this reconciliation was signified by public imposition of hands, followed by a public prayer, by the bishop acting as the recognised head of the Church, or a priest acting as the recognised officer of the congregation, not by virtue of any power personally attached to the priest, *quoad* priest; and perhaps this might have been accepted as a meaning sufficiently obvious, and satisfactory, and exhaustive to preclude the necessity of looking for anything farther: and our ordination formula might be taken to refer simply to the official remission of ecclesiastical censures and penalties, just as the analogous passage in St. Matthew refers to personal reparation by the person injuring and personal forgiveness by the person injured. The sin, in its relation to the Church, would be forgiven in heaven, even as it had been forgiven on earth by the Church against whom the sin had been committed; and I again put to my readers whether it is not perfectly clear that if this is the force of the passage, it can give no sanction to that which the Confessionalists contend for—private Confession, private penance as a condition of forgiveness—private absolution as the exercise of a personal sacerdotal power. *Our Lord's words refer to the remission of ecclesiastical censures.*

But though such an interpretation would satisfy all the definite requirements of the passage, yet, as in the primitive Church, reference is frequently made to it as the ground for expecting effective results from certain public ministrations of the clergy, other than the public reconciliation of notorious sinners by the laying on of hands and admitting them to the Lord's Table, it would seem that the interpretation above given does not exhaust the force of the passage. And as our Church (though ecclesiastical censures *But also to something more.*

have all but utterly disappeared from our system) still retains the words in the ordination formula, it would seem they are supposed to apply to some more particular exercise of the clerical functions : so that passing by the question whether their main reference was not to the remission of ecclesiastical censures, I will address myself to the point whether they contain any sanction to what is usually called Auricular Confession.

Comparison of the accounts in the Evangelists. If we compare the account given by St. Luke of what took place in the company which the two disciples from Emmaus found assembled at Jerusalem—viz. the eleven (or rather the ten), and others with them—we shall be struck by the absence of the commission which holds so prominent a place in the account given by St. John; there is not the smallest trace of it in St. Luke, in the shape at least in which St. John gives it; that it occurred, we must believe, without an atom of doubt, and we cannot suppose it to have been unknown to, or to have been forgotten by, St. Luke; the question is, whether he expressed the same thing under a different aspect, and in different terms. If so, this may give the key to the meaning of the passage in St. John. Thus we find in St. Luke that our Blessed Lord on that evening personally addressing the Church together with the Apostles distinctly ordered that repentance and remission of sins should be—not given or granted by the sentence of the Apostles—but preached among all nations; in other words, He instituted the same ministry of reconciliation, the same ministry of forgiveness of sins, as St. John records in the well-known passage. St. Luke, taking in what may be called its practical phase the commission, which, according to St. Matthew and St. Mark, was also conferred in the same way upon the eleven separately, gives the methods whereby the ministry of forgiveness of sins was to be exercised, while St. John, in a more doctrinal spirit, though not with more essential correctness and truth, records the words, whereby the commission was doctrinally, so to say, conferred, and in which the Holy Ghost was given for the execution thereof; just in the same way as, omitting the institution of Baptism and the Lord's Supper, he sets forth with more distinctness the theory and nature of both these sacraments. Hence, taking the two evangelists together, we find that on that evening our Lord conferred upon His Church, first, the power, 'receive ye the Holy Ghost,' secondly, the office or ministry of reconciliation, 'whosesoever sins ye remit, &c.,' and thirdly, He ordained the means whereby the office was to be executed the preaching authoritatively repentance and forgiveness, in other words, God's mercy in forgiving sins: to which St. Matthew and St. Mark add the administration of Baptism: and thus we get the whole ministry of reconciliation, whether we view it as conferred by Christ on the Apostles and continued to their successors, or as delegated by the Church to those who are ordained to the ministry. And this is the view which our Church seems to take in the matter. The absolution in the Daily Prayers recognises in the commandment to declare and pronounce, *i.e.* set forth by authority, St. Luke's statement of the powers given, namely, preaching repentance and remission of sins; in the Visitation office, the absolution puts forward St. John's practically identical commission for remitting sins. Again, the former takes St. Matthew's and St. Mark's account of this authority being given to the eleven personally, at another time and place: it is said that the power and commandment is given to the ministers: in the latter we have the account given by St. John and St. Luke (of course referring to the same occasion as St. John) of its having been given to the Church: and it is spoken of as only committed to the minister: the reason of this difference probably being, that in the one case both the pub-

[margin:] Our Church embodies both accounts.

licity of the ministration and the form of the absolution mark that the power is exercised by the ministers as officers of the Church and the congregation: where a more private, though not necessarily altogether private, exercise of this power is permitted, our Church has thought fit to state the fact, that the authority is given by the Church and only committed to the ministers, lest it should be supposed, either by the sinner absolved or by the priest absolving, that it was exercised in virtue of a sacerdotal power conferred directly on every single member of a priestly caste or order by Christ Himself.[1]

How it was exercised.

The point, however, practically resolves itself into the question how the power so conferred was exercised: for in the early ages of the Church, and especially in the Apostolic age, under the immediate supervision of those unto whom Christ had committed the organisation of the Gospel Kingdom, it is impossible to conceive that whatever Christ intended in those words should not have been definitely ordained, or should have lapsed into desuetude; impossible, that that which was instituted and ordained by the Apostles should not have been the exhaustive development of the commission: so that, by seeing what was taught by them, and practised in the really early Church, before error had time to establish itself, or forgetfulness to creep in unrebuked, we shall ascertain what the passage really does mean: while by observing what is not so taught and practised, we shall find out what it does not mean: we shall be able to detect the falsity of any modern theories and practices, which, pretending to rest on St. John's words, have, in reality, no such foundation.

---

[1] This use of the word 'commandment' would rather lead us to think that the power to be exercised is to be received as being imposed upon the Apostles as a command. Now, they are never commanded to forgive sins in the Confessionalist sense, but they are commanded to preach and baptize: these being ways which, as we shall see presently, the Early Church accepted as the legitimate exercise of the power of remitting sins.

The Confessionalists certainly lose nothing for want of assertion: if anything is needed to support their case, they immediately assert the fact of its existence; and there is no stronger instance of this than their prompt statement that, as might be expected, the powers thus given to the Apostles were not allowed by them to lie dormant: the matter of fact being that throughout the records of the Early Church as given in the Acts of the Apostles—throughout the records of the Church for three hundred years—there is not a single instance or the slightest trace of the exercise of the power claimed by the Confessionalists, though there are numberless occasions in which, had it existed, it must have been exercised and recorded. *[Assertion of Confessionalists.]*

Thus—had the Apostles believed themselves to have had this power, is it credible that in healing diseases they never once used the formula which our Lord had Himself consecrated to the exercise of this power, 'Thy sins be forgiven thee?' Again, if we look to Acts viii., we shall find that though Simon Magus was evidently anxious for forgiveness, he does not ask for absolution at St. Peter's hands, but requests his prayers; and though St. Peter is no less anxious for Simon Magus' restoration, he does not suggest to him auricular confession of his sins, and the receiving thereupon absolution, but prayer to God for forgiveness. Anyone who reads the Acts with a thoughtful eye can scarcely fail to observe how many cases there are in which, if the Confessionalist system were true, confession would have been enforced and absolution requested: and yet in no one of them is there the smallest hint of either the one or the other. *[Private confession and absolution not recognised by the Apostles.]*

There is, indeed, one case seemingly in their favour, which is disingenuously quoted as if it were one of many, and not a singular one. It is astonishing that men of any logical power whatever, should not see at a glimpse that even this tells directly against them. It is the case of the Corinthian penitent, in which St. Paul, after speaking of a punishment inflicted on him by many,[1] afterwards speaks of himself as forgiving it in the person of Christ.[2]

Case of Corinthian penitent.

First. The word used for 'forgive' ($\chi\alpha\rho i\zeta\epsilon\sigma\theta\alpha\iota$), whatever else it may signify, does certainly not signify forgiveness by St. Paul of a debt due to God, but of a debt due to the person forgiving. That is, it was forgiven by the Corinthian Church and by St. Paul as the head of that Church, as an ecclesiastical offence against the Christian Commonwealth in Corinth, and against St. Paul as the chief pastor thereof, who by his miraculous powers had inflicted a temporal punishment upon the sinner, in order to bring him to repentance: there is not the very smallest trace of any auricular confession submitted to by the penitent: and even the sorrow which is spoken of seems to have been principally that of the congregation themselves, who had allowed the sin to go unpunished and unnoticed.

Meaning of $\chi\alpha\rho i\zeta\epsilon\sigma\theta\alpha\iota$.

I confess it is with reluctance that I feel myself obliged to take this view of the force of the word translated 'to forgive,' for if St. Paul could be viewed as forgiving the offence as against God, it proves beyond a doubt that the power of forgiving sins, which the Confessionalists maintain every priest has, *suo jure et arbitrio*, was not possessed by the Corinthian priests, since they were obliged to have recourse to St. Paul to ratify what they had done; nothing could be more complete; and thus is disposed of the only instance in which they even pretend to find a recognition of a power which, if it existed at all, must have been of the utmost importance, and of perpetual occurrence in every one of the Churches.

Other passages alleged as giving power to

In spite, however, of the absence of any trace of the exercise of this power of forgiving sins by private priestly absolution, the Confessionalists think to make out their

[1] 1 Cor. v. 4. [2] 2 Cor. ii. 4.

case by alleging passages which they interpret as giving *forgive sins.* this power to the priests, forgetting (to repeat what I have said above) that if they are right the power must have been perpetually exercised; so that even if the passages were verbally as distinct as the well-known words of St. John, yet it would not follow from these passages, any more than from that, that the power given was to be exercised in the way in which they pretend to exercise it, but in which it never was exercised in the early Church; if there had been any trace of its exercise in the early Church, then these passages might be used as probably referring to it: but even if the meaning affixed to them was as clear as it is shadowy, they cannot, either separately or together, neutralise the fatal fact, that the practice, founded on this interpretation, was unknown to Primitive Christianity.

I have already considered the passage in St. John, and I would, in addition to what I have there said, suggest a complete answer to the stress which the Confessionalists lay on the naked literal meaning of the passage, saying that the literal meaning of our Lord's words cannot and may not be evaded. This sounds all very well; but, as a matter of fact, neither by themselves, nor by anyone else, are the words taken in their literal sense: for this gives the priest the absolute unconditional power of forgiving sins without one word of faith or repentance: and this I believe no one has ever claimed. Again, if the naked literal sense is to be adhered to, the priests forgive sins by their personal authority, whereas even most advanced Confessionalists disclaim, in words at least, any ascription of this power to any but Christ. *Literal meaning of the passage in St. John.*

Another passage is in St. Matthew ix. 8, where, after our Lord had healed the paralytic man by the formula, 'Thy sins be forgiven thee,' St. Matthew adds 'the multitudes saw it, and marvelled and glorified God who had given *Such power given unto man. St. Matt. ix. 8 such power unto man.'* From this the Confessionalists argue that the power of forgiving sins is given to the priests. Thus—the multitudes marvelled at the power of forgiving sins being given to men; and as there is no disapproval or correction of these thoughts of the multitude, therefore this expression of St. Matthew is to be taken as a revelation of the power of forgiving sins being given to man. I think the first impression of most of my readers must be that it is incredible that rational beings could, on so serious a subject, use reasoning, which savours of jesting; my own personal impression was that it was so silly that the only way of answering it was by letting it answer itself; gradually, however, one or two salient points disclosed themselves on which a definite refutation may be based.

What it was at which the Jews marvelled.

First, it is clear that the Jews marvelled not at the inner unseen power which, according to our Lord's words, was implied in the miracle which was worked by these words, but rather at the outward manifestation of the power of healing; and in the parallel passage in St. Mark ii. 3 it is said, '*We never saw it in this fashion,*' and in St. Luke v. 26, '*We have seen strange things to-day;*' both of them referring rather to what they *did* see—the healing of the man—than to the power of forgiving sins, which they did not see; at all events, it is clear that the common people were not familiarised with even our Lord possessing the power which, according to the Confessionalists, they recognised as commonly given to men: for on a later occasion (St. Luke vii. 49) we find them exclaiming, '*Who is this that forgiveth sins also?*'—what they marvelled at and glorified God for, was the power of curing incurable diseases by half-a-dozen words.

Unreproved utterances of the Jews' no indica-

Further, if the thoughts of the Jews, unless definitely reproved and contradicted, are to be taken as indicating revealed truth, strange consequences would follow; for our

Lord was not here recognised by the Jews as a man who, being God, had power to do what other men could not do, but at the most as a man endowed by God to work miracles; it struck them as wonderful that a man—one of the human race—should have had such power given him; and if their thought is to be recognised as establishing a truth, it follows that our Lord is not God and man, but only a man empowered by God.

Again, the principle on which this argument rests does not hold; it is not true that every opinion or saying of the multitude, which is not directly denied or reproved by the evangelists, is indicative of revealed truth; as my readers study the Gospels, they will find many instances to the contrary; here is one: '*We know that God heareth not sinners*' passes without comment. Is this true? Again, in St. John vii. 26, '*When Christ cometh, no man knoweth whence He is.*' Is this true?

But after all, what they want to establish is easily tested; they claim for certain men—ordained priests—that they have the powers at which the Jews, according to St. Matthew, marvelled, and spoke of as being given to men— the same powers in this respect as our Lord. Nothing can be easier than to try. Let them go to the Hospital for Incurables, or even any of the ordinary Hospitals, and pronounce over some bed-ridden person the words, 'Thy sins be forgiven thee,' and see whether he does take up his bed, arise, and walk; nothing can be easier; if they have the power, let them exercise it. In fact, if there had been any reality in the practice of touching for the king's evil, which survived the Reformation up to the reign of Queen Anne, the power attributed to our anointed kings would have been far more like a continuation of the Apostolic powers, than anything enjoyed by the spiritual successors of the Apostles.

Another passage is no less weak—more so, it cannot

be. St. Paul says, 'He has given unto us the ministry of reconciliation' (2 Cor. v. 18), and 'hath committed to us the word of reconciliation' (v. 19). Who doubts that the ministry of reconciliation is given to Christ's ambassadors? Nay, I will go farther, and say that it means the ministry of the forgiveness of sins—the forgiveness of sins by God,[1] and the acceptance and grasping thereof by man. But how does this prove that this ministry is to be exercised by the auricular Confession and private forgiveness of sins of the Confessionalists? that is, by a method of which there is no mention or instance in Scripture, nor in the early Church? In this fact we see what this ministry is not; what it is, or at least one method of it, is told us in the commission to preach the Gospel of repentance and remission of sins, and in the order to baptise, with the light thrown upon it by the text, '*Arise, and be baptised and wash away your sins.*' Another phase of this ministry we see in the next verse,[2] in which St. Paul speaks of himself and Timothy as in Christ's stead *praying them to be reconciled to God*, as though God or Christ Himself were beseeching them to listen to Him. It is significant that some of the most dishonest of the Confessionalist school leave out the notion *pray*, and paraphrase the passage,[3] as if St. Paul spoke of himself as reconciling them to God as Christ did, that is, by forgiving their sins; though if the passage did stand thus, and had that meaning, the reconciling men to God as Christ did must carry with it a good deal more than merely forgiving sins—death on the Cross, for instance. My readers will easily see that the interpolations and alterations that

---

[1] 'To wit, that God was in Christ reconciling the world unto Himself, not imputing their trespasses unto them.'

[2] v. 20.

[3] 'He' (the Confessor) 'is the ambassador for Christ, and is sent in Christ's stead to reconcile you to God.' 'Pardon through the Precious Blood.' Edited by a Committee of Clergy. Palmer, 32 Little Queen Street, 1870.

the Mediævalists are so fond of making in certain passages both of the Scriptures or the Prayer Book are unconscious, but unequivocal confessions, that the passages as they stand are against them. The break-down of such arguments not only deprives their position of the weight they would have added to it, but adds greatly to the weight of the other scale.

<small>Confessionalist arguments.</small>

It is true, that our Lord said to His Church, just before he breathed upon the assembled disciples, '*as my Father hath sent me, even so send I you*:' this text is sometimes used—or rather misused—to give a colouring to the interpretation of the Ministry of Reconciliation of which I have just spoken; but our Lord's power to forgive sins did not arise from His being sent by God, but from His own divine Prerogative and Being, whence it is held to be a proof, not of His Mission, but of His Divinity.

<small>As my Father hath sent me, so send I you.</small>

Nor does this prove that God's Mission of His Son, and Christ's Mission to His Church, are so identical that all the works and powers attached to the one are attached to the other; and without this being so, the text cannot be used to prove that because our Lord had this or that particular function or power, the Church or the Apostles had it also. The word *as* may signify only the fact of the Mission and not its details. In some points our Lord's Mission and that of His Church are the same: but the points of similarity must be proved each by itself, and cannot be deduced *en masse* from the passage alleged. For instance, our Lord's Mission was prophetic. He published the good tidings of the work He was about to work for the remission of the sins of the whole world: the Mission of the Church is prophetic, to publish the work which Christ has wrought, the remission of sins attached thereto; but Christ's prophecy was that of Omniscience, that of the Church is interpretative. Christ's Mission was sacerdotal to offer the one Sacrifice for the

<small>In what respects our Lord's Mission and the Church's mission are the same.</small>

sins of the whole world; the Church's Mission is not sacerdotal, but still prophetic, to publish Christ's death as the one sufficient satisfaction and oblation. Our Lord's Mission was regal; that of the Church is not. Our Lord came forth from the Father, Himself being God with all the powers of the world visible and invisible at His command. He came forth as a monarch to establish His kingdom—to set forth His Word as its Master—to ordain Sacraments—to attach grace to that Word and those Sacraments; the Church has only a ministerial and executive office, of ambassadors and stewards. Christ destroyed both the penal and moral consequence of disobedience to God—the Church can only remove the moral results thereof by the ministration of the Word and Sacraments, except so far as in the latter sin is washed away by virtue of Christ's ordinance; and here the office of the Church and its clergy is purely ministerial, offering and ministering the means whereby sin is by our Lord's special ordinance forgiven. In short, I doubt whether the word 'as' expresses much more than this—as Christ's Mission was divine and not human, so is the Mission of the Church.

<small>Fallacy in the arguments grounded on this passage of Scripture.</small>

The logical fallacy which marks the reasoning of the Confessionalists from the passages of Scripture which they allege, is this : they ought to prove that the particular commission which they claim was distinctly attached to their office, whereas their strongest passage only proves that some commission was given. They ought to prove that this commission can only be exercised, and was only exercised in the particular way they claim; instead of which, they merely assert that the words of the commission do so limit it to that method, which is a mere assumption, contradicted by the nature of the commission itself, and the facts of the case. It is just the same as if a Baptist were to call upon us to admit that our Lord's

FALLACY OF THE CONFESSIONALISTS. 159

commission to baptise enjoined baptism by immersion, as if this were the only way in which our Lord's command could be fulfilled. Of course, if this power which each priest claims for himself—this sacrament of penance, for such it really is—were the only method in which the ministers of Christ could effectually minister to men the forgiveness of their sins, it would be certain, from our Lord's words, that the ministration of this (would-be) sacrament was part of the clerical office. Further, if what they say is true, then St. John's words must mean what they say they do: and the fact of there being no mention in the Apostolic writings of any sacrament of penance, must be accounted for (however improbable the solution) by supposing it to be the result of accident. Again, if their system had been the only way of carrying out the commission, and the sacrament of penance had been incidentally mentioned in other parts of Scripture, it would of course have been referred to this passage of Scripture as the authority for it. But where there are other methods of carrying out the commission in St. John, and the sacrament of penance is not mentioned as an Apostolic institution, it does not follow that it was actually conferred by Christ, or included in the words of St. John, merely because it might have been so conferred and included. All these arguments proceed from certain possibilities which are negatived by the facts of the case, to a supposed actuality, depending on these possibilities being realised in those facts. *If the Confessionalist's system was the only way in which our Lord's commission could be conceivably carried out, then our Lord's words would give warrant for it.* *But there are other methods, then the words do not warrant this system.*

Nor will it do to establish the Confessionalist system on our Lord's words, and then to determine the sense of those words by the very system which they have just been used to establish. The meaning of our Lord's words must be determined by other evidence, even were it admitted that the *prima facie* force of the passage is in their favour. My readers need not be reminded that there are many other passages of Scripture in which the *Arguing in a circle.*

prima facie literal meaning, or that which is assumed or asserted to be such, is not the real one. It is true that they are most consistent and most logical who assert that this is the only way in which sins can be forgiven; then in order to disprove their inference from our Lord's words, we have only to show that this is not the only way in which this commission of forgiveness can be exercised: and their case utterly fails in its very foundation if we can show, not only so much as this, but also that the primitive Church never recognised it at all, and that our own Church follows the primitive Church.

Those who hold that it is the only method easily answered.

Those again who claim for this method that it is only one way among many, while they at once give up the only way in which the case can be maintained, I do not merely say logically, but consistently, are easily met by the same practical answer, that neither the Primitive Church nor our own Church recognise this particular method as included in or intended by our Lord's commission.

So also those who hold it to be one way out of many.

It is easy to test this argument of theirs in a very practical way. Supposing a number of fanatics or impostors were to revive among us a practice very similar to, if not the same as, that of indulgences before the Reformation, of remitting sins by papers under their hand and seal, they might if they liked, refer to 'Whosesoever sins ye remit, they are remitted,' and say that this mode of remitting sins was appointed by Christ: and they may justify it by arguments every bit as good as those used by the Ritualists—such as that when our Lord forgave the woman, He wrote on the ground; that St. Paul's forgiveness to the Corinthian penitent must have been conveyed in writing; really these are not one bit more absurd than some of those advanced by our 'Catholic' school, such, for instance, as the David and Nathan argument. And now how would any rational Churchman meet such a

Practical way of dealing with such arguments.

system? Would he not say that though not denying that a power of remission of sins was given in some way or other to the Church, yet he denied that *this* power was given? and he would appeal to the judgment of any reasonable being whether he could be accused of denying the former because he denied the latter—or whether the latter followed from the former. He would say that there was not a single instance of this particular exercise of this power in Scripture nor in the Primitive Church, and I think the argument would be absolutely conclusive, and far outweighing any supposed advantages which might be pleaded in its favour: and my readers will see that it is *verbatim* and *literatim* the argument I use against our Confessionalists.

CHAPTER XII.

Witness of the practice of the post-apostolic Early Church as to the meaning of our Lord's Words—As to what was not held—As to what was held—Interpretation put upon our Lord's Words—In their widest sense—Direct remission of ecclesiastical offences—Mediate and indirect commission—By preaching of repentance and remission of sins—Baptism—Intercessory prayer—Result of the power exercised—By the proclamation of God's promises—By baptism—Intercessory prayer—Retaining power—Exercise and results of—Power not to be exceeded—What is absolution—Not mere preaching—Not merely reading the Bible—Proclamation of the Gospel by the Church before the New Testament Scriptures existed—Under our Lord's special commission and authority—This proclamation afterwards embodied in the written Word—Authority of the Church and of the Scriptures—The written Word does not supersede the voice of the Church, but bears witness to it and protects it from corruptions—Essential duty of every Church still to publish the message which our Lord put into its mouth—This prophetic office of the Church exercised in absolution—Conferred in our own Church on the second order of ministers—Couched in a formula of words—Difference between this and preaching on the one hand, and the sacramental theory on the other—Not antagonistic to the written word.

Practice of early Church. WE have already seen what is the witness borne by the Apostles' practice as to their interpretation of our Lord's words; I will now consider the practice of the Early Church: and I am very much mistaken if the result will not be the same.

What it did not recognise. And first, negatively: we have already seen that there is no trace or hint, either in the Scriptures or in the Apostolic Church, of our Lord's words being recognised as giving authority to any priest to forgive sins privately, by virtue of any sentence or formula embodying or implying any such authority. Nor do we find any recognition of such practice in the Church of the three first centuries. We have seen that there is no trace of private Confession for the purposes of private absolution in these centuries (see page 57 sqq.). In explaining the office and the function of the Pænitentiarius, we have seen that the witness of the early Church is the same as that of Scripture; and that though confidential unbosoming of the soul to others was practised and occasionally recommended, yet it was not with a view to any remitting power to be privately and formally exercised by a priest, but either for the sake of comfort or counsel—which is the aim of Confidence as distinguished from Confession—or else to ascertain whether it was necessary or advisable to have recourse to public discipline; and therefore as far as the Confession of the Confessionalist is essentially connected with private absolution, the absence of the one bears witness against the recognition or practice of the other; and so far I think my readers will deem the question settled as to what was not held.

And when we turn from what was not held in the Church to what was, we shall, I think, arrive at such a clear and correct notion of what was believed to be included in and intended by our Lord's words, as will settle the special obligations towards the Church imposed on the English clergy by the use of these words in the Ordination office—in other words, what obligations our Church intended to be imposed and accepted. *What it did.*

In general terms, our Lord's words were held to give to those to whom they were addressed—the Church and the Apostles, and Christ's ministers and stewards in His Church—the power to proclaim and bring home the ministry of forgiveness—of the remission of sins on repentance—effectually to those to whom they speak in Christ's name as ministers; and our Lord meant to express that the mission of His Church carried with it divine authority even as His own had done; that this ministry was not merely a human one, but that whatever consciences were loosed from sin thereby, were loosed as effectually and surely as *Interpretation put upon our Lord's words.*

Their force.

when our Lord Himself preached the same opening of eyes to the blind, the same delivery from the guilt and power of sin by the work which He came on earth to accomplish.

<small>In their widest sense.</small>

We must not lose sight of the fact, that in their widest acceptation our Lord's words in the first clause of the sentence—'*whosoever sins ye remit, they are remitted*' (and this is the point to which I wish at present to confine our attention)—were loosely taken to include all those ministrations within the range of the Gospel scheme, which by bringing men to Christ, exhorting them to, and producing in them, repentance and faith, are thus mediately and instrumentally the means of their sins being forgiven. All these were held to fall under our Lord's promise, as by them men were loosed from their sins; this would hardly have been the case, had those words been conceived to institute a special and peculiar sacramental ordinance of immediate and direct forgiveness. The mere exhortation to virtue was held to be an act of loosing.[1] And this ministration of loosing might sometimes even be exercised by a layman, not only in the case of an injured man forgiving the injury done to him, in which case the forgiving of the injury on earth carried with it, according to Christ's promise, the remission of the guilt which was attached to it as a sin against a brother—but even by a layman praying for another man. A man is even said to break the bonds of his own sins[2] when by the energies of his own conscience and reason he is led to repentance and faith. But still the definite fulfilment of the promise—the formal carrying out the commission—was something more than this. The Church had a special function, as contrasted with the pious energies of individuals, in bringing the Gospel home to souls. The results might be the same, but there was in the one *ex officio*, a

---

[1] Usher, p. 121, note 133. [2] Bingham, vi. 578.

certainty and authority which was lacking in the other. Passing by then, what may be called the informal results of our Lord's words as scarcely apposite for our purpose, we shall find that those acts of official remission, which are limited to the Church in its corporate capacity, and to the clergy in respect of their ministerial office in that corporate body, were held to be:

1. A direct and immediate remission of sins committed against the Church, signified by a public imposition of hands before the congregation, and admission to the Lord's Table, exclusion from which had been part of the punishment inflicted. This public reconciliation was performed as an act of the Church and congregation by a presbyter or president thereof—always followed by a prayer.[1] This method of exercising the power given in the text of St. John is foreign to our subject, inasmuch as public discipline in the congregation has passed away, not only from our own Church, but from most of the Churches of Christendom.[2]

Direct remission of ecclesiastical offences.

---

[1] Bingham, vi. 533. This prayer must either have reference to the sins condoned by the Church as ecclesiastical offences, or to other sins which are not taken cognisance of by public discipline. In the one case the notion would be that the condonation of sins against the Church did not extend to the remission thereof as against God; in the other, the notion would be of secret sins which were left to each man's conscience. The words of the liturgical prayer seems to me to mean the latter, as it includes all sins. It is observable that our Lord's words are quoted as a warrant for the prayer, which seems to indicate that they were not conceived to confer the power of absolute remission as a *fait accompli*.

[2] On the disuse of the direct power of loosing from the ecclesiastical penalties and guilt, this direct forgiveness of sins against the Church, and for that phase of guilt against God arising from such sins—which was granted and consummated by the will of the clergy, and signified by the imposition of hands—was passed on to another class of sins, namely, those immediately against God, which had hitherto been left to other ministrations of the clergy in indirect discharge of our Lord's commission. The dispensation of the Word and sacraments, as an independent, though indirect, mode of remitting sins against God, was more and more merged in a direct sacerdotal prerogative of granting directly that forgiveness for these sins which had previously been given for sins against the Church. Thus sacerdotal absolution became the only way in which forgiveness was granted to repentance and faith, though the old precatory form

CONFESSION.

Mediate and indirect remission.

2. A ministry of mediate [1] and indirect remission of sins—of personal sins as against God—by proclaiming and pronouncing and presenting authoritatively, as the mouth-pieces and ministers of Christ, the Gospel promises of forgiveness of sin and sins against Himself to all the world on certain conditions of faith, repentance—not as a sentence of the minister's own will or word, but as God's will and offer to all mankind.[2]

Proclamation of repentance and remission of sins.

This consists in either the general proclamation of God's unlimited mercy, on certain terms prescribed by God, from which there is no authority for varying; set forth either by public ministration, by preaching, in the scriptural sense of the word, or ministration of the doctrines, facts, promises, and precepts of the Scriptures,[3] or by a more particular assurance thereof to individuals—such as to the jailor by St. Paul at Phillippi, and the eunuch by St. Philip.

Baptism.

Or, the administration of Baptism. As, for instance, when St. Peter, on the day of Pentecost, answered the question, 'What shall we do?' by the public proclamation of repentance and baptism, causing those who asked it to be baptised in the name of Christ for the remission of sins—there was repentance, faith, and acceptance on their part, and instant forgiveness on God's; not a word of confession or forgiveness of sins by formal absolution. And in accordance with this notion, we find Cyprian distinctly recognising baptism as one of the ways in which our Lord's commission was executed. Admission to the Holy

---

was retained as a witness and a relic of the primitive view that pardon of such sins was not granted by man, but though sought for by prayer from God (see p. 75).

[1] Usher, p. 109. Bingham, vi. p. 538, p. 546.

[2] If this indirect ministry had not been so recognised, it would follow that our Lord's commission would for the first four centuries have been held to warrant nothing more than public discipline, and then of course no warrant can be drawn from it for the private exercise of a sacerdotal power of private forgiveness.

[3] Usher, p. 121 sqq., notes 133, 134. Bingham, vi. 538.

Communion was also viewed as a mode of exercising this power, as being the consummation, or sign of it.[1] See page 129, note.

Or, the praying[2] ministerially in their public office, that God would pardon the sins of those for whom they prayed; and this is sometimes prefaced by the declaration of God's mercy as the foundation of the prayer. Sometimes it stands alone, but even when standing alone it virtually implies the former, inasmuch as prayer for pardon must be grounded on a belief in the possibility of God's mercy thus prayed for, just as baptism implies a firm belief in those promises of which it is the seal. *Intercessory prayer.*

Taking then this as the view of the early Church on the commission and powers conferred by our Lord's words, '*whosoever sins ye remit*,' we shall have not much difficulty in arriving at a clear view of the results expressed in the words '*they are remitted*.' *Result of the power exercised.*

First. If a man is moved to repentance and faith and acceptance of the mercy thus, either publicly or privately, proclaimed to him, the promise of forgiveness of sins, thus set before him as in God's name and by God's authority, becomes to him an actual offer on God's part. He may know that there is no power in his sins to bind him, but that he may come to God in full confidence that forgiveness of his sins awaits him in *foro cœli*, not by the virtue of the proclamation, but by the absolute certainty of the mercy which the proclamation tells him is prepared for his acceptance. *In the proclamation of God's promises.*

Secondly. If a man accepts Baptism in repentance and faith he may trust that his sins are forgiven him in this sacramental exercise of the ministry of reconciliation, combining the offer and the acceptance thereof, ordained and prescribed by Christ Himself, and specially committed to His Church and ministers. If he lacks repentance and *In baptism.*

---

[1] Bingham, vi. pp. 531 and 535.   [2] Usher, p. 110 sqq.

faith, then this exercise of the ministry of the forgiveness of sins by the Church is null and void, not by reason of the uncertainty or failure of the offer or promise, but by lack of the conditions necessary to its effectiveness.

Intercessory prayer.

Thirdly. If a man earnestly desires the fruition of God's mercy, and discerning in the formal prayer the exposition of that mercy in its full extent and reality, lays hold thereof by a corresponding act of intelligent faith, then he may trust that his sins are forgiven him in *foro cœli*. If he lacks repentance and faith, the prayer passes away ineffectively. It does not itself give him forgiveness of sins, though it may lead him to that change of mind to which the promise is made.

Retaining power.

Once more—with regard to the second part of the promise '*Whososoever sins ye retain, they are retained.*' If the Church finds men obstinately and hopelessly determined not to receive Christianity, as in the case of the Jews from whom St. Paul turned to the Gentiles, then the sins of these people are retained, the bonds of their sins are not loosed, they remain exactly as they were. Or if a man seeks for Baptism obviously from merely worldly motives, without either faith or repentance, then the Church, or the ministers of the Church, in refusing to baptise him, would be refusing to loose him from his sins: and the judgment of the Church, provided that it were true and just, would be only the echo of that truth which came down to us from heaven, that there is none other name under heaven whereby men can be saved but that of Jesus Christ. It would be in vain for a man to seek escape from his sins by any other way than that which Christ has proclaimed to be the only way. Or if there be reasonable evidence or a reasonable presumption, that a man is still in unrepented sin, then the refusal of the Church to pray for him, or to tell him formally that God's mercy is still applicable to his case, is a refusal to hold out to him officially, the Gospel message of remission of sins: such an act must of necessity give his sins a firmer hold over him, unless indeed it should awaken him to that repentance and faith, to which the Church could, without breach of trust, hold out God's promises. In each case the Church's judgment on earth, provided it be true and just, is the expression of what the sinner is sure to find in heaven, not by virtue of its being the Church's judgment, but by virtue of the nature of the Gospel thus ministerially, and not judicially, set forth.[1] If there are repentance and faith he is, on God's own promise and fiat, sure that pardon is prepared for him. If there are not, he remains in his sins—they are by the same fiat retained. Of course the Church or the ministers must not exceed their authority, and must proceed on no other consideration than that of the absence of repentance and faith. If other elements are introduced, then the authority is exceeded, and the judgment is null. Thus, for instance, if the Church refuses to proclaim God's promises to a nation on grounds of policy or revenge, or if a priest refuses to proclaim those promises except on the condition of confession to him, then the man who is thus repelled is none the worse for the refusal—the sin attaches to the priest.

Power not to be exceeded.

We have now, I think, examined sufficiently into the functions and powers committed by our Lord to His Church by His words in St. John to enable us to form a clear notion of what are the powers exercised by, and the benefit received from, absolution.

What then is Absolution? We have seen (page 132) what it is not—let us now see what it is. The Confessionalists try to make out that those who do not hold their sacerdotal theories on the subject must maintain that it is merely preaching; and since this would be generally denied, and is, moreover, contradicted by the

---

[1] Usher, p. 134, note 241; *Ibid.*, p. 107, note 48.

places which absolution and preaching severally hold in our services, they imagine that we are driven into the conclusion that it must be what they say it is. I think that they are mistaken; for though our Church—ignoring, in harmony with primitive usage, any direct exercise of a sacerdotal power of forgiving sins against God privately, by virtue of a form of words pronounced by the priest—has returned to primitive usage by taking the dispensation of the word and sacraments as the execution of the commission for the remission of sins, yet it does not follow that every such dispensation of the word is absolution in the eyes of the Church. It is true that the benefit of absolution (see page 111) may be, and often has been, produced by preaching, without any definite authority: by letters or books; but still we must not confound such ministrations of pious men, whether clergy or laity, with absolution. Neither is reading the Bible to a man in grief of conscience absolution, however decided and marked may be the spiritual result of such a dispensation of God's word. One obvious difference between such ministrations and absolution is, that the latter is always couched in a formula; but I think the real difference lies deeper than this, and that on examination we shall see that absolution is, in our theological language, confined to some peculiar declaration or dispensation of God's scheme of mercy, in which is called into play, not the power [1] (in the proper sense of the word), but the office and authority of the Church and its ministers as the warrant for the message really being God's word and will.

Commission to Church before the written word.

We shall, I think, best arrive at a clear notion of the nature and extent of that authority if we go back to the time at which that commission was first given, before the word of the New Testament existed in its written shape,

---

[1] See Usher, p. 107, note 48.

containing the full revelation of the Gospel scheme, as the complete source of all religious knowledge and the rule of all faith. In those days the Gospel message of the remission of sins was set forth to men on the personal authority of the Apostles, or of those whom they sent out to found churches in the several localities, or of the churches so founded; and to the reality of this authority witness was borne by miraculous powers, and the testimony of those who had seen and heard our Lord.

We must keep steadily in mind the existence of the authority of the Church under our Lord's direct commission, and then go on to the time when the written word was called into being by the formation of the canon of Scripture, containing the sum and substance of what fell from the Apostles' pens and lips under the immediate leading of the Holy Spirit of Truth; thus perpetuating and transmitting in all generations to the end of the world the teaching and guiding which they had received: whence men could draw by the aid of their spiritualised reason exactly the same message which the Church was authorised to pronounce—Repentance and Remission of Sins. We cannot fail to see that the written word embodies the same promise of remission of sins to individual faith, drawn from personal study of the word, as was attached in our Lord's commission to the authoritative declarations thereof by the Church. *The written word of the New Testament.*

There was then in those early times an authority distinct from that of the New Testament Scriptures, and yet substantially the same. It was the voice of the Church, and those whom the Church sent forth under the commission for the publication of the remission of sins, given, as we have seen, with a promise that the message published, though it was by mere men, would hold good in Heaven. *These two distinct.*

This voice and authority of the Church still exists

side by side with the voice of the written word, which perfectly embodies its utterances. The written word was not meant to cancel or supersede the personal office, or the authority or the message of the Church, but rather to establish it, to bear witness to its having been conferred, to stereotype it, to protect it against the danger of being perverted or altered, to which it is exposed by being committed—a treasure in earthen vessels—to the uninspired ministry and agency of men of strong passions, eager fancies, blind wills; and the real function of the written word ever since has been not only to enable men to read God's message for themselves, but to prevent, or at least to bear witness against, any misuse of the personal prophetic office of the Church, against perversions and distortions of the message committed to its authority which the best and most divine things are apt to suffer at the hands of men.

Relations between them.

As then before the publication of the written word it was part of the absolute duty of the Church and every branch thereof—the final cause and condition of its existence as a Church—to carry out our Lord's commission for the remission of sins by the publication of the message which He put into its mouth; as it was the office of every minister of that Church, according to his vocation and mission, to act on the authority which the Church gave him for this purpose; so now, the same commission and duty appertains to every Church and its ministers, to proclaim the remission of sins by the exercise of that authority, which was from the beginning, and is still, an essential attribute of the body which our Lord called into existence for this purpose; however much the message which the Church was commissioned to declare has been in some ages and countries added to and falsified, in spite of the protest of the written word; nor do I believe that there ever has been, in any country, a Church, whatever

The office of the Church still exists,

and is exercised in all Churches.

may have been its constitution, which has not, and, as far as it was a Church at all, claimed to act on this divine commission, and to exercise in some shape or other this prophetic office; distinct, indeed, from that of the written word, but still in subordination to it, derived from our Lord Himself, in an age anterior to that of the written word itself.

It is then the personal prophetic office of which I have been speaking, confined to, and bearing directly on, the remission of sins—that is the very Gospel itself—which our Church exercises in our absolution, by the authoritative declaration of that class of ministers whom we term presbyters or priests, to whom it has been thought fit to confine it, couched in a formula of words; the effect of such formula being to mark that it is not the energy of the individual will of the minister pronouncing it, but that the authority to put forth such a declaration belongs to the Body Corporate of the Church, and not to every individual priest *jure sacerdotale*. This differs both from preaching on the one hand, and the sacramental system of Rome and the Confessionalists on the other. From the former, in that though the message of the priest and the preacher is the same, yet in the one it rests on the prophetic office of the Church—on the individual, though official, responsibility of the minister; in the other, it rests directly on the written word set forth by those to whom this particular ministration is committed. And our Church, by thus claiming the mission and the prerogative with which our Lord Himself invested it, presents itself to the eyes of man as being what our Lord meant it to be, and doing what our Lord meant it to do, but does not place itself in any antagonism or rivalry to the written word, but rather in harmony and unison with it. For to the creation, the existence, the exercise of this prophetic office of the Church, the personal and prophetic office of the clergy so

[margin: This office exercised in absolution.]
[margin: Thus differs from preaching.]
[margin: Not in antagonism to or as independent of the written,]

authorised, the written word bears witness, as well as to the limits of the office, and the nature of the message to be proclaimed. And it is by reference to this written word, as fixing what was taught by the Apostles, that we are able to draw out most significantly the difference between our personal absolution, and that which bears the same name in the system of Rome, and of our Confessionalists. As absolution differs from preaching mainly in the difference of the authority in which the message of each comes forth, so in this last the difference is, that the utterance is different. In the one it is the proclamation of the remission of sins as God's free gift to all who repent and believe by virtue of Christ's atonement; or to any one who falls under that class : it is the witness of the Church, superadded, where needful, to the witness of God's word. In the other, it is the actual remission of sins, granted by the priest to those to whom he speaks certain words, by virtue of those words, in excess, if we are to believe apostolic and primitive practice, of the commission which our Lord conferred upon His Church; and therefore, contrary to its duty and office as a Church, and, *pro tanto*, destructive of its claims to be considered a sound and faithful branch of Christ's Body.

and also from the sacerdotalism of Rome.

CHAPTER XIII.

How this power is exercised in our own Church—In a formula expressing the unlimited mercy of God—In a formula of prayer—In a formula addressed personally to an individual—In the Morning and Evening Service—In the office of the Holy Communion—Confirmed by the comfortable words of Scripture—Visitation office—State of the man—Nature and result of the absolution—Not granting of pardon, not declaring it absolutely granted—Not a sealed pardon but a sealed offer of pardon—How far it affects the state of the individual—Illustrations—Not required by men of strong faith—Hence only permitted in cases of morbid doubt—How far an assurance of repentance—Doubt of God's mercy not to be suggested—Pardon not to be represented as given through the minister—Not to be suggested with a view to future influence—Absolution not to be pronounced over unconscious persons—Argument thence as to its nature—Confession and absolution not recognised as a preparation for the Holy Communion—Doubts not to be suggested or aggravated—Why absolution permitted on a death-bed.

Now let us see, a little more particularly, what is held and taught by our Church in this matter, and how this power or ministry committed to the Church is viewed and exercised. In other words, what is the absolution, formally and technically so termed, of our Church? *How this power is exercised in our Church.*

The authoritative dispensation of God's Word and its promises may be made in any one of three ways:

1. In a formula expressing the unlimited mercy of God on repentance and faith.

2. In a formula of prayer or invocation, implying the same promise, or prefaced by a declaration of the same.

3. In a formula addressed personally to an individual whose spiritual state is too morbid, and his faith too weak, to believe that God's mercy is greater than any sin he may have committed, and repented of: or to apply to himself the general dispensation of God's word and its

promises by either of the two preceding methods. Such a declaration is not in itself more absolute, or efficacious, or a more direct exercise of our Lord's commission than the other, but only to the man who stands in need of it.

<small>Absolution in Morning Service.</small> In the Morning and Evening Services the officiating priest (for the Church has in all cases thought fit to entrust the formal absolution to the two first orders of the ministry) is ordered to pronounce and declare God's unlimited mercy to all those who have repentance and faith. It is the message—the exercise of Christ's commission and commandment—in its widest and broadest shape: there is no application thereof to anyone: the promises are set forth as loosing the bonds of sin, and suggesting and authorising to all who repent and believe, an immediate access to God for forgiveness: and that in this message the priest views himself as included, is shown by the use of the words *us* and *we* in the concluding paragraph of the passage, in which, as I must again (see page 130) remind my readers that forgiveness is not supposed to be conveyed by the words pronounced, but, a certain condition, viz. repentance, being attached to the realisation of the proclaimed promise, it is suggested that we should all pray for the assistance of God's Holy Spirit to enable us to perform that condition, without which the forgiveness spoken of to us is only *in posse*—a possibility, not a reality.

I have already claimed (page 96) my reader's assent to the proposition, that this most abstract and undefined exhibition of the power, which the Church conceives our priests to have authority to exercise, must run through all the more defined and applied phases of it, unless there is some distinct provision to the contrary. If in the Morning Service absolution is pronounced in the words, '*He pardoneth and absolveth all those that truly repent*,' then the absolution in the Communion and Visitation offices must be essentially the same, however differing in certain accidents.

We now turn to the absolution in the Holy Communion office: and here we shall find that there is a more defined application of the promises than in the former case; there it was addressed to all, definitely applied to none: here it is addressed 'to you,' that is, those who intend to be partakers of the Holy Communion. We find first of all the same proclamation of God's promised forgiveness of sins to all them who with hearty repentance and true faith turn unto Him: and then assuming that those, who have drawn near and have made their confession to Almighty God, have the necessary faith and repentance to which they were exhorted, the priest is directed to use words which bring the promised forgiveness nearer, but do not actually put forgiveness into the hand—for such an invocation or prayer is the act, not of one who gives, but who seeks in hope that it may be given. I have already pointed out how this ancient form negatives the theory that the priest announces judicially sins to be forgiven, or does more than found on God's fiat of general forgiveness an invocation with regard to those who have confessed their sins to God; so as to quicken their faith for the effectual and personal reception thereof, by creating an assured conviction of God's merciful purposes towards them. And this is pointedly confirmed by what immediately follows: the minds of those addressed are immediately thrown back upon comfortable words of Scripture, containing the written promises and mercies of God in Christ as the foundation of assured forgiveness, and not referring to any power and authority of the priest absolutely to grant forgiveness, or declare it absolutely granted. If these had been believed to have been operative elements in the preceding absolution, surely the comfortable words quoted would have been, 'Whosesoever sins ye remit, they are remitted,' &c. &c.

Next, in the Visitation of the Sick, the application of

God's promises as a means of loosening sins is still more personal.[1] We may observe, too, that in this setting forth of God's mercy as directly applicable to an individual, the independent prophetic authority committed to the Church and to the clergy, is, by the use of the direct formula, 'I *absolve thee*,' prominently brought forward as the warrant for the man's putting his trust in God's mercy: while the message itself, which in the Morning Service forms the prominent part of the absolution, to the comparative exclusion of the office of the priest, is left in the background. We may remark further, that ecclesiastical history furnished such strong proof of the misuse to which the direct ambassadorial formula was liable, and the errors and superstitions into which both clergy and laity might be, as they have been, led by its use, that it is permitted only in that particular case, in which the ordinary means of producing trust in God's mercy are, from the state of the man's mind, combined with the urgency of the moment, ineffective. When grievous sin is weighing down a dying man's conscience with a burden that is not removed by the disclosing it (which has been suggested as possibly all that is wanted), but he earnestly and humbly desires something which may make him feel that his peace may be made with God as well as with man; then the priest is empowered to tell him that he, by the authority committed to him, looses him from the bond of his sins: does not *forgive* them, but absolves him from them by an ambassadorial declaration—sets before him God's

Marginal note: State of the man.

---

[1] Some persons think that the absolution here is the remission of ecclesiastical censures: it is an easy and therefore a tempting explanation. It is fairly urged in answer, that the sick person is not supposed to be under such censures, but only under the pressure of his own conscience. I think the answer is decisive, though it is conceivable that it is framed with a view to those who may feel that they have committed offences against the Church, and who wish to have this feeling removed before they die. This would be analogous to the practice in primitive times which led to the establishment of the Pænitentiarius (see page 70).

promises[1] in the form of an ambassadorial assurance—solemnly pronounced in the name of the Father, and of the Son, and of the Holy Ghost; so that the notion which he had of his sins being an impassable barrier between himself and God, is contradicted by the message of reconciliation of which the priest is the authorised minister: and he thus receives the comfortable assurance that he is as free to accept God's mercy as the man who has no such grievous sin on his conscience—as the man who has by God's grace believed and appropriated the promises of pardon, either set forth in Scripture, or in the more general proclamations thereof in the Church : that he may reject with absolute certainty—as absolute as if Christ Himself told him so—the notion that God will not grant him the pardon which he so earnestly desires; and for the granting of which a petition is presently offered up to God. But there is no actual or assured forgiveness of sins in all this, beyond the assurance which faith in God's promises, thus personally applied to his case, gives him. The assurance of forgiveness is not a talismanic effect of the priest's words, but is an act of the mind created by them, but which might have existed without them. *Nature and results of the absolution. Not granting of pardon. Not declaring it absolutely granted.*

It is sometimes said that absolution is not, indeed, the granting the pardon, but the declaring who are pardoned: and this, up to a certain point, is perfectly correct, if it means that it defines authoritatively the class who are within the limits of God's pardon—'God pardoneth and absolveth all them that truly repent and unfeignedly believe,' &c.—which may be called a major premiss ; but if it is meant that there is a judicial declaration or sentence that this or that man is actually pardoned, essential to

---

[1] Ferus, 'Comm. Matt.' cix. lib. ii. apud Usher, p. 149, note 313. *Annuncio tibi te habere propitium Deum, et quæcunque Christus in baptismo et evangelio nobis promisit nunc per me annunciat et promittit.* I announce to you that you have a God propitious to you. Whatever Christ in baptism and the Gospel hath promised to us, He now by me proclaims and promises.

the reality of the pardon, or making it more real than it would otherwise have been, then, as we have seen above, it goes beyond the possibilities of the case (see page 130), and the language of our own Church (see page 176). It is perfectly true that the absolution in the Visitation of the Sick may be viewed as an absolute minor premiss, stating that the person addressed is in the class whom God pardoneth and absolveth: but this is a totally different thing from granting him pardon, either as exercising an act of mercy in pardoning him, or judicially declaring him pardoned. The absolution may, indeed, be said to set the man free from his sins by assuring him that he is free, but not in the sense of making him free. The priest does not even open the door, he merely declares that the door is open: he opens the eyes which sin has blinded, so that the sinner can see clearly the way which hitherto he has been groping for in vain: with the sword of the Spirit he cuts the Gordian bandage which the sinner has hitherto been trying in vain to untie for himself. The priest does not by the formula of absolution present the sinner with a sealed pardon, but a sealed promise—an offer of pardon, sealed by his authority as a minister of Christ and His Church. It is applied to an individual without the least affecting the question of the actual remission of sins, for this is still a matter of prayer: without altering his state in any way, except the loosing his conscience from the fear of some weighty sin being unpardonable though repented of: even though the sincerity of his repentance is witnessed to himself by his confession, not necessarily private, of something, the concealment of which has hitherto rested as a burden upon his conscience; and which makes him fear that if the minister of God knew the extent of his transgression, he could not tell him that God's mercy was still open to him, and therefore makes him desirous of the formal

Not a sealed pardon, but a sealed offer of pardon.

How far it affects the state of the individual.

declaration, in the formula prescribed by the Church, that his sins, this grievous one included, do not shut him out from God's mercy.

It resembles nothing so much as the act of a steward or authorised agent who should declare to an assembled tenantry, his master's will and pleasure to remit all arrears of rent on certain conditions (say the presenting a petition pleading their inability to pay); and then finding a tenant, the amount of whose arrears prevents his believing that he is included in the offer, should go and say to him personally, 'In my lord's name, who offers to cancel all your debts, I absolve you from them, as far as they create any doubt of the reality of his offer as regards yourself—go and present your petition to my lord.' It is the answer of God's minister to the suggestions of despair—to the accusing voice of sin, that the sinner is his captive and bondsman. *[margin: Illustrations.]*

Another illustration may be found in commissioners authorised to settle a revolted province by promise of amnesty on certain conditions. For ordinary purposes a general proclamation, or general invitation would suffice; but to the leaders in rebellion, or those who were—in spite of the proclamation—disloyally distrustful of the merciful intentions, or the good faith of the sovereign, they might certify, not the pardon, but the promise under their hands and seals as commissioners, without exercising any authority different in kind from what had been exercised in the general proclamations. I hope I shall not be supposed to be guilty of the logical fault of adducing these illustrations as proofs, or for any other purpose than to put what I mean clearly before my readers: and I am inclined to think that the view implied in these illustrations will furnish a solution of this difficult subject.

The man whose faith is strong enough to realise for himself the fact of God's unlimited mercy, does not stand in *[margin: Not required by men of] strong faith.*

need of any such formal absolution; he is not thus bound in the chain of his sins, and therefore does not need in this sense to be loosed from them: and this is the reason why this 'I absolve thee' is reserved for those cases of troubled conscience, where the trouble arises not only from the sick man yearning after the relief of telling others his sin, but

Hence only permitted in cases of morbid doubt.

from the doubt whether his sin is not beyond pardon. If this formula conveyed the actual forgiveness of sins, which is equally needed by everybody, it would be equally enjoined for all; as it is, it is only where pardon seems out of a man's reach, that this absolution is permitted. And the whole of the absolution formula bears out this view of the case. The Church does not claim the power to forgive sins, but only to absolve and set loose the man; the power of the forgiveness of sins is reserved to our Lord Jesus Christ alone, and is not spoken of as given to the priests as a prerogative or function of their sacerdotal office.

Not to be suggested to a sick man to confess, with a view to gaining influence over him.

Again, when a man is troubled at the seeming approach of death, if the minister neglects or avoids putting before him the promises of God's free mercy in the hope of driving him to have recourse to the sacerdotal powers which he claims; if, instead of waiting for the sick man's humble and earnest desire for absolution, he tells him that he cannot hope to die in peace without absolution: or, at all events, that his peace and hope cannot be assured unless he is absolved: or even that he will be more assured and peaceful if he is absolved, and that absolution is out of the question unless he confesses his sins to him, promising to absolve him if he does so; then such a minister seems to me to exceed his office, to be untrue to Christianity, disloyal to his Church; and my impression is that something like this will be found at many death-beds at which Confessionalist clergymen minister. So again, where a clergyman finding a man on a bed of sickness, in his judgment not unto death, deals with him as if he were dying, and taking advantage of his weakness, gets him to confess his sins to him, in the notion that on his recovery he will be more amenable to his counsel and discipline: then, however good his intentions for the future may be, he would seem to me to be acting more like a Jesuit priest than an English clergyman; he would be hunting the man's soul with deceits which can hardly be justified by the way in which he hopes to deal with it when captured. There is another point which, I think, comes in here. The sick man, though he has testified his repentance by every means in his power, may yet feel, as he has no means of proving that repentance to himself by amendment of life, a doubt whether his repentance is such as to outweigh his sin; this doubt too is met by the authorised minister of God assuring him that it need not disquiet his soul, or keep him bound and tied by the chain of his sins. From these chains, as God's minister, he looses him, so that, his repentance being such as his circumstances admit of, he is within the sphere of God's mercy: and hence this special declaration of his state in God's sight is not conditioned by the man's repentance: this is assumed.

Effect of the absolution on doubt of the sufficiency of the repentance.

I think my readers will now see that the question which Confessionalists, with an epigrammatic arrogance, put to clergymen who deny their theory, 'Pray, have you ever been ordained?' may be easily answered to the confusion of the questioner: 'Yes, I have been ordained, and the
'power then committed to me, whatever it may be, I
'exercise, if the Church is to be trusted, every time I
'pronounce the absolution in the Morning Service, or use
'the form in the Communion office, and this without
'any other previous confession save to God; and I believe
'that I exercise my office in the visitation of the sick when
'I use the form the Church has prescribed, though I do not
'—could not—exercise the office, or claim the power, of
'forgiving the man's sins; therefore, though I deny auri-

'cular Confession, I do believe myself to have received a 'power in ordination, and exercise it accordingly.'

Doubt of God's mercy not to be created or suggested.

Further, it is quite clear that there is, in what is here prescribed, no warrant for the minister trying to create in the sick man's—in any man's—mind a doubt of God's mercy, by telling him that he cannot be saved without absolution: or suggesting to him its benefit, so as to lead him to avail himself of the special ambassadorial power committed to the priest by the authority of the Church, to be used in cases where sin obscures faith, and in no other. This were only to throw down a house to build it on a less sure foundation. On the contrary, that power is only to be exercised where the man's earnest desire shows that he cannot realise for himself the fact of God's mercy outweighing his sins. And, we may observe farther, that there is no authority given to the priest to refuse this exercise of his absolving power, except there should be any lack of earnestness and humility in the patient. He assures him of God's willingness to pardon him, undiminished, unhindered by the seeming inadequacy of his repentance.

Pardon not to be represented as given through the minister,

There are some other important points, which follow, I think, from what I have said. One is, that no minister thus officiating at what he believes to be a death-bed (and in no other case is he authorised thus to officiate) is justified in using this absolution without calling the sick man's attention to the prayer he is about to use, and the fact implied in it: not only, that the actual forgiveness of sins comes from Christ, not from him, but also that it is

but immediately from God to the sinner.

not through him that it comes from Christ; but is a distinct and separate gift of God immediately and personally to the sick man. The minister indeed prepares the sick man for seeking the promised pardon, but he does not interfere, either judicially or mediately, between the pardoned sinner and the pardoning God—he may absolve and loose him from his sins, but it is God who through Christ pardons them on the man's full trust in His mercy.

One thing seems to me to be almost axiomatic on the subject. It is this: That the conditions, on which God's mercy is proclaimed or prayed for, must not be added to or altered—the message must embody God's promises as He has actually set them forth to us. If these conditions are varied or altered, the authority is exceeded, the commission cancelled, and the message loses whatever value and power[1] it may have, or may be supposed to have, as an ambassadorial communication from God Himself. For instance, if a priest ventures to add to the conditions prescribed by God Himself—faith and repentance and confession to God—those of humiliation before, and confession to, himself; or if he assumes to himself the power of directly forgiving sin, or attributes to his word any power of removing by his fiat or sentence the penal consequences of sin; or of declaring by any such fiat that God has done that which in consequence of the man's lack of repentance He may not have done—then any formula of absolution in his mouth becomes a mere sounding phrase, without any of the power or virtue or effectiveness he may suppose to be attached, either in kind or degree, to the commission he believes himself to have received. Even supposing the Confessionalists to be right in holding that our Lord's words give them a judicial power of remitting sins, the conditions on which they exercise it being in excess of what God has laid down as the terms of forgiveness, deprive the sentence, they suppose themselves to have pronounced, of the power and virtue they suppose to have been inherent in it. The arrow which destroys their pretensions is winged with their own feathers.

Again, care is taken to provide against the superstitious use of this formula over persons who have already entered so far on the passage of death, as to be unconscious, and therefore incapable of knowing what is going

Absolution not to be pronounced over unconscious persons.

[1] Usher, p. 128, note 209.

on around them, or of seeking God's pardon by faith. This superstitious use is perhaps a reasonable development of the Confessionalist system: for it is not the body but the soul that is pardoned: and if a priest can pronounce judicially and effectively the actual pardon of sins, there is no reason why it should not take effect after the soul has departed from the body as well as before. The care that the Church has taken to guard this point by inserting the words 'if he humbly and earnestly desire it,' marks that absolution is not to be regarded as a judicial pardon pronounced over the soul, for in that case it might be with as great propriety pronounced over an unconscious as a conscious man. The conditions prescribed by the rubric imply that the effect of the absolution is moral and not judicial, so that an unconscious state, where no such moral effect is possible, precludes the possibility of its application.

Argument thence as to its nature.

I must again call my readers' attention to the fact that there is only one other case in which the Church suggests to a person in spiritual trouble to have recourse to a clergyman: and that is before the Holy Communion, when a person, in spite of his repentance, lacks faith or trust in God's mercy, in consequence of his conscience being unduly disquieted by the pressure of sin: here neither confession nor absolution are recognised. I have already gone through this so much at length (see page 100 sqq.) that I may content myself with a very brief statement of it; less than this I cannot do, because it is necessary to a complete comprehension of the part of my subject of which I am now treating. The grief is a doubt of the extent of God's mercy—the disquiet is caused by the presence of scruple and doubtfulness, produced by sin: not only hindering belief in God's mercy, but disquieting the mind by the apprehension of the punishment of unforgiven sin. The theory of the Confessionalists admits this to be the

Confession and absolution not recognised as a preparation for the Holy Communion.

source of the disquiet, otherwise their pretended forgiveness of sin would not quiet the conscience. We agree so far—but they meet the doubt by asserting their own power—we by magnifying and enforcing God's mercy out of God's word. The person applied to is a minister of God's word; whereas all the formal acts of absolution—that is of absolution technically so called—are not entrusted to anyone below the second order of the clergy. The sin is not to be confessed: in fact, it need not be, for the hue and the circumstances of the sin do not set the least limit to God's mercy short of the unpardonable sin; that, in any such case, this does not exist is clear, from the fact of the man himself desiring forgiveness, and having repented of his sin. What the troubled sinner is to do is perfectly clear; what the minister who is applied to is to do, is also perfectly clear; he is not to give absolution, for this, as we have seen before, is confined to the cases where a formula is put into his mouth. He is to strengthen doubting faith by the ministry of God's word, and the result will be that he will receive the same benefit, though by a different method, which is conferred either in the Morning and Evening Services, the Holy Communion, and the Visitation of the Sick. It is, too, perfectly clear that the minister consulted is not to pry into the particulars of the sin, to aggravate it, to put it before the sinner in its worst colours, to make him doubt whether he is fit for the Holy Communion. For the object of the further comfort or counsel which he may give him is not to increase the sense of his sin being of too heinous a dye to allow of it being pardoned: not to keep him back from the Holy Communion till his confession to God and his general repentance already performed is supplemented by confession to the priest personally; but it is to make that repentance effectual to the laying hold of the promises of God's word by adding to it the faith which it lacks. No one

Doubts not to be suggested or aggravated.

word which ministers utter to the sinner who consults them ought to be such as to increase his scruple and doubtfulness, but to the avoiding thereof. Nor have they any power to refuse the Holy Communion to such a man; their part is to persuade him to draw near without scruple or doubtfulness, having, *ex hypothesi*, gone through the means required.

I have in another place pointed out how carefully the alterations in the passage are framed to exclude the system which the Confessionalists ground upon it—a claim to which many Churchmen have inconsiderately assented. Nor can there be the smallest doubt that the Church does not intend the doubting man to be relieved in the same way as the dying man; and the reasons of this may be easily seen, the man whose time on earth is short, and whose mental vision is perplexed by the coming change, and perhaps also distracted by pains and weakness, often needs to be dealt with more rapidly and more distinctly, and to have the power of his sins broken more swiftly and briefly—more palpably so to say—than the man, who in health and strength has time to take in the meaning of the word of God put before him, and to let it do its work on his soul. At all events, it is absolutely certain that no form of absolution is permitted to the minister; there was, as I have before said, formerly the rubric in the Visitation Office recognising such a practice, and prescribing a form for it (see page 112); but it was deliberately struck out; and Laud, who saw that its absence from the passage, combined with its having been expunged, was fatal to the Confessionalist view, tried to have a form prescribed in the exhortation paragraph, but failed. Hence it is not unreasonable to suppose that when the Church took away the form of absolution, and used 'minister' in place of a 'priest,' it was to guard against the very thing which the modern school are trying to establish.

[margin: Why absolution is permitted on a deathbed.]

[margin: No absolution permitted in the preparation for Holy Communion.]

CHAPTER XIV.

Summary of the proofs and arguments on each side—Case of the Confessionalists—Case on the other side—Practical conclusions—Difference between Rome and Confessionalists one of degree not of kind—Between Confessionalists one of kind not of degree—Powers conferred by ordination—How exercised in our Church—Absolution does not convey pardon—Not even in *I absolve thee*—Confession—Confession as viewed by the Confessionalists and in the Church of England—Special confession in the Visitation Office—Recognised nowhere else—Difference between confidence and confession—Between what is suggested in the Communion Office and that permitted in the Visitation Office—The question is not between habitual and occasional confession—How this notion arose—Flaw in the theory of occasional auricular confession—Solution of the difficulty in which Ritualists plead they are placed by the importunity of applicants—Unreality of the plea—Danger of even confidential consultations in these days—Laity not responsible for the revival of the practice—How clergymen may deal with those who consult them—For relief of mind—For disclosing a doubt—Auricular confession a misuse of the clerical office—Cannot be claimed by the laity as a right—How such an applicant to be dealt with—This method pursued since the Reformation—Distinction between mortal and venial sin—Does not authorise auricular confession—Nor do the Confessionalists confine the practice to mortal sin—Plea for absolution as a restitution to a state of grace.

My readers are now in possession of the proofs and arguments which are urged on each side the question, and will be able to decide for themselves whether auricular confession, or sacramental confession—call it which you will—as held by our Confessionalists (see pages 19-91), is or is not a part of the revealed economy of God for the salvation of souls; whether it is ordained, or recommended, or recognised by our Church; whether it is in accordance with the mind of our Church to restore the system to the place which it held before the Reformation. I cannot help thinking that men of calm judgments and clear thought will have not much difficulty in making up their minds on the matter.

Case of the Confessionalists. On the one side there is adduced a passage of Scripture, taken professedly in its strictest literal sense, as giving to priests personally the power which they claim to exercise *jure divino*—one or two other passages of Scripture which they interpret with still less reason in the same sense—a certain number of passages in writers of the third and fourth centuries, which, taken apart from the context and the facts of the time, may be understood in its favour—its universal recognition and adoption in the Mediæval Church up to the time of the Reformation—the use of our Lord's words in the ordination formula of our Church—the directions given for preparation for the Holy Communion—the prescribed use of a definite formula in the office for the Visitation of the Sick—and some expressions in a canon and a homily which do not fairly or reasonably bear the interpretation put upon them. I believe this fairly exhausts the case of the Confessionalists, as far as concerns its being an ordinance of God, or recognised as such by our Church.

Case on the other side. On the other side, there is the fact that the Confessionalists themselves do not take in its simple literal sense the very passage in St. John, the literal meaning of which they maintain it is impossible to disguise or evade: and that the other passages cannot be, and, in the judgment of sound divines of all ages, do not admit of being, thus applied. The fact, too, that there is not in Scripture the smallest trace of this sacerdotal power being exercised by the presbyters, or even by the Apostles themselves, except once in the remission of ecclesiastical censures by St. Paul, which, of course, is entirely beside the question; that the passages which are quoted from the Fathers in support of the practice, refer without exception to the public discipline, in no case to private absolution, in no case to private confession as an ordinance of God: these too are clearly beside the question: that there are, at least, un

equal number of passages in Patristic writers of that age
denouncing private confession to man of sins against God;
that, whereas early writers mention several methods of
exercising the commission given in St. John, the power
of giving absolute forgiveness of sins on private confession to a priest is not among them; that the growth and
prevalence of this practice in the Church was coincident
with the decadence of Christianity into Mediævalism, so
that its recognition and adoption in those corrupt times,
so far from being any proof of its being from God, is
exactly the reverse. That even when private confession
had taken the place of public discipline, the power, technically termed that of the keys, was exercised not in a judicial form, but in one which implied not the actuality,
but the possibility of pardon. That our Church in the
Ordination formula must be held to use our Lord's words
as He used them, and that they cannot be held or intended to confer a greater power on the priest of the
present day than the Apostles believed themselves to be
invested with; and that this *à priori* view is confirmed
by the fact that the Church does not claim the power
to forgive sins, but only to absolve, the former being
reserved to Christ Himself; and consistently with this,
in no one of the cases in which the clergy are allowed to
pronounce absolution, is it represented as conveying or
declaring absolute forgiveness of sins, not even in the
Visitation office; that in the exhortation to the Holy
Communion it is so far from being the fact that private confession of sins to a priest for its own sake is recommended or suggested, that a formerly existing direction to that effect was expunged, and the communication
to the priest confined to the opening to him some particular grief, not with a view to its forgiveness, but to its
solution—to comfort and counsel; and the method directed
to be used by the minister to remove any such doubt of

God's mercy is not a formal absolution, but the ministry of God's word. This is the case which my readers will have to decide—for myself, I cannot conceive any theory to have more completely broken down than that of the Confessionalists'.

Summary of conclusions.

The practical conclusions which I wish to put before my readers, or rather the conclusions, to which I trust the foregoing pages may have led them, may be summed up as follows:—

Difference between Rome and Confessionalists in degree not in kind.

1. The difference between the Romanists and the Confessional School among ourselves is one only of *degree*, not of *kind*. In the former, auricular confession (that is, private confession and private absolution, together forming a Divine ordinance and spiritual discipline for the salvation of souls and for the forgiveness of sin after baptism) is canonically necessary and indispensable: in the latter, it is—in theory at least—not canonically necessary, but only morally—only optional, not obligatory—occasional, not habitual; though from the way in which it is put forth and insisted upon it is, to all practical intents and purposes, necessary, obligatory, and habitual.

Between Confessionalists and Church of England in kind.

2. That the difference between the system and practice of the Confessionalists and the authorised teaching and practice of the Church of England is one not of *degree* only, but of *kind*. Auricular confession being in the one *a*—sometimes *the*—divinely appointed method of absolute and direct forgiveness of sin, and absolute assurance of individual sins being actually pardoned: in the other no such method is recommended or recognised.

Power conferred by ordination,

3. That the powers conferred by our Lord on His Church by the commission given in St. John, and committed to the second order of our clergy in Ordination, are exercised by the faithful dispensation, whether general or special, of the Word and Sacraments, and public intercessory prayer, as in the early Church; while in the Con-

fessionalist system they are held to be exercised by a divinely conferred privilege of hearing confessions, and a divinely conferred power of forgiving sins, actually and immediately, or pronouncing them to be actually forgiven, by virtue of certain prescribed words pronounced sacerdotally by a priest, which did not exist in the early Church. *[according to Confessionalists.]*

4. That the exercise of the power specially conferred on the second order of the clergy is by our Church confined to cases in which the promise of God's mercy on repentance and faith is to be set before and offered to a congregation or individual, by being declared or prayed for in a prescribed formula by a minister authorised by Christ and His Church to do so; which formula is not, however, conceived to convey that actual forgiveness of sin or that actual assurance of having received pardon, which are essential elements of the Confessionalist theory. *[How exercised in our Church.]*

5. That while confession in the Confessionalist method of dealing with individuals is always the recounting of sins, as part of a supernatural ordinance for the forgiveness thereof, and therefore always with a view to formal absolution, and necessary to it—always, where held to be complete, sufficient, and effective, followed by it, in our Church's system—in the single case in which it is recognised—it is the disclosure, not necessarily private, of some particular pressing sin or sins, or doubt or scruple—primarily with a view to relief by unbosoming a secret burden, or to the reception of spiritual comfort from the minister, without consequent absolution being necessary to its completeness or effectiveness; nor yet to be followed by absolution, except where it has failed of producing its proper effects of relieving the man's conscience from a distrust of God's mercy and a despair of pardon. *[Confession.]*

6. That absolution in the Church of England is in no case held to convey actual forgiveness of sins or the *[Absolution does not convey pardon.]*

actual assurance of pardon as a *fait accompli*: and that while in the Confessionalist theory, absolution is *virtute signi*—by virtue of the words used—held to do away with the penal consequences of sins previously confessed, in the Church of England it is not so; but with us, it is only held to remove the *moral* consequences of sin—*i.e.* the doubts of the possibility of pardon which sin naturally produces in the human mind: and this result is produced not by any inherent virtue in the priest's words, but by virtue of the certainty of God's promise thus expressed—*virtute significati*, and not *virtute signi*.

<small>Not even in 'I absolve thee.'</small>

7. That the words '*I absolve thee*' do not, as in the Confessionalist system, convey the actual pardon of sins, or the actual assurance of sins being coincidently pardoned, but only, where necessary, put before a despairing sinner the offer and promise of that pardon sealed by the personal exercise on the part of the presbyter of the authority—given by Christ to His Church, and committed to such presbyter at ordination—to declare authoritatively and definitely to all and singular, as need may be, the message of the remission of sins—that God pardoneth and absolveth all those that truly repent; and that this case is no exception to the message so committed to his ministration. That there is no power in the priest to grant pardon—no power to assure pardon, except so far as the Divine faithfulness, justice and mercy are pledged to the message which He has entrusted to His Church and its ministers—from which the minister officially declares to the doubting man that his sins do not exclude him.

<small>Special confession in Visitation Office</small>

8. Hence the special confession in the Visitation Office differs from the Confession of the Romanists and the Confessionalists essentially and invariably; it is not that, when used, it is the same as that of the Confessionalists; but, even when used, it differs from it in nature, aim, and result—in nature, as not being an act of disci-

pline, or part of a sacramental ordinance; but very little removed from confidence, and that only in the accident of being sometimes followed by absolution—in aim, as not necessarily or primarily contemplating absolution— in result, as not, even when followed by absolution, having anything directly to do with the actual pardon of sin, but only with the dispelling, on the common principles of man's moral nature, that morbid distrust in God's mercy, which, taking into account the nature of the message, the evidence of its reality, and the ambassadorial character of those who officially bear witness to it, it is a violation of right reason to entertain.

9. That in no case, except that of a sick bed, is special confession recognised or recommended, whether with or without absolution, even limited as above; and that in the exhortation to the Holy Communion the opening of the grief, suggested by the Church, differs in kind from the confession of the Confessionalists, inasmuch as in no case is it more than what I have termed Confidence, generally followed by the remedial ministry of God's Word. Special confession nowhere else recognised.

10. That Confidence differs from the Confession of the Confessionalist in not being an act of discipline or humiliation or penitence, or a preliminary to, or an essential condition of, an ordinance or rite of pardon, but only the opening of a grief, or a burden, or doubt, or difficulty to a minister, with a view to receive counsel: or in certain cases, that comfort and release from a distrust of God's mercy, which in the Visitation service, and only there, are sometimes conveyed, as I stated above, by formal absolution, when the mere unbosoming of the burden does not produce the desired result. Difference between Confidence and Confession.

11. The difference between what is suggested as an occasional resource in the preparation for the Holy Communion, and what is permitted in the Visitation Office is not, that, absolution being given in both, in the one it is Difference between what is suggested in the Communion Office

and what is permitted in the Visitation Office.

ministerial and pastoral, while in the other it is judicial, sacerdotal, and sacramental: so that this latter, being confined to a deathbed, is not contemplated as a preparation for the Holy Communion. It seems to me that we cannot exclude from the preparation for the Holy Communion that which is permitted in the Visitation of the Sick, by any such distinction. The facts are misstated, and the distinction seems arbitrary and illusory. I think the point may be more truly established on less slippery ground. The difference between them is, that in the one absolution is never permitted, in the other it occasionally is. The doubt and distrust are the same in both, but the way of meeting them is different. In the one a sinner is led and encouraged to draw what he needs by the energies of his own repentant reason from God's own words, placed before him by His minister, without this one interposing his special authority. In the other, the priest, formally and by absolution, puts before the doubting soul the same message on the warrant of the authority which the Church and the clergy have received, thus to minister to those who need it. In the one the written promises of God are placed before the man as applicable to himself; the other is a special application, or rather the authoritative declaration of the *applicability* (if I may venture to coin a word), of those promises on the authority committed to the Church; and so far this is an exercise of a priestly office which is wanting in the other.[1] In the one the convictions of reviving faith are more immediate, fresh, and personal; in the other, these convictions are mediate and second hand, so to say. Nothing comes to the sinner which might not have come to him in a better way—for I venture to think that the faith which comes to a sinner from the

---

[1] Why this is permitted to a dying man we have already considered (page 188).

active energies of his own inner man is better and higher than that which he takes in passively from the formal utterance of another man—had it not been for that extreme lack of faith, caused by his great sin, which made him distrust either God's will or power to forgive him. The distinction between the two is thus real and intelligible. They both indeed differ from the Confession of the Romanists and of our own Confessionalists—the one, inasmuch as no absolution is pronounced: the other because the absolution, when pronounced, is different in kind and essence from that of the Romanists, in not being sacramental, judicial, or effective, set forth as a grant, or as an assurance, of actual pardon.

It is not, therefore, merely against the extreme view of the Confessionalists that the Church bears witness—that Sacramental Confession is the only or the surest appointed means of obtaining pardon; nor yet merely against its being practised habitually: but actually there is no case in which the Church either contemplates confession to a priest, as part of an ordained rite for the forgiveness of sins, necessarily followed by absolution: nor yet any case in which the absolute judicial forgiveness of sins is attributed to absolution, as a result implied and contained in, and granted by, the priest's words—a *fait accompli* when those words have been spoken. In fact, those who in defining that which our Church recognises in individual cases—whether it be the Confidence of ordinary spiritual life, or the Confession in the Visitation Office—make the difference between the Romanists and us to consist in the habitual and the occasional use thereof, are either confounding technical Confession with Confidence, or Confession essentially joined to absolution with Confession essentially independent of it: or are taking a superficial view of the passage in the exhortation in the Communion Office; or fail to realise the fact that the absolution and pardon are different things.

Not merely the extreme view which our Church does not recognise.

The question is not between habitual and occasional Confession.

How this Confession has come to pass.

It is true, indeed, that in Auricular Confession, and in that which our Church recognises, there are points of external and accidental identity, and one of these is that both *may* be viewed as occasional. In the Church of England, both confidence and special confession are only occasional, and it is possible to form an illogical conception of Auricular Confession as being only occasional. This, perhaps, has suggested the too general solution of the difficulty, which supposes that the former is only a modified use of the latter; but I trust that I have shown that this accidental resemblance does not justify anyone in arguing an identity, which is contradicted by a comparison of the nature and use of the two systems; and that Auricular Confession is so utterly alien to the Church of England that if it were used but once, it would be as real a contravention of what the Church teaches as if it were used habitually.

Flaw in the distinction between habitual and occasional confession.

Those who admit occasional and deny habitual Confession are in reality playing the game of the most advanced school: for in the view which admits the occasional use of confession as a means of forgiveness of sin, there is a fatal flaw. If Confession and Absolution be in any case a divine ordinance for the forgiveness of sins, it must be so in all, or at the very least no one can wisely or safely dispense with it. It can only be needless or useless where there is no sin—that is never. The occasional use of Auricular Confession is a solecism—if true at all, it must be habitual and universal, and the system which asserts its occasional use is a negative of the whole claim. But in the view which I have endeavoured to show to be that of our Church, no such difficulty arises. For if absolution be viewed as a formal way of setting God's promises and offers, distinctly and absolutely before men, as by special authority committed to our Presbyters, then it is clear that, according to the temperaments of different men, the most formal and direct mode of so doing, such as the form in the Visitation service, may be very useful for some sick men, and entirely out of place in others: it cannot be habitual; it must be occasional. If it is identified with Auricular Confession, it must be habitual, or it is a delusion.

This will furnish a ready solution of the difficulty in which the Confessionalists sometimes represent themselves as being placed, and by which they often puzzle the authorities who expostulate with them: pretending that this practice is, as it were, taken from them by force by the numbers who come to them demanding to be confessed and absolved. 'What are we to do'—such is their touching question—'when a sinner comes to us in distress of mind, and prays us to hear the tale of his sins, and to give him forgiveness by absolution?' Of course the unsoundness of this plea is easily seen through, even where it is *bonâ fide* and not a mere sophistical pretence. There would be no confession, say they, among the clergy if the laity did not come to be confessed. The truth is, that there would have been no desire for confession among the laity, had there been no persons who set themselves up for confessors; if the doctrine and the practice had not been recommended and carried out, at first secretly among the young and inexperienced of either sex, and afterwards more boldly, as the system took root, among older men of mediæval mind. It *may* be perfectly true that it began by one or more young men coming to some one who had a high reputation for sanctity and spiritual-mindedness, to ask his advice in spiritual matters; but the responsibility and the sin of the system does not rest with these, but with those whose answer was 'Let me confess you'; especially the men whose restless spirit of innovating Mediævalism have produced so much evil within the last thirty years. Had they, at the very beginning, chosen to deal with those who applied to them, as English clergy-

<small>Plea that Auricular Confession is forced upon the clergy by the laity.</small>

men, and not as Romish priests, the evil (of which at pres
we only see the beginnings), would have been checked in
its bud. The superstitious cravings of inexperienced minds
would have been directed towards those more true and
Scriptural methods of relieving their consciences and laying
hold of pardon, which the Church of England has carefully,
and to those in health and strength exclusively, set forth.
Faith in the act of a priest would not have taken the place
of faith in the promises of Christ. But then the priestly
temper in which superstition, delusion, and ambition are
strangely mingled, would not have placed its foot upon the
first step of the ladder.

<small>Unreality of such a plea.</small>

It seems perfectly clear that such a plea cannot be
accepted as *bonâ fide*, except when it comes from men,
who are not accustomed to urge the practice upon
those who are placed in their charge or subject to their
influence; and yet I am afraid that in very many, if not
most cases, the plea is urged by those who have lost no
opportunity by sermons, or conversations, or the circu-
lation of tracts, to represent it as an ordained means
of grace, an institution of the Church, if not absolutely
necessary, at least very useful for the development and
preservation of the spiritual life; who never lose an opportunity of preaching and teaching it in season and out of
season, continually exhorting and inciting to it, putting
temptations and facilities in the way of the people, especially the young, and more especially young girls. The
whole system of confessional boxes, of particular appointments for time, and place for hearing confessions,
the opening offices and consulting rooms (to use their
favourite illustration of the lawyer and the physican) for
the purpose, are as much suggestions and encouragements
and temptations to the practice of Confession, addressed
to those who never would have thought of it, as betting
offices are temptations to bet. Mind, I am drawing no

parallel between the two evils, but merely showing that what is encouragement and temptation in the one case is also temptation and encouragement in the other. And more than this—the suggesting confidential communications—distinguished though they be essentially from Confession—is in these days almost an invitation and an encouragement to the evil from which it is very properly distinguished. It is opening the door by which our Jesuit clergy will not fail to try to lead men on. When a well-meaning, short-sighted clergyman in the present day proclaims to his congregation that he will be ready in the vestry to hear what people have to disclose to him, he ought to add that probably it will be the first step toward the *soi-disant* sacrament of penance. I am saying nothing against the practice itself in ordinary times; except that it is good only as a remedy against a morbid state—a morbid state which it is better to prevent than to cure—better to remedy in some other way than this one so full of danger. It is like restoring the health by stimulants rather than by nourishing wholesome food. *Danger of confidential communications in these days.*

 I have seen an argument to the effect that as absolution is only given to those who humbly and earnestly seek it, it could not have been given to the laity, unless the laity had sought it; this has the usual flaws of Ritualistic reasoning—a suicidal unconsciousness that if the weapon were sharp, it would wound themselves, combined with a logical incapacity of seeing the flaw which makes it harmless. The very terms of the plea give up at once half the position, for it contemplates Confession as confined to a sick bed, which is one of the points which they are least willing to concede. Passing by, however, this mistake, we may observe that it loses sight of the consideration of how, and by whom this appetite was created. Is it pretended that the ritualistic clergy did not—do not—suggest it, recommend it, urge it, or that they ever tried to prevent or *Laity not responsible for it.*

persuade the laity from it? of course they could not force it on those who were not willing to receive it, but if this willingness was created by suggestions, arguments, exhortations, representations of its necessity or benefit, then the source of the evil is to be sought in those who set the stone rolling. It is much the same as if the man who gave the stone the first push from the top of the hill were to say that it was the law of gravitation which was to be blamed for the result. A vender of poisonous nostrums cannot get ignorant people to swallow them against their will; to have recourse to a gipsy fortune-teller is a piece of voluntary folly; but the one would not be relieved from criminal responsibility by the plea that his victims took them willingly; or the other by the plea that the dupes came to the gipsies, and not the gipsies to them. Now that, thanks to the exertions of the ritualists, the practice has taken root, I have no doubt that persons who have listened to Confessionalist preachers, or otherwise fallen into Confessionalist hands, do occasionally come to a clergyman and ask to be confessed: there is an old proverb about the rapid propagation of folly that is nowhere more *à propos* than here; and this is one thing among many which should make fathers of families very cautious how they allow their daughters to frequent ritualistic services, or to cultivate the society of ritualising friends.

How a clergyman may deal with those who consult him, unbosoming a burden.

I confess I cannot help thinking that those who are really unwilling to see it revived amongst us will find a very easy way of dealing with such applicants as I have referred to above. For instance, if a troubled conscience thus presents itself, it would be easy to ascertain whether the trouble arose for that yearning for sympathy which unburdens itself in that to which I have given the distinctive name of Confidence, or from a doubt of its being possible to obtain pardon for some sin or some course of sin, which seeks for solution in that same Confidence.

In the former case it is perfectly easy to warn the applicant that this Confidence must not be considered as an act of religion forming a characteristic feature in the Christian scheme: that though for many reasons the pastor is, humanly speaking, the natural person for such disclosures, yet he must not be considered as the minister, but as the friend; that it is not in his power to give any other relief or consolation than that which it would be equally in the power of any other faithful, discreet, and learned Christian to give.

If it be the second case, it would be easy to tell him that this Confidence must not be looked upon as an act of religion, in the sense in which confession to God is an act of religion; nor yet as an act of discipline in the sense in which public confession was an act of discipline in the primitive Church: but simply as an application for the solution of a spiritual doubt on a point, which the ministers of Christ and of His word and sacraments, are specially commissioned and authorised to solve: but he must be told that they are to be looked upon, not as judges, but as ministers and ambassadors. He may, indeed, in certain cases be examined as to whether he has repented him of the secret sins with which his soul is burdened: such a general examination into his repentance may be conceivably modelled on the way and means which are prescribed in the preparation for the Holy Communion; but this is no encouragement to Auricular Confession (see page 92). In the case of those who come to a minister on the suggestion contained in the exhortation to the Holy Communion, even this examination is needless, inasmuch as they come to him, after having gone through the repentance prescribed in the preceding paragraphs; but even in any other cases, it seems to be worse than unnecessary to enquire into the nature and particulars of the sin, inasmuch as the question is, not whether the sins which the

Disclosing a doubt

How to be dealt with.

person has committed are scarlet or not, but whether he has repented of them. And the mere fact of the man coming to a minister with such a doubt on his mind and such a desire for its solution, is in itself a proof of there being a change of mind, which, as every one knows, is the proper meaning of repentance. I say 'worse than unnecessary,' because the insisting on knowing all the details and circumstances of sin before it can be pronounced within the limits of God's mercy, is to suppose that there is in this respect a difference between the debt of the five hundred pence and the debt of fifty—the Gospel message being that the same mercy is ready freely to forgive both.

<small>Auricular Confession an abuse of the clerical office</small>

Is it not strange that men, the very men authorised to set forth God's mercy in the light of day, should dare to conceal, alter, or disguise it for a moment? For myself, I no more dare do it—I no more dare tell a man that God's mercy waits on my sentence, than I dare tell him that Christ died for our sins, only if I say He did, or that He is the sinner's Advocate with the Father, only if I say that He is so. When to a man standing in the position of an ordained priest of the Church of England there comes a person in the bond of his sins, bound by a morbid distrust of God's mercy—an unreasonable, because faithless fear of God being unwilling or unable to pardon his sins—does that priest fulfil the holy office which God has put into his hands—does he perform his duty to his Church, which puts Christ's commission into his hands, when he tells such an one that there is no hope to be found by him in God's pledged word, no well of comfort open for him in the Scriptures—that turning to a priest and trusting to him, to his sentence and his word, is the only or the surest way? Is it not his bounden office to tell him that, though actual recovery from habits of sin may be difficult and tedious, yet that the forgiveness of past sin is not so—that forgiveness of his sins is absolutely ready for him on certain terms? And on what terms? Confession to a priest? humble acceptance of his sentence? humble obedience to what he enjoins? Surely not; but confession to God, faith in Christ, acceptance of pardon, resolution to amend.

And as for pressing for formal absolution, or as some put it, insisting on it as a right, even in the Visitation office, the word '*humbly*' seems to negative the notion of any such rightful claim to the particular exercise of the ministerial commission in formal absolution; as far as the minister is under any obligation to give it, this arises from his duty to the Church who has directed it. And when it comes to the practical question of dealing with such a clamorous applicant, in any case save that of the dying man, it seems to me perfectly easy for a clergyman to answer— as he would answer a man who asked to be re-baptised for the remission of post-baptismal sin—by telling him plainly that he is not authorised to reassure him by the pronouncing of any form of absolution; he may tell him that formerly there was such a form provided, but that it was deliberately struck out, and that the remedy substituted was the ministry of God's word; that even were he authorised to pronounce any such form, it would not be accompanied by the absolute forgiveness of sins; that it would simply be a declaration on his ambassadorial authority, that the bond of sin, if repented of, could not really bind his soul to itself; that no sin, if repented of, was any barrier between the sinner and God's mercy, or any limit to its infinite extent: and that this assurance was not more attainable by the use of a formal absolution than by the remedy which is here directed: perhaps less so, except in the only case in which he was authorised to use it, when a soul was on the river's brink. And then he might administer the prescribed remedy—read to him those parts of Scripture which set forth God's mercy most unmistakingly and touchingly—the parable of the prodigal son, for instance, the restoration of St. Peter, the forgiveness of David, and all those other passages with which a minister of God's word ought to be furnished (see page 115 note).[1] And this, in fact, is the way in which for three centuries in the English Church these doubts and difficulties have been solved, and sick souls led to comprehend and accept the infinite mercy of God. This is the way in which the ministry of reconciliation in such cases has been exercised by successive generations of the clergy, among whom were thousands upon thousands of ordained men, not less devoted, not less faithful to their God, their Church, and the trust committed to them at their ordination, not less honest, not less learned, not less clear-sighted and far-sighted, not less successful in bringing souls to God, and in quieting troubled, and reassuring doubting, consciences, than those innovating Mediævalists of the present day, who pretend to have rediscovered, not a royal, but a sacerdotal road to heaven.

Distinction between sins mortal and venial. The Confessionalists, though most usually they speak of Auricular Confession as the proper remedy for all sins, are sometimes driven to draw a distinction between sins which do require it, and sins which do not. It is true that the distinction drawn by Mediæval and patristic theology between venial sins and mortal sins may have some ground; indeed, our Church seems to recognise the distinction when deadly sin is spoken of in the Litany and in the Articles, where it appears to be used to express sins, humanly speaking, of a more heinous dye; but the distinction can hardly be maintained with reference either to their guilt or their pardon; for St. James tells us that he who is guilty of the least is guilty also of all; and

---

[1] It is recorded of Bossuet that he adopted this method of dealing with the Duchesse d'Orléans (daughter of Charles I.) on her bed of sudden death, even though she had been confessed and absolved by her confessor.

even if it were not so, it would hardly be possible or fitting for man to judge what were mortal sins in God's sight, and what venial: nor yet as to the possibility or method of forgiveness; for we are expressly told that the sin of five hundred pence is the object of the same free mercy as the sin of fifty pence. The distinction probably arose in the days in which some sins were held by the Pœnitentiarius to require public satisfaction to the Church, and others were not. A mortal sin is clearly not the same as the sin unto death, for that is so unpardonable that it may not even be prayed for: and what it is—its very nature and indications—is hid in the secret judgments of God's knowledge; and even if it were otherwise, it could not be the subject of the Confessionalists' absolution, for this concerns the pardon of sin, and, where the sin is unpardonable, this could find no place. The distinction may hold with reference to one sin being more fatal in its effects on the soul than another, or as being a stronger evidence of a soul being spiritually dead than another: but this has nothing to do with the forgiveness of the sin, which the Confessionalists pretend is the essence of private absolution; though it has something to do with private absolution viewed as the authoritative offer of God's mercy, which removes the obstacles and looses the bands whereby grievous sins keep the soul in bondage from God; and thus our Church wisely reserves private absolution for the case of such exceptionally weighty or heinous matter. But the mercy which is proclaimed, and the message of proclamation is essentially the same in itself and in its results, in the case of all sins, whether mortal or venial—God's will to forgive which God's ministers proclaim in the Morning and Evening Prayer. *Does not authorise Auricular Confession*

Besides which the Confessionalists are very far from following the directions of the Church in restricting the uses of private absolution to those cases of grievously *This not confined by Confessionalists to mortal sin.*

disturbed consciences, which supposing themselves to be out of the sphere of God's mercy, do without any priestly admonitions, or suggestions, or promptings, humbly and earnestly desire it at their hands.

<small>Absolution as a restoration to a state of grace.</small>

They sometimes, however—losing hold for a time of their real doctrine that absolution is the forgiveness of sins—take occasion from this distinction between mortal and venial sin to put it before us as merely a restoration to that state of grace which had been lost by mortal sin: thus thinking to steer clear of some of the difficulties in which they are placed by their claim to pardon sin absolutely. But this cannot be held to be more tenable than the other: for this restoration to a state of grace follows coincidently, either on the forgiveness of sins, or on repentance, or on the recovery of the gift of the Holy Spirit by some of God's appointed means. Of these pardon is excluded by the view which they for the nonce profess to take of absolution: and Auricular Confession is certainly not repentance, nor does it carry with it any special gift of the Spirit. The sinner is not restored to a state of grace by virtue of the act or words of the priest, as the penitent was restored to church fellowship and privileges by the imposition of hands. In fact, it can only be viewed as a restoration to a state of grace as being the means to that restoration, by encouraging or creating a full trust in that mercy, for the acceptance of which it sets the soul free, loosing the bonds of fear and distrust, by an official declaration thereof.

CHAPTER XV.

Catena alleged in favour of it—Value of a catena overrated—Especially when not contrasted with practice—Opposite catenæ—Variety of views in English divines—This caused by the want of a clear idea of truth—By a rapid and fertile thought—Especially under pressure of opposition—This very perceptible in English writers—Passages often taken without the context—Conditions of value for a catena—All authorities to be struck out of the catena who are speaking of something different to the point alleged—And those whose views are based on probably erroneous grounds—Or where they are at variance with the Church of England or with history, or with each other—On the other side, a large catena of practice—Occasional instance of absolution—Not always in harmony with the Church teaching—Catena of authorities on the other side—What the catena is worth at its highest and best—Catena cannot supply evidence—Nor can any amount of vague assumptions—Nor counterbalance the lack of it—Limitations introduced by these divines fatal to their theory—Benefits alleged as arising from the practice—See-saw argument of the Confessionalists—Testimony to its benefits—From personal experience—From parochial experience—Not necessary to parish work properly carried on—Perhaps necessary to public discipline if it existed among us—Possibly useful for direction, but this not recognised in our Church—Confidential intercourse admits neither sacramental confession nor direction—Confession and absolution are not to be directed as a condition of pardon, or used to get the secrets of a man's soul—Alleged benefits counterbalanced by known evils—Question whether it is not an intrusion on the revealed scheme of salvation—This the great question—The evil of this not counterbalanced by any great benefits—What God has given us is exhaustive and sufficient—Clergy not physicians, but only errand-boys of the Great Physician—Have no licence to alter or add to His panaceæ—Certainty of methods prescribed by God—Danger of human devices—Auricular confession implies disbelief in God's promises—The importance of this principle makes me defer the consideration of the benefits of confession—Argument for toleration is a sign of conscious weakness—Not likely to succeed—Apathy on the point quite unintelligible—Important results of the confessional: Theologically—Evangelically—Ecclesiastically—Religiously—Personally—Nationally—Socially—Danger of again allowing it to take root.

WE must now turn to another point alleged by the Confessionalists, viz. that there is a strong catena of *Catena alleged in favour of it.*

English divines in its favour. They bring forward a list of names in successive generations who have advocated Confession, or at least tolerated it as allowable. Some advocates of the system rest their case on this ground almost exclusively; and its influence is felt by a still greater number who, without themselves teaching it or practising Confession, yet allow the occasional use of it.

Value of a catena generally over-rated.

It seems to be a thing much needed that some accurate notion should be formed of the worth of a catena, both in its intrinsic value as embodying truth, and its bearing on any particular points as an evidence in support thereof. I think that many persons on reflection will be inclined to think that very often more value is given to it than it deserves. A beam of iron is made by a celebrated firm. There is an *à priori* probability of its bearing a certain amount of pressure in a vital part of the building, but I should be sorry to employ an architect who took it for granted that it would be so. If it bends, its being of this or that manufacture does not prove that it is strong or elastic enough. This is an illustration of my position with regard to catenæ. They very often, indeed, only evidence the opinion of a particular school, the adherence of a particular party to a notion which reflects some of its peculiar characteristics. It often happens that a man, of learning and power of a peculiar kind, lays down a proposition or an argument which, recommending itself to minds of a kindred tone, is accepted by those who follow him, either for its own plausibility, or on the faith of the name with which it is associated, without being tested or weighed. It is repeated generation after generation in the same way—gathering weight and substance more rapidly and solidly as it rolls on from one man to another, until at last it seems to be as substantial as the truth itself, or at least seems to embody the judgments of many minds, whereas in reality it is only the notion of the single mind whence it first sprung. It is therefore no disrespect to the eminent men, whose names are cited as authorities to test any position or notion by the evidence which we should apply to it, if it were proposed to us for the first time.

A curious illustration of how little trust can be safely placed on a catena is to be found in the almost universally received notion that the sufferings of our Lord on the Cross are represented at the consecration of the elements by the breaking the bread and pouring out the wine. There is perhaps no point for which there is a longer or more universal catena than this; and yet the wine is not thus poured out during the office of the Lord's Supper; in most cases not at all; in none, at the moment at which the representation is supposed to be made. *Illustration of this.*

And such opinions are all the more likely to be received on the credit of the names who sanction them, or of the school with whose system they are connected, when, the practice itself having either altogether or almost fallen into disuse, theologians are not bound to test an abstract opinion by its practical working and tendency: when they are able to hold an opinion without being led by its practical importance to look into the grounds upon which it is based, or to define its exact nature as carefully as they might and ought, and perhaps with as much care as they would have thought themselves bound to use, had it presented itself to their minds in its practical bearings. Thus, till within the last twenty years a theologian who held the Divine authority of the ordained clergy would naturally in general terms maintain, in opposition to the school which denied it, that the clergy had a power of remitting sins: and his language might possibly seem to include the Confessionalist system, in consequence of his taking no care to exclude a point which practically did not present itself to him. In such circumstances again men are often be- *Especially when not contrasted with practice.*

trayed by a spirit of opposition, to which even a theological mind is liable, into using exaggerated terms, in maintenance of some theory, while the practical difficulties which might have led them to modify such terms, do not present themselves to their minds; and surely to assert that these expressions necessarily express an opinion in favour of a development or application of that theory, in a way which was not present to their minds when they wrote, is, I think, to misinterpret and misrepresent them.

Opposite catenæ.

Again, it results from the very nature of catenæ, being as they are, a reflection of the changing shades of human judgment, that it is possible to draw out opposed catenæ on both sides the question, not only from the writings of leading men in the same Church and in the same generation, but even from different writings of the same man, sometimes even from different pages of the same book.

Variety of views in English divines.

I do not think that anyone can study the writings of our English divines, who are adduced in favour of Confession, without being struck by the fact that their language, taken as a whole, does not exhibit clear and definite views on the subject: they seem to be vibrating between two notions, each of which they alternately wish to assert, without denying the other so absolutely as to be precluded from giving it prominence when its turn comes. This would seem to arise partly from the general laws of human thought, partly from the circumstances in which controversialists are for the most part placed.

This caused by the want of a clear idea of truth,

There are very few men who have so distinct and complete an idea of truth in the whole and in all its parts, as to be always consistent with themselves; and of course the more fanciful and mystical the mind—the more abstruse and abstract the subject—the more voluminous the writer—the greater is the chance, or rather the certainty, that his authority can be quoted on both sides the question.

Men of fertile genius and rapid thought, especially if words flow quickly from their lips or their pens, and there is, as I said above, no practical point to act as a drag, are apt, when treating of some point in a particular aspect, to press it to the utmost, to exhibit it in all possible positions and colours; and in another treatise handling a different point to press that, too, to the utmost—to exhibit it in all its relations and colours, and thus to say at one time what is out of harmony with what is said at another. And this is more likely to be the case when there is a pressure from opposite sides, against one or other of which it was necessary to take up a strong position, and perhaps to advance a little beyond the right line. Thus our divines since the Reformation have been subjected to pressure on the one side from the Puritans, who denied altogether that the office and powers of the clergy were of divine origin and authority: and against these that office and those powers were magnified, since the denial or the limitation of the power of the keys, which was of course one of the points denied by the Puritans, would have been up to a certain point allowing them to have been right—a concession which it requires a, perhaps, unusual amount of controversial clearness to be able to make without carrying it too far; and a still more unusual amount of controversial fairness to be willing to make. The Romanist, too, asserted that we had with the Reformation lost the office and powers of the old priesthood, and this led on the defenders of the Reformed Church to claim the possession thereof more strongly than they otherwise would; while the Puritans, again, by asserting that the Church of England differed nothing from Rome, made it necessary for our divines to draw in their horns a little, to reduce what they claimed for the priesthood within more modest limits, and to use language essentially opposed to the pretensions and practices of Romish sacerdotalism. I think no one can

This very perceptible in English writers.

read our Mediævalistic divines without seeing traces of this see-saw, not only on the subject of Confession, but on others of an analogous nature. For myself, I confess that, for these reasons, catenæ have very little weight with me in determining any disputed point. Nor can I accept any such as even an indirect proof of the mind of the Church, otherwise than is laid down in the Prayer Book and Articles, or as interpreting the silence of the Prayer Book, or as giving to the language thereof a scope and meaning which it would not naturally and reasonably have. In fact, I rather take it as an evidence that the persons adducing it are conscious of the lack of that direct proof on which such a system ought to rest its claims for acceptance.

Passages often taken without the context.

Again, the way in which this particular catena is formed from isolated passages in the several writers, detached from the context, and without any notice being taken of the modifications or limitations elsewhere, creates an *à priori* suspicion of its value, which ripens into actual distrust, when it is subjected to the rigorous examination which, if it were worth anything, it ought to be able to bear.

Conditions of value for a catena.

For when we come to weigh the actual value of any catena, alleged as a support of any system, it is evident that there are certain obvious conditions which are necessary to its having any value at all, even in the eyes of those who are willing to give it weight. For instance, we must make ourselves sure that the authorities are speaking of the same point, in the same sense, in the same relations, as the system in support of which it is adduced. It is clear that those authorities who speak of the same thing differently at different times have no real value. Thus a writer who, maintaining Confession, alleges the disclosure of sins, as used in the early Church, preparatory to public discipline, must be at once struck out of the list, inasmuch as what the Confessionalists advocate is something which did not exist in the early Church. So again, all those must be struck off, who by confession mean only that which I have termed Confidence, for that which the Confessionalists recommend is, as we have seen, essentially different. Thus Bishop Andrewes, walking up and down in St. Paul's to listen to those who wished to consult him, is no evidence in favour of anything more than of Confidence. So again, those who hold absolution to be merely the remission of ecclesiastical censures must be struck off, inasmuch as the Confessionalists hold it as the actual channel of absolute forgiveness of sins committed against God. And when all these are struck off, the list is woefully diminished; and when again we exclude those who only held it in theory and never practised it themselves, or recommended it practically to others, I suspect that the catena will be found to consist of marvellously few links.

All to be struck out of the catena alleged, who are speaking something different from the point alleged.

Again, where a writer lends the sanction of his name to a theory which, adopted from others, rests on insufficient grounds, his name, however weighty it may be, does not add much strength to the chain. A curious instance of this may be found in Bishop Wilson—whose name, if that of any man, would be of great authority. Writing on the office for the Visitation of the Sick (for to this point alone he seems to confine his approval), he quotes Usher and Andrewes. The first he introduces as saying, that the Church of England refuses not any confession, whether public or private, which is necessary for the exercise of the power of the keys: forgetting to add that Usher[1] distinctly speaks of the power of the keys as exercised by the clergy solely in applying those means whereby God does remit sins, viz. the ministration of the word of God,

And those whose views are based on palpably erroneous grounds.

---

[1] Usher, p. 109.

and the sacraments, properly so called, to which he adds intercessory prayer and the remission of ecclesiastical censures; whereas what is meant by sacramental confession in the ordinary sense of the term is a power exercised by the clergy besides and beyond these: so that Bishop Wilson is either not speaking of what the Confessionalists mean, or he misrepresents Usher's meaning.

And again, he quotes Bishop Andrewes as another authority whom he follows: 'It is not said by Christ, 'whose sins ye wish and pray for and declare to be remitted, 'but whose sins ye remit.' Now if it be true, that the exercise of prayer be no true exercise of the keys, then there was no such thing in the Church till the indirect form was changed into the direct 'I absolve.' If to 'declare' is only a gloss upon the authority given by Christ, then our Church is wrong in saying that authority is given to declare and pronounce. If absolute remission of sins be the power conferred in the formula of Ordination, then nowhere does the Church authorise the clergy to exercise that power—certainly not in the Morning and Evening Service: and yet, where it is distinctly said that the authority is there exercised.

When they are at variance with our Church, or with history, or with each other.

The same principle I think applies to those writers who, in their defence of sacramental confession, have laid down [1] something which is at variance with, or in excess of, the manifest teaching of the Church of England, or with the known facts of history,[2] or even with what other writers alleging the same catena, have laid down.

The two first cases almost speak for themselves. Where a writer exceeds or contravenes the teaching of

---

[1] For instance, Bishop Cosin, 'if he has committed mortal sin, then we *require* confession of it to a priest.'

[2] *The duty of confession from the penitent to the priest has been commended by the Church in the purest times of antiquity.*—Dean Pierce.

our Church, his value in a catena on a point of Church teaching is proportionably diminished. With regard to the third, the value of a catena must depend on the virtue of the harmonious utterances of the several writers: so that contradictory utterances mutually affect the value of each other, and the catena perishes beneath the authorities produced. *Mole ruit suâ.* For instance, the man who says, *that the power must be used with great tenderness and discretion, and the rather because the sentence duly pronounced on earth will be ratified in heaven, and determine their future and final state,*[1] cannot be esteemed a very high authority by the man who speaks of an absolution as only declaratory, conditional, and ministerial.[2]

And further, against this shaky catena of theory, we are able to oppose a far larger unvaried catena of practice.[3] I suppose that there can be no doubt that up to the last thirty years it would be easy to count the cases in which there is any mention or evidence of a person having sought forgiveness of sins by means of sacerdotal absolution, or of any clergyman having taught it in the pulpit, or urged it in private; where mentioned, it is as something remarkable. The ordinary way in which a man made his peace with God was by the reception of the Holy Communion after the ordinary self-preparation; and though there have been instances in which divines have refused this to criminals who would not confess their guilt, yet this was required rather as a reparation to society and to justice, than as a condition to the exercise of any supposed sacerdotal power.

_{Catena of practice on other side.}

---

[1] Dr Hole, 1730.
[2] Dr. Hakewill. These quotations are all taken from the catena put forth by Mr. Gray.
[3] The Laudian divines admit that in their days the practice they recommend was all but extinct. This shows what must have been the tenor, not only of popular feeling, but of the practical teaching of the Church since the Reformation.

Occasional instances of its use.

Occasionally, indeed, there is mention of it in the cases of one or two political criminals, to whom absolution was ostentatiously administered by sympathising divines of the Laudian or Jacobite school; this was rather as an exhibition of political religious feeling, than as securing to the person absolved the spiritual benefits which it professed to convey.

I doubt very much whether many of the divines who are alleged in its favour availed themselves of it, or used it in their ministrations. We have the records of the last hours of many of these men, and, with a few exceptions,

Not always in harmony with the Church's teaching.

there is not the smallest trace of it. And even where it is recorded that certain learned men did avail themselves of it, we must stop for a moment to consider whether the controversial value of their practice is not affected by their betraying a manifestly fanciful or incorrect notion of what the Church permitted or recognised. Thus, for instance, it is recorded of Saunderson and Hooker that they both sought for and received absolution at the last, though it is not recorded that they felt themselves under that heavy pressure of mind which the Church recognises as a condition of special confession and, of course, of formal absolution; on the contrary, Saunderson, two days before, received the Holy Communion from his chaplain's hands; and of Hooker it is recorded that throughout his illness he had that submission to God's will which makes the sick man's bed easy by giving rest to his soul; and surely the practice of such men cannot be considered as the exponent of the views of the Church, the plainest restrictions of which it ignores or disregards.

Catena of authorities on the other side.

I cannot help thinking that these considerations will induce my readers to be slow in assigning to the alleged catena much weight on the point in question; but even were the catena much more perfect in all its links than it is, still we should be able to bring forward on the other side no less weighty authorities, who either disapprove sacramental confession, or entirely omit it from their teaching.

And again—lose sight of all I have been saying—take the value of the catena at the highest—allow all the authorities which Confessionalists urge as advocating that which they advocate—what does it amount to? That in every generation since the Reformation, there have been men, of learning and piety if you will, mostly, if not exclusively, of what is called the Laudian school, who like our Ritualists had a hankering after certain Mediæval doctrines and practices which were dropped, or rather excluded, from our Church as it came forth from the crucible of the Reformation; and who, in particular, were unwilling that the hold which sacramental confession gave the clergy over the common people should be loosened by its abrogation, and would, like our modern Confessionalists, have been glad to see it reintroduced, though not to the extent to which these men carry it? I doubt whether many authors can be found among those Anglican writers who speak of it as our modern Laudian school do. *What the catena is worth at its highest and best.*

And again, it must never be forgotten that a catena, however weighty and perfect it may be, cannot alter the facts of the case: cannot insert into the Scriptures a single instance of the practice: cannot turn confession to the Pænitentiarius, as a preliminary to public discipline, into confession as a discipline of grace—a condition of, and followed by, absolute forgiveness; it cannot alter the method prescribed by the Church in ordinary cases into a form of absolution instead of the ministry of God's word; it cannot even make the absolution in the Visitation service grant that forgiveness of sins, which is in the next prayer spoken of as a thing yet to be granted; in short, it cannot alter one jot or tittle of what the Scripture has spoken, or what the Church has laid down. *Catena can not supply evidence.*

Nor any amount of vague assumptions can.

No amount of vague generalities as to its being an ordained rite for the forgiveness of sins—of its being recognised and sanctioned by primitive antiquity, or its being prescribed or recommended by our own Church—however dogmatically conceived and expressed—however plausibly seasoned by pious denunciations of the sin and folly of declining what is thus assumed to have been ordained by God; practised from the earliest times, ordered by our own Church, used by pious men of all ages—none of these plausible and well-sounding assumptions can create for the system of sacramental confession that clear scriptural authority—that continuous use in all ages of Christianity —that well-defined recognition by our own Church—which alone can justify an English clergyman in assuming to himself, and telling people that he has, that power of forgiving individual sins, or declaring that they are forgiven, sacramentally, sacerdotally, and absolutely, compared with which all other powers conferred on, or claimed by, the priesthood in any age or country are as nothing: which alone can justify a minister of Christ in claiming to be anything more than a faithful minister and dispenser of the promises and offers of the remission of sins set forth in God's word, and of those sacraments, which Christ has unmistakably ordained, as means whereby we receive such spiritual gifts, and as pledges to assure us thereof. Nay, more; nothing less than positive proof can justify those who take their views of Christianity from Christianity itself, in admitting or accepting such a claim, or allowing themselves to be misled by a system which, finding no sure ground whereon securely to rest, either in Scripture or antiquity, takes refuge in a catena. If men in such a matter choose to put their trust in a catena for that which they cannot find in Scripture—that which the ancient Church did not find in Scripture—it is much the same as if one were to try to walk on the water, or fly in the air, on the strength of the plausible demonstrations of the professors thereof, that such performances must in the nature of things be possible and practicable: or as if a merchant were to trust to the axioms of alchemy for making his fortune, or a statesman frame his policy on the predictions of astrology.

Nor can the absence of all those points of evidence, which, had the system been true, must have existed, be counterbalanced by any of these generalities and assumptions, any more than the lack of proofs in a legal case can be fairly balanced by the vague rhetoric of a counsel, who tries to throw dust in the eyes of the jury, in the hope of getting a verdict, which after all would not satisfy honest men of the justice of his client's cause, or be secure of not being set aside as against evidence. Nor counterbalance the lack of it.

Nay, even supposing the catena alleged to be more favourable than it really is to Auricular Confession, as an occasional sacramental ordinance for the forgiveness of sins, it would but bring out more decidedly the fatal flaw which arises from the endeavour to steer a middle course between those who magnify the priestly power to the utmost, and those who would reduce it to something less than a minimum. They find themselves compelled to limit to merely occasional use that commission and function, which, had it been given and instituted by Christ in a sacramental and sacerdotal phase, must from its very nature have been universally necessary—*semper, ubique, et ab omnibus*, as it has been from the beginning in its ambassadorial and ministerial phases of the dispensation of the Word and Sacraments. If there is a special ordinance for the forgiveness of sins, it must be universal, so that the very limitations which are forced on the writers of this catena disprove the very point which it is adduced to establish. Whereas the clerical power viewed as the dispensation of the Word and Sacraments, though as a whole The limitation introduced by these divines fatal to their theory, universally necessary, may vary in the details of application, without any limitation as to its universality (see page 198). The same follows from viewing the position advanced by the Confessionalists in relation to the words on which they profess to found it. They take the words in the most literal, unlimited sense, and finding it impossible to maintain this, they limit the words in a way which shows that the interpretation, on which their case is built, is untenable.

and to their interpretation of certain passages of Scripture.

There remains only one plea to be examined, and that is the spiritual benefits which result, or are said to result, from the system. The Confessionalist proposition on this point in its mildest and meekest form—the form in which it is often urged on inexperienced boys and girls—is this: that it is not forbidden, that great spiritual benefits had been found to result from it, and therefore it is no harm to try it.

Benefit alleged as arising from the practice.

Some persons, perhaps, if they watch the Confessionalists, will perceive something very like juggling in argument, of which I hope most of them are perfectly unconscious. When they are driven out of their position of sacramental confession being a divinely appointed ordinance of God, they bring forward the benefits of it as a prudential motive for adopting it; then, when this is answered by showing that the alleged benefits of it are more than doubtful, and that even if not doubtful they are more than counterbalanced by the evils of it, they urge its claims being an ordinance of God: and thus by this sort of logical see-saw they manage to keep themselves going, and to evade the grasp of that common sense which, sharp enough in judging rightly of a single point, is often confused when two are thus shaken in our faces alternately.

See-saw argument of the Confessionalists.

The benefits which are alleged in its favour, rest on the testimony of two kinds of witnesses: one speak from the results of their own experience of it, the other from their

Testimony to its benefits:

observation of its results on others. With regard to the
first, I am not certain whether it argues much depth of
the spiritual life, when a man comes forward in public as
I have heard men do, to bear evidence to the value of a
system as having made him spiritually what he is, and
therefore, indirectly but really, sets forth his own spiritual
state, as something to be admired and imitated by others; *from personal experience of it.*
such evidence, practically in one's own favour is, I think,
suspicious, especially when the *soi-disant* model man is
known to have thrown in his lot with an innovating school,
of which this is one of the nostrums. It is a natural instinct
which pervades all religionists, from the Romanists to the
Mormons, from the Agapemone to the Trappist, to believe
in and to magnify the blessings which they find in the
religious system which they have adopted. Generally
speaking, the falser any modern phase of Christianity, the
more positive is the verbal evidence of its professors to its
spiritual powers and excellences, as realised in themselves,
for the simple reason that such pretenders lack that humble
estimate of themselves which prevents them thinking of
themselves as model specimens of spirituality: such evidence, speaking generally, is of little value: of none at all,
when compared with facts patent in the thing itself. The
Confessionalist system must not be judged by the estimate
formed by those who are pledged to it, but must be tested
in all its parts, by its own merits and characteristics and
history.

There are others, however, whose evidence in its favour *from experience of its results in parish work.*
is grounded on their own external experience, in the
working of their parishes, and dealing with individual
souls. What these men say in its favour is entitled to
much respect, especially at first sight. I hope I shall not
be held to mean any disrespect to them—I hope that they
will pardon me—if I say that it strikes me that they can
hardly be masters of their art, if they cannot exercise their

ministry of reconciliation without using methods which those who were entrusted with the same ministry in the early Church never had recourse to, or thought of; they seem to me to be like men who have lost the key, and are obliged to have recourse to a picklock. It would indeed be a totally different thing if, as in the early Church, they were required to decide, not whether the sin could be pardoned by God, but whether it was one which required public discipline, before the person could, without detriment to the Church, be admitted to the privilege of Church fellowship. Private confession might then have its use, in order that the priest might know the extent of the offence, and that the offender might not escape the punishment due to his offences, and thus deprive the Church of its security against its being injured and scandalised by the offender's relapse.

Not necessary to parish work properly carried on.

Might be necessary for public discipline.

But there is no such system as this recognised in our Church; the essence of the Gospel scheme of pardon surely is, that we are not dealt with according to our sins, or rewarded after our iniquities. That change of mind, which is called repentance, and confession to God, and faith in Christ, are the conditions on which God's ministers are empowered, and instructed, and commanded to tell a man that he may enter, or re-enter, into the Kingdom of Heaven. It may be useful indeed in, even necessary to, the system which is called Direction—and it is for this purpose that the Jesuits principally make use of it: but then it is evident that this assumes that Direction is a benefit to the Church, and to the individual souls that are under it, and does not testify to Confession being in itself good. And Direction, as part of the sacrament of Penance— sacramental direction it might perhaps be called—does not enter into the system of our Church, and he who uses it or recommends it is doing what his Church does not authorise him to do—is transgressing the bounds which the

Useful for Direction; but not recognised in our Church.

Church has set up to secure the laity against the undue interference and control of the clergy. Nor, as I have ventured to say before, is he justified, who, without holding the extreme view of the Confessionalists, yet uses Confession as a means of unlocking a sick man's soul and heart, so as to enable him to deal more effectively with the man should he recover.

It is true, indeed, that confidential intercourse between the parish priest and members of his flock may, as I have said elsewhere, be necessary to his giving them comfort and counsel. It may be used as a remedial benefit, provided that it be not represented as being, or believed to be, an act of religion or of discipline, or of obedience, or of duty, or a part of repentance, or a preliminary of pardon—in short, if care is taken to exclude from it all the features which the Confessionalists give it. A pastor may indeed do well to win the confidence of a troubled soul, may invite it, may even urge it, but he may not force it—he may not obtain it on false pretences, or represent it as the only or the surest way to pardon, or so use it as to make it a possible stepping-stone to Confession. If, indeed, a man has been guilty of some notorious sin, the pastor may examine him specially whether he has repented of it; but, as it seems to me, he is not authorised to suggest to him a doubt of God's mercy, or to trouble an untroubled conscience by the possibility of some weighty matter being yet unrepented of, or urge him to confession in order to discover whether it is so. Or, if instead of waiting for the sick man's earnest desire for absolution he represents to him that he cannot die in peace and hope without it; or at all events that it is a safe precaution—that his peace and hope will be better founded if he is absolved—that absolution is out of the question unless he confesses his sins to him, while he promises to absolve him if he makes a full confession—then it seems to me that

Confidential intercourse admits neither sacramental Confession nor Direction.

Pastors may invite confidence but not represent Confession and Absolution as a condition of pardon, or use it to get at the secrets of a man's soul.

Q

such a mode of treatment does not differ much from that of the extreme Confessionalists, who tell men that they will die in their sins unless they disclose them to a confessor: who hold out private personal absolution as a necessary and a certain channel of pardon. He is putting into the man's mind a delusion which may, and if it is rested on, will, end in the omission of those acts of personal faith in our Lord on which the promised pardon waits; he is luring him on by false pretences to lay bare his soul to him; he is turning Confidence into a Confession, which differs only from that of the Confessionalists, in that pardon is not definitely attached to the formula spoken by the priest: and again I venture to express my conviction that such misrepresentation is scarcely justified by the hope or the notion that, if the man recovers, the knowledge of those details of his inner being and outer life will enable the pastor to mould his advice so as to be more applicable to the man's case, or make him more amenable to pastoral advice.

Alleged benefits counterbalanced by known evils.

At all events, it is clear, that against whatever benefits may be supposed to result from it, must be placed its disadvantages and evils: the witness of those, who in foreign countries, where it has had its full swing, have tried it, or who have witnessed the evil influence it has exercised on society, and on individual souls: all these must be placed against the statements of those, who in its favour bear witness, either that they have themselves personally found the benefit of it, or that they have seen the good results which it has produced in others.

Previous question.

Before, however, I enter on this branch of the subject, there is a previous question to which I must again call attention. It is this—whether in matters relating to the spiritual life and salvation of souls, any, humanly speaking, possible or even probable benefits can justify us in adopting any other method or rule than what has been revealed to us as a definite part of the scheme of salvation?

I am not, of course, speaking of minor details, such as are left to every Church to decide and adopt for itself: but of essential principles and weighty practices, which must exercise great influence on the system which adopts them: on the character and temperament and spiritual life and spiritual hopes of those who use them: under the auspices and influences of which Christianity becomes a different religion from what it is without them. In such matters—and surely the forgiveness of sins by sacramental Confession is one of these—it is more than doubtful whether that which is adopted on the ground of its seeming, humanly speaking, likely to be beneficial, may not in some way or other obstruct or neutralise the work of God's revealed scheme in God's appointed ordinances. The Gospel scheme of salvation is not an outline sketch, which is to be filled up in detail by the clergy, or even by the Church; it is not a skeleton map in which the mountains and rivers and roads and cities are to be filled in by the guesses of human wit; but it puts before us, exhaustively and yet minutely, in their completeness the great principles and powers of the Redemption of the world and of every individual in it. In the efficacy—in the certain result—of these principles and powers, it is the part of faith implicitly to trust—nay, it is the part of mere human wisdom. To introduce into it movements and powers of our own, as if we could supplement what God has given us, savours to my mind of human folly and human pride. I confess I think there can be discerned a tendency in the clergy, strongly developed in the Mediæval and Romish systems, of late years reviving among ourselves, to think of themselves as the physicians of the souls of men, instead of what they really are, the errand-boys and dispensers of the one Great Physician—having received from Him a panacea of life—sent into the world by Him, as He was sent by the Father, to do His work

Marginalia: Intrusion on revealed scheme of salvation. The danger of this not counterbalanced by any alleged benefits. What God has given us is exhaustive and sufficient. Clergy not physicians but only errand-boys of the great Physician.

in the ministry of reconciliation—not in acts of confession to them, not in words of absolution from them; but in the preaching the Gospel of their Lord, dispensing His sacraments, in exhorting, warning, teaching: licensed by Him to minister the Gospel in His name, with the promise that to those who receive it and its offers from their hands it shall be as effectual to cure them, as if He Himself had ministered it—as it was to those to whom He did minister. They indeed are bound to use all their energies, all their talents, all their industry, in short, all that God has given them, some in one way, some in another, in getting men to accept the remedy committed to their dispensation; but with that remedy they have no authority or licence to tamper, or to alter or change it: they have no warrant to practise for themselves, or to vend nostrums of their own, or to add to their Lord's panacea ingredients of their own, in the notion of making it more agreeable or beneficial. If they do so, they do it not only at their own peril, but the peril of those on whom they try their experiments, at the risk of neutralising the healing effects of that which they have thus adulterated.

Have no licence to add to or alter His panacea.

That God will Himself work in what He has prescribed and promised we are certain—that He will work in these inventions of our own we have no reason to think; on the contrary, those who study most accurately the growth of the errors and the corruptions which have made Christianity almost a by-word among the nations, will be most convinced, that these can be traced to the rashness of well-intentioned men, who chose to be wise above that which is written. There are persons who talk very glibly and frequently of Christ's presence in His Church, and the Spirit's work in the Church, but who forget that this twofold presence guarantees the effectual working of what He has ordained for His Church, and forbids men to work in their own devices, and in ways which He has not or-

Certainty of methods prescribed by God.

dained, as if what He has ordained would not do His work without the aid of these human devices. It seems to me to be a phase of disbelief. There are those, who think that men cannot be saved without their exercising functions and powers which belong to God alone. Like Korah and his company, they seem to think it a small thing that God hath made them to stand before the congregation to minister to them, they seek Christ's priesthood also. Nor is there anything surprising in this; it is the natural working of the perverse, proud, will of man on the knowledge and the system which He has given them. For myself, I confess that I look upon these inventions and additions with distrust and alarm: and when a man has nothing more to say for a religious nostrum than that it is not forbidden, and may be beneficial, I think it wiser and safer to trust to God's wisdom in what He has prescribed for us, than in our own wisdom and in what we prescribe for ourselves. *Danger of human devices.*

Of course all this is heightened when the theory of this supposed beneficial addition contradicts, or is inconsistent with, some leading principle or fact or injunction or ordinance or promise of God's revealed scheme: or when its supposed benefits are counterbalanced tenfold by the evils which are inherent in it, or which history bears witness to it, having produced. And under both these aggravations the Confessionalist system falls. If—to take one instance out of many that could be alleged—it is necessary to the obtaining pardon of sins committed against God, to confess them privately to a priest, then the promise that 'If we 'confess our sins to God, He is faithful and just to forgive 'us our sins,' is held of no account. The believing the one is an act of disbelief in the other, and I know of no reason to think that it will not bring with it the penalties of disbelief. And the pages of history—the memories, nay, even the experience of living men, ring with the evils, *Auricular Confession implies disbelief in God's promises.*

spiritual, political, social, domestic, moral, of the Confessional.

The importance of this principle makes me defer the question of the benefits of Confession.

For myself, I place so much importance on the principle that the absence of any authority or warrant or precedent in Scripture for the practice of what is technically called Confession cannot be counterbalanced by any possible benefits resulting from it, that I am unwilling to mix up the two questions together: and therefore confining myself in my present publication to the former question, I shall defer for the present entering on the latter point; it will form the subject which it is my intention to consider in the second part of my work. At present I will only add that this mode of treating the subject furnishes a ready answer to those Confessionalists who urge that those who have not tried their system cannot form a fair or trustworthy judgment against it. It is the old argument of the Romish Proselytizers. It is about as reasonable to say that none but opium-eaters can reasonably condemn or dissuade from opium-eating. But setting this aside, we answer that the Confessional is not on its trial with respect to the benefits which may conceivably flow from it, or from the spiritual enjoyments it may confer. We are willing to join issue with its advocates on this point: but at present the question is whether it is ordained by God, recognised by the really Primitive Church, or accepted by our own. This is to be decided by the tests whereby we have tried it—if the answer is in the negative, then its benefits must be delusive, its enjoyments dangerous.

Argument for toleration.

There is a plea of the Confessionalists, savouring somewhat of an *argumentum ad misericordiam*, which finds a ready acceptance with many, who do not accept their system on grounds either of logic or expediency; the plea is, that their system should meet with toleration instead of opposition.

A writer on the subject expresses a hope that the solution of the difficulty may be found in the practical adoption of the requirement of mutual forbearance given in the first book of Edward VI. (see page 109). The proposition is practically this: that whereas the difficulty consists in one party maintaining that Confession is permissible, and another party maintaining that it is not permissible, the latter should admit the permissive formula which the Church has struck out. Verily, they must have a very low estimate of the energy and discernment of those with whom they have to deal. There is no greater proof of a man being himself wanting in the faculty of discerning what is true and honourable and reasonable and of good faith, than his proposing what is unfair and unreasonable, in utter unconsciousness of its absurdity and trickery.

The advantage of the plea (self-condemning though it be) consists in this, that it is in harmony with that theoretical indifference to truth, which holds that anything may be true, and with that practical opposition to truth which holds that no error is to be opposed. This chimes in well enough with the liberalism of the age; but one would hardly expect it to be put forth by a school who profess themselves ready to go to the stake in defending what they believe to be true, or opposing what they believe to be false. It is clear they do not give their opponents credit for the same amount of discernment and firmness for which they take credit to themselves. In reality, their plea betrays their consciousness that their cause cannot stand against the convictions and instincts of the nation. They feel that their chance is to be able to stifle the instincts and master these convictions, by gradually bringing men's reason and men's feelings under the influence of a sacerdotal power which should forbid men to think or feel except as the priest should bid them: and for this all that

_{This proposition, though in harmony with the age, is a sign of conscious weakness.}

they want is what they call 'fair play.' It is the judgment of Solomon over again—they are willing to cut the truth as it were into two halves, provided one half may fall to their share, it will be to them so much gain. But if we, who know the truth to be wholly on our side, consent to any such compromise, the loss will be on our side. It is a proposition that those who occupy a vantage ground shall descend from their stronghold, and give the invaders a fair chance of conquering their country—a proposal wearing a fair enough semblance of chivalry and valour, admissible, perhaps, in mimic contest for a laurel crown, but not likely to be accepted, or even listened to, by reasonable men, engaged in the momentous interest at stake between us and the Confessionalists.

Not likely to succeed.

I confess there is nothing which more excites my astonishment, not to say apprehension, in this matter, than the toleration which is conceded by some men to the endeavours which are now being made to revive this pre-Reformation practice: the indulgence, with which it is pleaded that everyone should be allowed to do as he likes herein: the complacency with which men see the system gaining ground as long as it does not actually touch themselves. In fact, I cannot conceive how such a course of apathy, indifference, indulgence, toleration, and even connivance, which the Confessionalists kindly recommend to their opponents as the proper way of meeting them, can be listened to by anyone who is aware of the greatness of the danger, of the gravity of the crisis. They have scarcely realised the full nature and the full results of the confessional in its theological, evangelical, ecclesiastical, religious, political, social, personal bearings.

Apathy on the point quite unintelligible.

Importance of the results of the Confessional:

Theologically, it puts before us as necessary to salvation, or at least highly beneficial to our spiritual state, that for which we find no warrant or sanction in Revelation. It claims our acquiescence in and adoption of a

Theologically.

system of man's invention, plausible enough and effective enough, perhaps, had there been no revelation of God's nature, and counsels, and scheme of salvation, which overrides, or rather supersedes, whatever man may have guessed or dreamt on these matters, whatever man may have devised or arranged.

Evangelically, it is an alteration of the condition of the Gospel message—of the channels whereby forgiveness is conveyed from God under the Gospel scheme—of the means whereby man is to lay hold of what God provides for him. It is an infringement of the charter of our salvation as children of grace, having the right, each of us, of free access to God by virtue of the freedom whereby Christ has made us free. *Evangelically.*

Ecclesiastically, it is a setting at naught of the teaching and practice of the early Church, the teaching and practice of our own. It is the setting up a sacerdotal order to be not only ambassadors from God to man, but mediators between man and God, as lords over God's heritage, judges of their brethren—the attorneys, so to say, of their spiritual interests, empowered to arrange with each man the terms on which God's free mercy shall be his—dealing out spiritual life or spiritual death according to the issues of their weak judgments. *Ecclesiastically.*

Religiously, it is opening in this our hitherto happy country that same source of superstition which has flooded so many Papal countries—notably France, Spain, and Italy—with infidelity, even in minds not naturally indisposed to religion, by pressing Christianity on men's homes and hearts in a form deeply repulsive and utterly untrue. Christianity has no greater enemy than the Confessional, perhaps none so great. Infidelity has no greater friend, perhaps none so great, as the Confessional. In its bearing, too, on individual religion its work of demoralisation is complete. It dries up the springs of real *Religiously.* *Personally.*

religion, fills up its wells with rubbish; it paralyses the energies of individual spirituality, and makes faith nothing more than reason limping in a priest's footsteps, or reluctantly dragged along by a heavy chain—nothing more than reason bowing its neck to the ground and letting a priest put his foot upon it, instead of walking in the knowledge of God, with the uplifted face and the firm, free, step of spiritualised, evangelised intelligence.

Nationally. Nationally, it turns that which should be the light of a nation, its religion, into darkness; and if so, how great is that darkness? It destroys the very nerves of a nation, sucks out its life-blood, places the lives, the consciences, the interests of the people at the mercy of a Father Confessor, who may by the means of the Confessional have gained dominion over the soul and the conscience of a weak or a wicked king or minister. It places the fortune, the strength, the destinies of the nation in the hands of the priest. To all this history bears witness in the records of the crimes, and the follies, and the disasters which were brought about by the Confessional, the echoes of which, long passed though they be, still ring with a painful clearness, and ever will, ring, in the ears of the civilised world as long as that world lasts—in vain it would seem for those men who sit quietly by and smile, sometimes approvingly, sometimes disdainfully at its progress among us. And *Socially.* when to these we add the social, the personal evils in the family—in the heart—which have always waited, and ever must wait upon it, it seems to me inconceivable, incredible, unintelligible, that anyone should watch its revival with satisfaction, or even indifference, on the ground that this revival is but partial, and its success or triumph unlikely.

Danger of allowing it again to take root. Such men need to be reminded of that pretty water-plant which was welcomed so warmly a few years ago as a charming addition to the flora of our streams. A few years passed, and it was found that wherever it had taken root it had choked the waters, and made them a mass of impenetrable herbage; it cost much time and expense to remove the evil. And what would be thought of, what would now be said to, the man who re-planted it in a flowing river or a glassy pool?

INDEX.

Absolution, ancient forms of, 95; what they indicate, 95; 'I absolve thee,' what does it convey? 96; to be distinguished from pardon, 97; benefit of, 111; meaning of, 111; not to be pronounced over unconscious persons, 185; what it is not, 132; what it is, 169; not mere preaching or reading the Bible, 170; private, not recognised in the Scriptures or Apostolic Church, 162; practical use of, 175; in the Morning and Evening Services, 176; in the Holy Communion Office, 177; in the Visitation Office, 178; why the direct form 'I absolve thee' is used, 178; why permitted to the dying man, 179, 182; nature and results of, 179, 180; how far it may be said to be a declaration as to who are pardoned, 179; illustrations of, 181; not to be suggested to every sick man, 182; may clear away doubt of repentance, 183; why limited to a death-bed, 188; is it a restoration to a state of grace? 208

Advice, following Confidence differs from Direction, 45

Analogies of lawyer and physician, 27; examined, 28 *seq.*

Ancient writers, contradictory language of, 63; solution of, 68

Anxiety for salvation, not the point at issue, 15

Apostles, why they may have been conceived to forgive sins absolutely, 142

Applicants, how clergy may deal with them, 202, 205

Auricular Confession, different modes of administering it, 25; even voluntary, no sanction for in primitive Church, 86; what is meant by, 19; Confessionalists' teaching thereon, 91; several notions wrongly identified with, 20; not recognised as a preparation for Holy Communion, 188; plea that it is forced upon the clergy, 199 *seq.*; that laity are responsible for it, 201; an abuse of the clerical office, 204; cannot be claimed by a layman, 205; benefits alleged as arising from the practice, 222; this evidence in its favour not to be trusted, 222 *seq.*; this not the primary question, 226; real question whether ordained by God, 226; objections to it on this score, 227; why not to be tolerated or connived at, 230 *seq.*

Benefit of Absolution, meaning of, 111

Canons, passage alleged from, in favour of Confession, 117

Carter, Mr., his admission as to Confession in the early Church, 57

Catena—alleged by the Confessionalists, 209; examination of, 209 *seq.*; of practice is against the Confessionalists, 217; on the other side of authorities, 218; logical value of, at the highest, 219

Christ's words in St. John, meaning of, 138; questions involved therein, 141; to whom addressed, 141; are they, if addressed to the Apostles, necessarily carried on to their successors, 142; bearing of our Lord's promise, 'I am with you always,' on this point, 143; not addressed to the Apostles only, 144;

CHU

bearing of this point on the question, 145; what were the powers given? evidently forgiveness of sins against the Church, 147; why they cannot be limited to this, 147; comparison of the Evangelists on this point, 148; account given by St. Luke and St. John of the commission given, 149; both recognised by our Church, 149—taken by no one in their literal meaning, 153; how interpreted by the practice of the early Church, 162; how not interpreted, 162; what taken to include, 164

Church's mission, how it differs from our Lord's, 157

Church s office before the canon of the New Testament, 170; still exists in Absolution, 173; relations between it and the written word, 172

Clerical office and authority not the point in question, 14, 120, 139

Commission to remit sins, how exercised in early Church, 150; Confessionalist assertion thereon, 151

Confession—importance of, 1; subject forced upon us, 3; aspects and results. 1; nature, 282; revolution in religion, 2;—aversion to, not unreasonable—not the ground for opposing it, 3; Ritualistic argument from, 10; supersedes revelation, 3; indistinct views about, 4;—two phases of, 21; differences between, 21; how identified by the Confessionalists. 22; links in the process, 23; ending in Auricular Confession, 24;—the two pleas for, 26;—confounded with the human yearning after sympathy, 26; how it differs from confidence, 44; how girls are led to, 49; its connection with Absolution, 50;—might be useful if there had been no revelation, 51; real objection against, that it is not revealed, 52; no trace of it in Scripture, 54; unknown in early times, except in connection with public discipline, 56; totally different from modern Confession, 57; witness of the primitive Church as given in the note to Tertullian, 58 *seq.*;—as permitted in Visitation Office, generally only confidence, 98;—cannot under any circumstances be a precedent for other cases, 100;—not necessary to the exercise of the priest's

FOR

office, 133; not to be suggested to every sick man, 182; habitual and occasional flaw in the assumed difference between, 197, 198

Confidence only once suggested by the Church, 46; transition from Confidence to Confession, 47;—existed in early Church, 82; changed into private Confession, 85;—how it may slip into Confession, 43; care to be taken against this, 43;—danger in it at present day, 44, 201; how it differs from Confession, 44

Confidential communications not the point at issue, 16

Corinthian penitent, case of, 151

Cyprian, passage from, 70

Differences of view briefly considered, 17; causes of, 19

Direction differs from advice given in confidence, 45

Discipline of the Church—meaning of the phrase in the Ordination Service, 125; not mentioned among the particulars of the clerical office, 126; falls under faithful dispensation of the Sacraments, 126; does not support the Confessionalist point, 126

Early Church practices, retained by our Church, 82

Exhortation to the Holy Communion, passage in, considered, 102; wrongly claimed by the Confessionalists, 102; their language about, 103;—does not suggest recourse to a minister as the usual or best method, 103; case in which it is suggested, 104; directions for it, 105; all go to exclude Auricular Confession, 105; object of, not absolution, but benefit of absolution, 10; how the contrary interpretation has been accepted, 106;—counter-balanced by general disuse, 107; —need not be read by a priest, 107; alterations in the passage, 109-111; —what is suggested in, distinguished from that which is permitted in the Visitation Office, 195

Extravagancies not used to disprove Confession, 16

Forgiveness of sins not recognised by our Church in the Confessionalist sense, 129; reason of this, 130

INDEX. 239

FOR

Forgiveness, threefold method of, 65, 70

Formula for private absolution expunged from the Prayer-Book, 110

Girls, how led to Confession, 49

God's mercy, doubt of, not to be created or suggested, 184; conditions of, not to be altered or exceeded, 185, 187

Homilies, passage of alleged in favour of Auricular Confession, 118

Human yearning after sympathy confounded with Confession. See under 'Confession.'

Leo I., changes introduced by, 64

Ministry of God's Word, meaning of, 113

Morbid spiritual state, not to be encouraged, 42

Noctarius, discipline contemplated by, 84

Ordination formula, meaning and force of, 119, 128; real issue involved in the question, 120;—does not prove the Confessionalist point, 121; paragraphs in, 122; two powers conveyed by. 122; positive power exhausted by dispensation of the Word and Sacraments. 123; retaining power by the faithful dispensation thereof, 124;—no other exercise of the clerical office in this respect recognised by our Church, 125; or mentioned in the ordination exhortation, 125; no private exercise of retaining for secret sins recognised in the Rubrics or in the Canons, 127; arbitrary exercise of retaining powers not contemplated in the exhortation to the Holy Communion or in the Visitation Office, 124

Pænitentiarius, appointment and office of, 79; a step towards mediæval confession, 80; abolished, 81; no

PRI

warrant for modern Confession, 81

Pardon to be distinguished from Absolution, 97; comes directly from God, 184

Pastoral confidence, no sanction for confession, 38; natural and allowable, 39; nature of, 40; for relief or advice, 40; beneficial, 41; for solution of doubts, 41; cure for morbid state, 41; to be received under certain limitations, 42

Penance not recognised by our Church, 135

Penitence not recognised by our Church, 137

Penitential discipline, 65; prominence given to, 67; difference between this and modern confession in theory, 71; and details, 72; decay of, 82; public changed into private, 83; matter of canonical arrangement, and therefore not of divine obligation, 87

Power of forgiving sins, as claimed by Confessionalists, practical test of, 155

Practical conclusions, 192

Prayer after Absolution in Visitation Office, 93; affects the force of the absolution formula, 94;—after public reconciliation in early Church, 165

Priest, struck out of the Rubric in the exhortation to the Holy Communion, 108

Primitive Church, witness of, 59 seq.

Private Confession, not commanded in Scripture, 32; examination of passages alleged to the contrary, 32; how it sprung from public discipline, 74; unknown at first, 75; changes introduced after pænitentiarius, 83; authorised by Leo I., 84; still different from modern Confession, 85; plea that it may be adopted by any Church, 88; proves it not to be of divine obligation, 89; question whether it is recognised by our Church considered, 89 seq.; mistaken assumption of the Confessionalists on this point, 90; arguments advanced in support of, 90; not practised or recognised by the Apostles, 151

Private personal discipline in early Church, 81; retained by our Church, 82

INDEX

REM

Remission of sins—direct, 165; indirect, 166; results of, 167
Retaining power, results of exercise of, 168; power not to be exceeded, 169

Scripture, precedents alleged, 9; passages alleged, as giving power of forgiving sins, 152
Sin, threefold phases of, against a brother, against the Church, and against God, 65; against the Church, 65; condoned in public discipline and reconciliation, 66; against the Church, distinguished from sins against God, 69; secret disclosure of, 76; not made necessarily to a priest, 78; object of, 78; remission of by God and man, difference between, 97; prevalence of, 77; did not go beyond confidence, 77
Sins, mortal and venial, distinction between, does not authorise Auricular Confession, 207
Sophistries, and petty arguments of the Confessionalists, 7; instances of, 7;

VIS

logical value of, 12, 157; practical way of testing, 160
Spiritual life, Ritualistic argument from, in favour of Confession answered, 10
St. James, passage alleged from, 32; examined, 32 and *seq.*
St. John's words, 'As my Father hath sent me,' &c., Confessionalist argument from, examined, 157
St. Matthew, ix. 8, Confessionalists' arguments from, examined, 154
St. Paul, 2 Cor. v. 18, examination of argument alleged from, 156
Summary of the arguments on both sides, 189 *seq.*

Tertullian, note on, 58; evidence contained in, as to primitive practice, 59 *seq.*

Visitation Office, Confessionalist argument therefrom, 91; the Confession here permitted shown to be not that of the Confessionalist, 92, 98

39 Paternoster Row, E.C.
London, *November* 1874.

GENERAL LIST OF WORKS

PUBLISHED BY

MESSRS. LONGMANS, GREEN, AND CO.

	PAGE		PAGE
Arts, Manufactures, &c.	25	Mental & Political Philosophy	8
Astronomy & Meteorology	17	Miscellaneous & Critical Works	12
Biographical Works	6	Natural History & Physical	
Chemistry & Physiology	23	Science	18
Dictionaries & other Books of Reference	14	Poetry & the Drama	35
		Religious & Moral Works	28
Fine Arts & Illustrated Editions	24	Rural Sports, Horse & Cattle Management, &c.	36
History, Politics, Historical Memoirs, &c.	1	Travels, Voyages, &c.	32
		Works of Fiction	34
Index	41 to 44	Works of Utility & General	
Knowledge for the Young	40	Information	38

HISTORY, POLITICS, HISTORICAL MEMOIRS, &c.

Journal of the Reigns of King George IV. and King William IV.

By the late Charles C. F. Greville, Esq. Clerk of the Council to those Sovereigns. Edited by Henry Reeve, Registrar of the Privy Council.

3 vols. 8vo. price 36s.

The Life of Napoleon III. derived from State Records, Unpublished Family Correspondence, and Personal Testimony.

By Blanchard Jerrold.

Four Vols. 8vo. with Portraits from the Originals in possession of the Imperial Family, and Facsimiles of Letters of Napoleon I. Napoleon III. Queen Hortense, &c. Vol. I. price 18s.

⁎⁎ Vol. II. will be published in the Autumn, and Vols. III. and IV. completing the work, in the Spring of 1875.

A

Recollections and Suggestions of Public Life, 1813-1873.
By John Earl Russell.
1 vol. 8vo.　　　　[*Nearly ready.*

Introductory Lectures on Modern History delivered in Lent Term 1842; with the Inaugural Lecture delivered in December 1841.
By the late Rev. Thomas Arnold, D.D.
8vo. price 7s. 6d.

Essays on the English Government and Constitution from the Reign of Henry VII. to the Present Time.
By John Earl Russell.
Fcp. 8vo. 3s. 6d.

On Parliamentary Government in England: its Origin, Development, and Practical Operation.
By Alpheus Todd.
2 vols. 8vo. £1. 17s.

The Constitutional History of England since the Accession of George III. 1760-1870.
By Sir Thomas Erskine May, K.C.B.
Fourth Edition. 3 vols. crown 8vo. 18s.

Democracy in Europe; a History.
By Sir Thomas Erskine May, K.C.B.
2 vols. 8vo.　　　[*In preparation.*

The History of England from the Fall of Wolsey to the Defeat of the Spanish Armada.
By J. A. Froude, M.A.
CABINET EDITION, 12 vols. cr. 8vo. £3. 12s.
LIBRARY EDITION, 12 vols. 8vo. £8. 18s.

The English in Ireland in the Eighteenth Century.
By J. A. Froude, M.A.
3 vols. 8vo. £2. 8s.

Estimates of the English Kings from William the Conqueror to George III.
By J. L. Sanford.
Crown 8vo. 12s. 6d.

The History of England from the Accession of James II.
By Lord Macaulay.
STUDENT'S EDITION, 2 vols. cr. 8vo. 12s.
PEOPLE'S EDITION, 4 vols. cr. 8vo. 16s.
CABINET EDITION, 8 vols. post 8vo. 48s.
LIBRARY EDITION, 5 vols. 8vo. £4.

Critical and Historical Essays contributed to the Edinburgh Review.
By the Right Hon. Lord Macaulay.
Cheap Edition, authorised and complete, crown 8vo. 3s. 6d.
STUDENT'S EDITION, crown 8vo. 6s.
PEOPLE'S EDITION, 2 vols. crown 8vo. 8s.
CABINET EDITION, 4 vols. 24s.
LIBRARY EDITION, 3 vols. 8vo. 36s.

Lord Macaulay's Works. Complete and uniform Library Edition.
Edited by his Sister, Lady Trevelyan.
8 vols. 8vo. with Portrait, £5. 5s.

Lectures on the History of England from the Earliest Times to the Death of King Edward II.
By W. Longman, F.A.S.
Maps and Illustrations. 8vo. 15s.

The History of the Life and Times of Edward III.
By W. Longman, F.A.S.
With 9 Maps, 8 Plates, and 16 Woodcuts. 2 vols. 8vo. 28s.

History of England under the Duke of Buckingham and Charles the First, 1624–1628.
By S. Rawson Gardiner, late Student of Ch. Ch.
2 vols. 8vo. [*In the press.*

History of Civilization in England and France, Spain and Scotland.
By Henry Thomas Buckle.
3 vols. crown 8vo. 24s.

A Student's Manual of the History of India from the Earliest Period to the Present.
By Col. Meadows Taylor, M.R.A.S.
Second Thousand. Cr. 8vo. Maps, 7s. 6d.

The French Revolution and First Empire; an Historical Sketch.
By W. O'Connor Morris, sometime Scholar of Oriel College, Oxford.
With 2 Maps. Post 8vo. 7s. 6d.

The History of India from the Earliest Period to the close of Lord Dalhousie's Administration.
By John Clark Marshman.
3 vols. crown 8vo. 22s. 6d.

Indian Polity; a View of the System of Administration in India.
By Lieut.-Colonel George Chesney.
Second Edition, revised, with Map. 8vo. 21s.

Waterloo Lectures; a Study of the Campaign of 1815.
By Colonel Charles C. Chesney, R.E.
Third Edition. 8vo. with Map, 10s. 6d.

Essays in Modern Military Biography.
By Colonel Charles C. Chesney, R.E.
8vo. 12s. 6d.

The Imperial and Colonial Constitutions of the Britannic Empire, including Indian Institutions.
By Sir E. Creasy, M.A.
With 6 Maps. 8vo. 15s.

The Oxford Reformers—John Colet, Erasmus, and Thomas More; being a History of their Fellow-Work.
By Frederic Seebohm.
Second Edition. 8vo. 14s.

The History of Persia and its present Political Situation; with Abstracts of all Treaties and Conventions between Persia and England.
By Clements R. Markham, C.B. F.R.S.
8vo. with Map, 21s.

The Mythology of the Aryan Nations.
By Geo. W. Cox, M.A. late Scholar of Trinity College, Oxford.
2 vols. 8vo. 28s.

A History of Greece.
By the Rev. Geo. W. Cox, M.A. late Scholar of Trinity College, Oxford.
Vols. I. and II. 8vo. Maps, 36s.

The History of Greece.
By C. Thirlwall, D.D. late Bp. of St. David's.
8 vols. fcp. 8vo. 28s.

The Tale of the Great Persian War, from the Histories of Herodotus.
By Rev. G. W. Cox, M.A.
Fcp. 8vo. 3s. 6d.

The History of the Peloponnesian War, by Thucydides.
Translated by Richd. Crawley, Fellow of Worcester College, Oxford.
8vo. 21s.

Greek History from Themistocles to Alexander, in a Series of Lives from Plutarch.
Revised and arranged by A. H. Clough.
Fcp. 8vo. Woodcuts, 6s.

History of the Romans under the Empire.
By the Very Rev. Charles Merivale, D.C.L. Dean of Ely.
8 vols. post 8vo. 48s.

The Fall of the Roman Republic; a Short History of the Last Century of the Commonwealth.
By Dean Merivale, D.C.L.
12mo. 7s. 6d.

The Sixth Oriental Monarchy; or the Geography, History, and Antiquities of Parthia. Collected and Illustrated from Ancient and Modern sources.
By Geo. Rawlinson, M.A.
With Maps and Illustrations. 8vo. 16s.

The Seventh Great Oriental Monarchy; or, a History of the Sassanians: with Notices Geographical and Antiquarian.
By Geo. Rawlinson, M.A.
8vo. with Maps and Illustrations.
[*In the press.*

Encyclopædia of Chronology, Historical and Biographical; comprising the Dates of all the Great Events of History, including Treaties, Alliances, Wars, Battles, &c. Incidents in the Lives of Eminent Men, Scientific and Geographical Discoveries, Mechanical Inventions, and Social, Domestic, and Economical Improvements.
By B. B. Woodward, B.A. and W. L. R. Cates.
8vo. 42s.

The History of Rome.
By Wilhelm Ihne.
Vols. I. and II. 8vo. 30s. Vols. III. and IV. in preparation.

History of European Morals from Augustus to Charlemagne.
By W. E. H. Lecky, M.A.
2 vols. 8vo. 28s.

History of the Rise and Influence of the Spirit of Rationalism in Europe.
By W. E. H. Lecky, M.A.
Cabinet Edition, 2 vols. crown 8vo. 16s.

History of the Early Church from the First Preaching of the Gospel to the Council of Nicæa, A.D. 325.
By Miss E. M. Sewell.
Fcp. 8vo. 4s. 6d.

Introduction to the Science of Religion: Four Lectures delivered at the Royal Institution; with two Essays on False Analogies and the Philosophy of Mythology.
By F. Max Müller, M.A.
Crown 8vo. 10s. 6d.

The Stoics, Epicureans, and Sceptics.
Translated from the German of Dr. E. Zeller, by Oswald J. Reichel, M.A.
Crown 8vo. 14s.

Socrates and the Socratic Schools.
Translated from the German of Dr. E. Zeller, by the Rev. O. J. Reichel, M.A.
Crown 8vo. 8s. 6d.

The History of Philosophy, from Thales to Comte.
By George Henry Lewes.
Fourth Edition, 2 vols. 8vo. 32s.

Sketch of the History of the Church of England to the Revolution of 1688.
By the Right Rev. T. V. Short, D.D. Bishop of St. Asaph.
Eighth Edition. Crown 8vo. 7s. 6d.

The Historical Geography of Europe.
By E. A. Freeman, D.C.L.
8vo. Maps. [In the press.

Essays on the History of the Christian Religion.
By *John Earl Russell.*
Fcp. 8vo. 3s. 6d.

History of the Reformation in Europe in the Time of Calvin.
By the Rev. *J. H. Merle D'Aubigné, D.D.*
Vols. I. to V. 8vo. £3. 12s. Vols. VI. & VII. completion. [*In the press.*

The Student's Manual of Ancient History: containing the Political History, Geographical Position, and Social State of the Principal Nations of Antiquity.
By *W. Cooke Taylor, LL.D.*
Crown 8vo. 7s. 6d.

The Student's Manual of Modern History: containing the Rise and Progress of the Principal European Nations, their Political History, and the Changes in their Social Condition.
By *W. Cooke Taylor, LL.D.*
Crown 8vo. 7s. 6d.

The Era of the Protestant Revolution.
By *F. Seebohm,* Author of 'The Oxford Reformers.'
With 4 Maps and 12 Diagrams. Fcp. 8vo. 2s. 6d.

The Crusades.
By the Rev. *G. W. Cox, M.A.*
Fcp. 8vo. with Map, 2s. 6d.

The Thirty Years' War, 1618–1648.
By *Samuel Rawson Gardiner.*
Fcp. 8vo. with Maps, 2s. 6d.

The Houses of Lancaster and York; with the Conquest and Loss of France.
By *James Gairdner.*
Fcp. 8vo. with Map, 2s. 6d.

Edward the Third.
By the Rev. *W. Warburton, M.A.*
Fcp. 8vo. with Maps, 2s. 6d.

BIOGRAPHICAL WORKS.

Autobiography.
By *John Stuart Mill.*
8vo. 7s. 6d.

Life and Correspondence of Richard Whately, D.D. late Archbishop of Dublin.
By *E. Jane Whately.*
New Edition in 1 vol. Crown 8vo. [*In the press.*

Life and Letters of Gilbert Elliot, First Earl of Minto, from 1751 *to* 1806, *when his Public Life in Europe was closed by his Appointment to the Vice-Royalty of India.*
Edited by the Countess of Minto.
3 vols. post 8vo. 31s. 6d.

Memoir of Thomas First Lord Denman, formerly Lord Chief Justice of England.
By Sir *Joseph Arnould,* B.A. K.B.
With two Portraits. 2 vols. 8vo. 32s.

The Life of Lloyd First Lord Kenyon.
By Hon. G. T. *Kenyon,* M.A.
With Portraits. 8vo. 14s.

Recollections of Past Life.
By Sir Henry *Holland,* Bart. M.D. F.R.S.
Third Edition. Post 8vo. 10s. 6d.

Isaac Casaubon, 1559–1614.
By Mark *Pattison,* Rector of Lincoln College, Oxford. 8vo. [*In the press.*

Life of Alexander von Humboldt.
Edited by Karl *Bruhns,* and translated by *Jane* and Caroline *Lassell.*
With 3 Portraits. 2 vols. 8vo. 36s.

Biographical and Critical Essays, reprinted from Reviews, with Additions and Corrections.
By A. *Hayward,* Q.C.
Second Series, 2 vols. 8vo. 28s. Third Series, 1 vol. 8vo. 14s.

The Life of Isambard Kingdom Brunel, Civil Engineer.
By I. *Brunel,* B.C.L.
With Portrait, Plates, and Woodcuts. 8vo. 21s.

Lord George Bentinck; a Political Biography.
By the Right Hon. B. *Disraeli,* M.P.
Eighth Edition. Crown 8vo. 6s.

Memoir of George Edward Lynch Cotton, D.D. Bishop of Calcutta; with Selections from his Journals and Correspondence.
Edited by Mrs. *Cotton.*
Second Edition. Crown 8vo. 7s. 6d.

The Life and Letters of the Rev. Sydney Smith.
Edited by his Daughter, Lady *Holland,* and Mrs. *Austin.*
Crown 8vo. 2s. 6d. sewed; 3s. 6d. cloth.

Essays in Ecclesiastical Biography.
By the Right Hon. Sir J. *Stephen,* LL.D.
Cabinet Edition. Crown 8vo. 7s. 6d.

Leaders of Public Opinion in Ireland; Swift, Flood, Grattan, O'Connell.
By W. E. H. *Lecky,* M.A.
Crown 8vo. 7s. 6d.

Life of the Duke of Wellington.
By the Rev. G. R. Gleig, M.A.
Popular Edition, Crown 8vo. with Portrait, 5s.

Felix Mendelssohn's Letters from Italy and Switzerland, and Letters from 1833 to 1847.
Translated by Lady Wallace.
With Portrait. 2 vols. crown 8vo. 5s. each.

The Rise of Great Families; other Essays and Stories.
By Sir Bernard Burke, C.B. LL.D.
Crown 8vo. 12s. 6d.

Dictionary of General Biography; containing Concise Memoirs and Notices of the most Eminent Persons of all Countries, from the Earliest Ages to the Present Time.
Edited by W. L. R. Cates.
8vo. 21s.

Memoirs of Sir Henry Havelock, K.C.B.
By John Clark Marshman.
People's Edition. Crown 8vo. 3s. 6d.

Vicissitudes of Families.
By Sir Bernard Burke, C.B.
New Edition. 2 vols. crown 8vo. 21s.

MENTAL and POLITICAL PHILOSOPHY.

The System of Positive Polity, or Treatise upon Sociology, of Auguste Comte, Author of the System of Positive Philosophy.

Translated from the Paris Edition of 1851-1854, and furnished with Analytical Tables of Contents.

[*In preparation.*

In Four Volumes, 8vo. to be published separately, and each forming in some degree an independent Treatise:—

Vol. I. The General View of Positive Polity and its Philosophical Basis. Translated by J. H. Bridges, M.B. *formerly Fellow Oriel College, Oxford.*

Vol. II. The Social Statics, or the Abstract Laws of Human Order. Translated by Frederic Harrison, M.A. *of Lincoln's Inn.*

Vol. III. The Social Dynamics, or the General Laws of Human Progress (the Philosophy of History). Translated by E. S. Beesly, M.A. *Professor of History in University College, London.*

Vol. IV. The Ideal of the Future of Mankind. Translated by Richard Congreve, M.D. *formerly Fellow and Tutor of Wadham College, Oxford.*

Political Problems, Reprinted chiefly from the Fortnightly Review, revised, and with New Essays.
By Frederick Harrison, of Lincoln's Inn.
1 vol. 8vo. [*In the press.*

Essays Critical & Narrative, partly original and partly reprinted from Reviews.
By W. Forsyth, Q.C. M.P.
8vo. 16s.

Essays, Political, Social, and Religious.
By Richd. Congreve, M.A.
8vo. 18s.

Essays on Freethinking and Plainspeaking.
By Leslie Stephen.
Crown 8vo. 10s. 6d.

Essays, Critical and Biographical, contributed to the Edinburgh Review.
By Henry Rogers.
New Edition. 2 vols. crown 8vo. 12s.

Essays on some Theological Controversies of the Time, contributed chiefly to the Edinburgh Review.
By the same Author.
New Edition. Crown 8vo. 6s.

Democracy in America.
By Alexis de Tocqueville. Translated by Henry Reeve, C.B. D.C.L. Corresponding Member of the Institute of France.
New Edition. 2 vols. post 8vo. [*In the press.*

On Representative Government.
By John Stuart Mill.
Fourth Edition, crown 8vo. 2s.

On Liberty.
By John Stuart Mill.
Post 8vo. 7s. 6d. crown 8vo. 1s. 4d.

Principles of Political Economy.
By John Stuart Mill.
2 vols. 8vo. 30s. or 1 vol. crown 8vo. 5s.

Essays on some Unsettled Questions of Political Economy.
By John Stuart Mill.
Second Edition. 8vo. 6s. 6d.

Utilitarianism.
By John Stuart Mill.
Fourth Edition. 8vo. 5s.

A System of Logic, Ratiocinative and Inductive. By John Stuart Mill.
Eighth Edition. 2 vols. 8vo. 25s.

Examination of Sir William Hamilton's Philosophy, and of the principal Philosophical Questions discussed in his Writings.
By John Stuart Mill.
Fourth Edition. 8vo. 16s.

The Subjection of Women.
By John Stuart Mill.
New Edition. Post 8vo. 5s.

Dissertations and Discussions.
By John Stuart Mill.
Second Edition. 3 vols. 8vo. 36s.

B

Analysis of the Phenomena of the Human Mind. By James Mill. New Edition, with Notes, Illustrative and Critical.
2 vols. 8vo. 28s.

A Systematic View of the Science of Jurisprudence. By Sheldon Amos, M.A.
8vo. 18s.

A Primer of the English Constitution and Government. By Sheldon Amos, M.A.
New Edition, revised. Post 8vo. [In the press.

Principles of Economical Philosophy. By H. D. Macleod, M.A. Barrister-at-Law.
Second Edition, in 2 vols. Vol. I. 8vo. 15s.

The Institutes of Justinian; with English Introduction, Translation, and Notes. By T. C. Sandars, M.A.
Sixth Edition. 8vo. 18s.

Lord Bacon's Works, Collected and Edited by R. L. Ellis, M.A. J. Spedding, M.A. and D. D. Heath.
New and Cheaper Edition. 7 vols. 8vo. £3. 13s. 6d.

Letters and Life of Francis Bacon, including all his Occasional Works. Collected and edited, with a Commentary, by J. Spedding.
7 vols. 8vo. £4. 4s.

The Nicomachean Ethics of Aristotle. Newly translated into English. By R. Williams, B.A.
8vo. 12s.

The Politics of Aristotle; Greek Text, with English Notes. By Richard Congreve, M.A.
New Edition, revised. 8vo. 18s.

The Ethics of Aristotle; with Essays and Notes. By Sir A. Grant, Bart. M.A. LL.D.
Third Edition, revised and partly re-written. [In the press.

Bacon's Essays, with Annotations. By R. Whately, D.D.
New Edition. 8vo. 10s. 6d.

Elements of Logic. By R. Whately, D.D.
New Edition. 8vo. 10s. 6d. cr. 8vo. 4s. 6d.

Elements of Rhetoric. By R. Whately, D.D.
New Edition. 8vo. 10s. 6d. cr. 8vo. 4s. 6d.

An Outline of the Necessary Laws of Thought: a Treatise on Pure and Applied Logic.
By the Most Rev. W. Thomson, D.D. Archbishop of York.
Ninth Thousand. Crown 8vo. 5s. 6d.

An Introduction to Mental Philosophy, on the Inductive Method.
By J. D. Morell, LL.D.
8vo. 12s.

Elements of Psychology, containing the Analysis of the Intellectual Powers.
By J. D. Morell, LL.D.
Post 8vo. 7s. 6d.

The Secret of Hegel: being the Hegelian System in Origin, Principle, Form, and Matter.
By J. H. Stirling, LL.D.
2 vols. 8vo. 28s.

Sir William Hamilton; being the Philosophy of Perception: an Analysis.
By J. H. Stirling, LL.D.
8vo. 5s.

The Philosophy of Necessity; or, Natural Law as applicable to Mental, Moral, and Social Science.
By Charles Bray.
Second Edition. 8vo. 9s.

Ueberweg's System of Logic, and History of Logical Doctrines.
Translated, with Notes and Appendices, by T. M. Lindsay, M.A. F.R.S.E.
8vo. 16s.

The Senses and the Intellect.
By A. Bain, LL.D. Prof. of Logic, Univ. Aberdeen.
8vo. 15s.

Mental and Moral Science; a Compendium of Psychology and Ethics.
By A. Bain, LL.D.
Third Edition. Crown 8vo. 10s. 6d. Or separately: Part I. Mental Science, 6s. 6d. Part II. Moral Science, 4s. 6d.

Hume's Treatise on Human Nature.
Edited, with Notes, &c. by T. H. Green, M.A. and the Rev. T. H. Grose, M.A.
2 vols. 8vo. 28s.

Hume's Essays Moral, Political, and Literary.
By the same Editors.
2 vols. 8vo. 28s.

*** *The above form a complete and uniform Edition of* HUME'S *Philosophical Works.*

MISCELLANEOUS & CRITICAL WORKS.

Miscellaneous and Posthumous Works of the late Henry Thomas Buckle. Edited, with a Biographical Notice, by Helen Taylor.
3 vols. 8vo. £2. 12s. 6d.

Short Studies on Great Subjects.
By J. A. Froude, M.A. formerly Fellow of Exeter College, Oxford.
2 vols. crown 8vo. 12s.

Lord Macaulay's Miscellaneous Writings.
LIBRARY EDITION, 2 vols. 8vo. Portrait, 21s.
PEOPLE'S EDITION, 1 vol. cr. 8vo. 4s. 6d.

Lord Macaulay's Miscellaneous Writings and Speeches.
Students' Edition. Crown 8vo. 6s.

Speeches of the Right Hon. Lord Macaulay, corrected by Himself.
People's Edition. Crown 8vo. 3s. 6d.

Lord Macaulay's Speeches on Parliamentary Reform in 1831 and 1832.
16mo. 1s.

The Rev. Sydney Smith's Essays contributed to the Edinburgh Review.
Authorised Edition, complete in One Volume, Crown 8vo. 2s. 6d. sewed, or 3s. 6d. cloth.

The Rev. Sydney Smith's Miscellaneous Works.
Crown 8vo. 6s.

The Wit and Wisdom of the Rev. Sydney Smith.
Crown 8vo. 3s. 6d.

The Miscellaneous Works of Thomas Arnold, D.D. Late Head Master of Rugby School and Regius Professor of Modern History in the Univ. of Oxford, collected and republished.
8vo. 7s. 6d.

Manual of English Literature, Historical and Critical.
By Thomas Arnold, M.A.
New Edition. Crown 8vo. 7s. 6d.

Realities of Irish Life.
By W. Steuart Trench.
Cr. 8vo. 2s. 6d. sewed, or 3s. 6d. cloth.

Lectures on the Science of Language.
By F. Max Müller, M.A. &c.
Seventh Edition. 2 vols. crown 8vo. 16s.

Chips from a German Workshop; being Essays on the Science of Religion, and on Mythology, Traditions, and Customs.
By F. Max Müller, M.A. &c.
3 vols. 8vo. £2.

Families of Speech.
Four Lectures delivered at the Royal Institution.
By F. W. Farrar, M.A. F.R.S.
New Edition. Crown 8vo. 3s. 6d.

Chapters on Language.
By F. W. Farrar, M.A. F.R.S.
New Edition. Crown 8vo. 5s.

Southey's Doctor, complete in One Volume.
Edited by Rev. J. W. Warter, B.D.
Square crown 8vo. 12s. 6d.

A Budget of Paradoxes.
By Augustus De Morgan, F.R.A.S.
Reprinted, with Author's Additions, from the Athenæum. 8vo. 15s.

Recreations of a Country Parson.
By A. K. H. B.
Two Series, 3s. 6d. each.

Landscapes, Churches, and Moralities.
By A. K. H. B.
Crown 8vo. 3s. 6d.

Seaside Musings on Sundays and Weekdays.
By A. K. H. B.
Crown 8vo. 3s. 6d.

Changed Aspects of Unchanged Truths.
By A. K. H. B.
Crown 8vo. 3s. 6d.

Counsel and Comfort from a City Pulpit.
By A. K. H. B.
Crown 8vo. 3s. 6d.

Lessons of Middle Age.
By A. K. H. B.
Crown 8vo. 3s. 6d.

Leisure Hours in Town.
By A. K. H. B.
Crown 8vo. 3s. 6d.

The Autumn Holidays of a Country Parson.
By A. K. H. B.
Crown 8vo. 3s. 6d.

Sunday Afternoons at the Parish Church of a Scottish University City.
By A. K. H. B.
Crown 8vo. 3s. 6d.

The Commonplace Philosopher in Town and Country.
By A. K. H. B.
Crown 8vo. 3s. 6d.

Present-Day Thoughts.
By A. K. H. B.
Crown 8vo. 3s. 6d.

Critical Essays of a Country Parson.
By A. K. H. B.
Crown 8vo. 3s. 6d.

The Graver Thoughts of a Country Parson.
By A. K. H. B.
Two Series, 3s. 6d. each.

Principles of Education, drawn from Nature and Revelation, and applied to Female Education in the Upper Classes.
By the Author of 'Amy Herbert.'
2 vols. fcp. 8vo. 12s. 6d

From January to December; a Book for Children.
Second Edition. 8vo. 3s. 6d.

The Election of Representatives, Parliamentary and Municipal; a Treatise.
By Thos. Hare, Barrister.
Fourth Edition. Post 8vo. 7s.

Miscellaneous Writings of John Conington, M.A.
Edited by J. A. Symonds, M.A. With a Memoir by H. J. S. Smith, M.A.
2 vols. 8vo. 28s.

DICTIONARIES and OTHER BOOKS of REFERENCE.

A Dictionary of the English Language.
By R. G. Latham, M.A. M.D. F.R.S. Founded on the Dictionary of Dr. S. Johnson, as edited by the Rev. H. J. Todd, with numerous Emendations and Additions.
4 vols. 4to. £7.

Thesaurus of English Words and Phrases, classified and arranged so as to facilitate the expression of Ideas, and assist in Literary Composition.
By P. M. Roget, M.D.
Crown 8vo. 10s. 6d.

English Synonymes.
By E. J. Whately. Edited by Archbishop Whately.
Fifth Edition. Fcp. 8vo. 3s.

A Practical Dictionary of the French and English Languages.
By Léon Contanseau, many years French Examiner for Military and Civil Appointments, &c.
Post 8vo. 10s. 6d.

Contanseau's Pocket Dictionary, French and English, abridged from the Practical Dictionary, by the Author.
Square 18mo. 3s. 6d.

New Practical Dictionary of the German Language; German-English and English-German.
By Rev. W. L. Blackley, M.A. and Dr. C. M. Friedländer.
Post 8vo. 7s. 6d.

A Dictionary of Roman and Greek Antiquities. With 2,000 Woodcuts from Ancient Originals, illustrative of the Arts and Life of the Greeks and Romans.
By Anthony Rich, B.A.
Third Edition. Crown 8vo. 7s. 6d.

The Mastery of Languages; or, the Art of Speaking Foreign Tongues Idiomatically.
By Thomas Prendergast.
Second Edition. 8vo. 6s.

A Practical English Dictionary.
By John T. White, D.D. Oxon. and T. C. Donkin, M.A.
1 vol. post 8vo. uniform with Contanseau's Practical French Dictionary.
[*In the press.*

A Latin-English Dictionary.
By John T. White, D.D. Oxon. and J. E. Riddle, M.A. Oxon.
Third Edition, revised. 2 vols. 4to. 42s.

White's College Latin-English Dictionary; abridged from the Parent Work for the use of University Students.
Medium 8vo. 18s.

A Latin-English Dictionary adapted for the use of Middle-Class Schools.
By John T. White, D.D. Oxon.
Square fcp. 8vo. 3s.

White's Junior Student's Complete Latin-English and English-Latin Dictionary.
Square 12mo. 12s.

Separately { ENGLISH-LATIN, 5s. 6d.
{ LATIN-ENGLISH, 7s. 6d.

A Greek-English Lexicon.
By H. G. Liddell, D.D. Dean of Christchurch, and R. Scott, D.D. Dean of Rochester.
Sixth Edition. Crown 4to. 36s.

A Lexicon, Greek and English, abridged for Schools from Liddell and Scott's Greek-English Lexicon.
Fourteenth Edition. Square 12mo. 7s. 6d.

An English-Greek Lexicon, containing all the Greek Words used by Writers of good authority.
By C. D. Yonge, B.A.
New Edition. 4to. 21s.

Mr. Yonge's New Lexicon, English and Greek, abridged from his larger Lexicon.
Square 12mo. 8s. 6d.

M'Culloch's Dictionary, Practical, Theoretical, and Historical, of Commerce and Commercial Navigation.
Edited by H. G. Reid.
8vo. 63s.

The Post Office Gazetteer of the United Kingdom: a Complete Dictionary of all Cities, Towns, Villages, and of the Principal Gentlemen's Seats, in Great Britain and Ireland, referred to the nearest Post Town, Railway & Telegraph Station; with Natural Features and Objects of Note.
By J. A. Sharp.
In 1 vol. 8vo. of about 1,500 pages.
[In the press.

A General Dictionary of Geography, Descriptive, Physical, Statistical, and Historical; forming a complete Gazetteer of the World.
By A. Keith Johnston, F.R.S.E.
New Edition, thoroughly revised.
[In the press.

The Public Schools Atlas of Modern Geography. In 31 Maps, exhibiting clearly the more important Physical Features of the Countries delineated.
Edited, with Introduction, by Rev. G. Butler, M.A.
Imperial quarto, 3s. 6d. sewed; 5s. cloth.

The Public Schools Manual of Modern Geography Forming a Companion to 'The Public Schools Atlas of Modern Geography.'
By Rev. G. Butler, M.A.
[In the press.

The Public Schools Atlas of Ancient Geography.
Edited, with an Introduction on the Study of Ancient Geography, by the Rev. G. Butler, M.A.
Imperial Quarto. [In the press.

ASTRONOMY and METEOROLOGY.

The Universe and the Coming Transits; Researches into and New Views respecting the Constitution of the Heavens.
By R. A. Proctor, B.A.
With 22 Charts and 22 Diagrams. 8vo. 16s.

The Transits of Venus; A Popular Account of Past and Coming Transits, from the first observed by Horrocks A.D. 1639 *to the Transit of* A.D. 2112.
By R. A. Proctor, B.A. Cantab.
With 20 Plates and numerous Woodcuts. Crown 8vo. [Nearly ready.

Essays on Astronomy. A Series of Papers on Planets and Meteors, the Sun and Sun-surrounding Space, Stars and Star Cloudlets.
By R. A. Proctor, B.A.
With 10 Plates and 24 Woodcuts. 8vo. 12s.

The Moon; her Motions, Aspect, Scenery, and Physical Condition.
By R. A. Proctor, B.A.
With Plates, Charts, Woodcuts, and Lunar Photographs. Crown 8vo. 15s.

The Sun; Ruler, Light, Fire, and Life of the Planetary System.
By R. A. Proctor, B.A.
Second Edition. Plates and Woodcuts. Cr. 8vo. 14s.

Saturn and its System.
By R. A. Proctor, B.A.
8vo. with 14 Plates, 14s.

The Orbs Around Us; a Series of Familiar Essays on the Moon and Planets, Meteors and Comets, the Sun and Coloured Pairs of Suns.
By R. A. Proctor, B.A.
Crown 8vo. 7s. 6d.

Other Worlds than Ours; The Plurality of Worlds Studied under the Light of Recent Scientific Researches.
By R. A. Proctor, B.A.
Third Edition, with 14 Illustrations. Cr. 8vo. 10s. 6d.

Brinkley's Astronomy. Revised and partly re-written, with Additional Chapters, and an Appendix of Questions for Examination.
By John W. Stubbs, D.D. Trin. Coll. Dublin and F. Brunnow, Ph.D. Astronomer Royal of Ireland.
With 49 Diagrams. Crown 8vo. 6s.

Outlines of Astronomy.
By Sir J. F. W. Herschel, Bart. M.A.
Latest Edition, with Plates and Diagrams. Square crown 8vo. 12s.

C

A New Star Atlas, for the Library, the School, and the Observatory, in 12 Circular Maps (with 2 Index Plates).
By R. A. Proctor, B.A.
Crown 8vo. 5s.

Celestial Objects for Common Telescopes.
By T. W. Webb, M.A. F.R.A.S.
New Edition, with Map of the Moon and Woodcuts. Crown 8vo. 7s. 6d.

Larger Star Atlas, for the Library, in Twelve Circular Maps, photolithographed by A. Brothers, F.R.A.S. With 2 Index Plates and a Letterpress Introduction.
By R. A. Proctor, B.A.
Second Edition. Small folio, 25s.

Magnetism and Deviation of the Compass. For the use of Students in Navigation and Science Schools.
By J. Merrifield, LL.D.
18mo. 1s. 6d.

Dove's Law of Storms, considered in connexion with the ordinary Movements of the Atmosphere.
Translated by R. H. Scott, M.A.
8vo. 10s. 6d.

Air and Rain; the Beginnings of a Chemical Climatology.
By R. A. Smith, F.R.S.
8vo. 24s.

Nautical Surveying, an Introduction to the Practical and Theoretical Study of.
By J. K. Laughton, M.A.
Small 8vo. 6s.

Schellen's Spectrum Analysis, in its Application to Terrestrial Substances and the Physical Constitution of the Heavenly Bodies.
Translated by Jane and C. Lassell; edited, with Notes, by W. Huggins, LL.D. F.R.S.
With 13 Plates and 223 Woodcuts. 8vo. 28s.

NATURAL HISTORY and PHYSICAL SCIENCE.

The Correlation of Physical Forces.
By the Hon. Sir W. R. Grove, F.R.S. &c.
Sixth Edition, with other Contributions to Science. 8vo. 15s.

Professor Helmholtz' Popular Lectures on Scientific Subjects.
Translated by E. Atkinson, F.C.S.
With many Illustrative Wood Engravings. 8vo. 12s. 6d.

Ganot's Natural Philosophy for General Readers and Young Persons; a Course of Physics divested of Mathematical Formulæ and expressed in the language of daily life.
Translated by E. Atkinson, F.C.S.
Cr. 8vo. with 404 Woodcuts, 7s. 6d.

Ganot's Elementary Treatise on Physics, Experimental and Applied, for the use of Colleges and Schools.
Translated and edited by E. Atkinson, F.C.S.
New Edition, with a Coloured Plate and 726 Woodcuts. Post 8vo. 15s.

Principles of Animal Mechanics.
By the Rev. S. Haughton, F.R.S.
Second Edition. 8vo. 21s.

Weinhold's Introduction to Experimental Physics, Theoretical and Practical; including Directions for Constructing Physical Apparatus and for Making Experiments.
Translated by B. Loewy, F.R.A.S. With a Preface by G. C. Foster, F.R.S.
With numerous Woodcuts. 8vo. [Nearly ready.

Text-Books of Science, Mechanical and Physical, adapted for the use of Artisans and of Students in Public and other Schools. (The first Ten edited by T. M. Goodeve, M.A. Lecturer on Applied Science at the Royal School of Mines; the remainder edited by C. W. Merrifield, F.R.S. an Examiner in the Department of Public Education.)
Small 8vo. Woodcuts.

Edited by T. M. Goodeve, M.A.
Anderson's *Strength of Materials*, 3s. 6d.
Bloxam's *Metals*, 3s. 6d.
Goodeve's *Mechanics*, 3s. 6d.
———.— *Mechanism*, 3s. 6d.
Griffin's *Algebra & Trigonometry*, 3s. 6d.
   Notes on the same, with Solutions, 3s. 6d.
Jenkin's *Electricity & Magnetism*, 3s. 6d.
Maxwell's *Theory of Heat*, 3s. 6d.
Merrifield's *Technical Arithmetic*, 3s. 6d.
   Key, 3s. 6d.
Miller's *Inorganic Chemistry*, 3s. 6d.
Shelley's *Workshop Appliances*, 3s. 6d.
Watson's *Plane & Solid Geometry*, 3s. 6d.

Edited by C. W. Merrifield, F.R.S.
Armstrong's *Organic Chemistry*, 3s. 6d.
Thorpe's *Quantitative Analysis*, 4s. 6d.
Thorpe and Muir's *Qualitative Analysis*, 3s. 6d.

Address delivered before the British Association assembled at Belfast; with Additions and a Preface.
By John Tyndall, F.R.S. President.
8vo. price 3s.

Fragments of Science.
By John Tyndall, F.R.S.
Third Edition. 8vo. 14s.

Heat a Mode of Motion.
By JOHN TYNDALL, F.R.S.
Fourth Edition. Cr. 8vo. with Woodcuts, 10s. 6d.

Sound; a Course of Eight Lectures delivered at the Royal Institution of Great Britain.
By JOHN TYNDALL, F.R.S.
Portrait and Woodcuts. Cr. 8vo. 9s.

Researches on Diamagnetism and Magne-Crystallic Action; including the Question of Diamagnetic Polarity.
By JOHN TYNDALL, F.R.S.
With 6 Plates and many Woodcuts. 8vo. 14s.

Contributions to Molecular Physics in the domain of Radiant Heat.
By JOHN TYNDALL, F.R.S.
With 2 Plates and 31 Woodcuts. 8vo. 16s.

Lectures on Light, delivered in the United States of America in 1872 and 1873.
By J. TYNDALL, F.R.S.
Crown 8vo. 7s. 6d.

Notes of a Course of Seven Lectures on Electrical Phenomena and Theories, delivered at the Royal Institution.
By J. TYNDALL, F.R.S.
Crown 8vo. 1s. sewed, or 1s. 6d. cloth.

Notes of a Course of Nine Lectures on Light, delivered at the Royal Institution.
By J. TYNDALL, F.R.S.
Crown 8vo. 1s. sewed, or 1s. 6d. cloth.

A Treatise on Magnetism, General and Terrestrial.
By HUMPHREY LLOYD, D.D. D.C.L. Provost of Trinity College, Dublin.
8vo. price 10s. 6d.

Elementary Treatise on the Wave-Theory of Light.
By H. LLOYD, D.D. D.C.L.
Third Edition. 8vo. 10s. 6d.

Professor Owen's Lectures on the Comparative Anatomy and Physiology of Invertebrate Animals.
2nd Edition, with 235 Woodcuts. 8vo. 21s.

The Comparative Anatomy and Physiology of the Vertebrate Animals.
By RICHARD OWEN, F.R.S.
With 1,472 Woodcuts. 3 vols. 8vo. £3. 13s. 6d.

Light Science for Leisure Hours; a Series of Familiar Essays on Scientific Subjects, Natural Phenomena, &c.
By R. A. PROCTOR, B.A.
First and Second Series. 2 vols. crown 8vo. 7s. 6d. each.

Kirby and Spence's Introduction to Entomology, or Elements of the Natural History of Insects.
Crown 8vo. 5s.

Strange Dwellings; a Description of the Habitations of Animals, abridged from 'Homes without Hands.'
By Rev. J. G. Wood, M.A.
With Frontispiece and 60 Woodcuts. Crown 8vo. 7s. 6d.

Homes without Hands; a Description of the Habitations of Animals, classed according to their Principle of Construction.
By Rev. J. G. Wood, M.A.
With about 140 Vignettes on Wood. 8vo. 21s.

Out of Doors; a Selection of Original Articles on Practical Natural History.
By Rev. J. G. Wood, M.A.
With 6 Illustrations from Original Designs engraved on Wood. Crown 8vo. 7s. 6d.

The Polar World: a Popular Description of Man and Nature in the Arctic and Antarctic Regions of the Globe.
By Dr. G. Hartwig.
With Chromoxylographs, Maps, and Woodcuts. 8vo. 10s. 6d.

The Sea and its Living Wonders.
By Dr. G. Hartwig.
Fourth Edition, enlarged. 8vo. with many Illustrations, 10s. 6d.

The Tropical World; a Popular Scientific Account of the Natural History of the Equatorial Regions.
By Dr. G. Hartwig.
With about 200 Illustrations. 8vo. 10s. 6d.

The Subterranean World.
By Dr. G. Hartwig.
With Maps and many Woodcuts. 8vo. 21s.

The Aerial World.
By Dr. George Hartwig.
With 8 Chromoxylographs and about 60 other Illustrations engraved on Wood. 8vo. price 21s.

Insects at Home; a Popular Account of British Insects, their Structure, Habits, and Transformations.
By Rev. J. G. Wood, M.A.
With upwards of 700 Woodcuts. 8vo. 21s.

Insects Abroad; being a Popular Account of Foreign Insects, their Structure, Habits, and Transformations.
By Rev. J. G. Wood, M.A.
With upwards of 700 Woodcuts. 8vo. 21s.

A Familiar History of Birds.
By E. Stanley, D.D. late Ld. Bishop of Norwich.
Fcp. 8vo. with Woodcuts, 3s. 6d.

Rocks Classified and Described.
By B. VON COTTA.
English Edition, by P. H. LAWRENCE (with English, German, and French Synonymes), revised by the Author. Post 8vo. 14s.

Primæval World of Switzerland.
By Professor OSWALD HEER, of the University of Zurich. Translated by W. S. Dallas, F.L.S. and edited by James Heywood, M.A. F.R.S.
2 vols. 8vo. with numerous Illustrations. [*In the press.*]

The Origin of Civilisation, and the Primitive Condition of Man; Mental and Social Condition of Savages.
By Sir J. LUBBOCK, Bart. M.P. F.R.S.
Third Edition, with 25 Woodcuts. 8vo. 16s.

A Manual of Anthropology, or Science of Man, based on Modern Research.
By CHARLES BRAY.
Crown 8vo. 5s.

A Phrenologist amongst the Todas, or the Study of a Primitive Tribe in South India; History, Character, Customs, Religion, Infanticide, Polyandry, Language.
By W. E. MARSHALL, Lieut.-Col. Bengal Staff Corps.
With 26 Illustrations. 8vo. 21s.

The Ancient Stone Implements, Weapons, and Ornaments of Great Britain.
By JOHN EVANS, F.R.S.
With 2 Plates and 476 Woodcuts. 8vo. 28s.

The Elements of Botany for Families and Schools.
Tenth Edition, revised by Thomas Moore, F.L.S.
Fcp. 8vo. with 154 Woodcuts 2s. 6d.

Bible Animals; a Description of every Living Creature mentioned in the Scriptures, from the Ape to the Coral.
By Rev. J. G. WOOD, M.A.
With about 100 Vignettes on Wood. 8vo. 21s.

The Rose Amateur's Guide.
By THOMAS RIVERS.
Tenth Edition. Fcp. 8vo. 4s.

A Dictionary of Science, Literature, and Art.
Fourth Edition, re-edited by the late W. T. Brande (the Author) and Rev. G. W. Cox, M.A.
3 vols. medium 8vo. 63s.

Loudon's Encyclopædia of Plants; comprising the Specific Character, Description, Culture, History, &c. of all the Plants found in Great Britain.
With upwards of 12,000 Woodcuts. 8vo. 42s.

The Treasury of Botany, or Popular Dictionary of the Vegetable Kingdom; with which is incorporated a Glossary of Botanical Terms.
Edited by J. Lindley, F.R.S. and T. Moore, F.L.S.

With 274 Woodcuts and 20 Steel Plates. Two Parts, fcp. 8vo. 12s.

Handbook of Hardy Trees, Shrubs, and Herbaceous Plants; containing Descriptions &c. of the Best Species in Cultivation; with Cultural Details, Comparative Hardiness, suitability for particular positions, &c. Based on the French Work of Decaisne and Naudin, and including the 720 Original Woodcut Illustrations.
By W. B. Hemsley.

Medium 8vo. 21s.

A General System of Descriptive and Analytical Botany.
Translated from the French of Le Maout and Decaisne, by Mrs. Hooker. Edited and arranged according to the English Botanical System, by J. D. Hooker, M.D. &c. Director of the Royal Botanic Gardens, Kew.

With 5,500 Woodcuts. Imperial 8vo. 52s. 6d.

Forest Trees and Woodland Scenery, as described in Ancient and Modern Poets.
By William Menzies, Deputy Surveyor of Windsor Forest and Parks, &c.

In One Volume, imperial 4to. with Twenty Plates, Coloured in facsimile of the original drawings, price £5. 5s.

[*Preparing for publication.*

CHEMISTRY and PHYSIOLOGY.

Miller's Elements of Chemistry, Theoretical and Practical.
Re-edited, with Additions, by H. Macleod, F.C.S.

3 vols. 8vo. £3.
PART I. CHEMICAL PHYSICS, 15s.
PART II. INORGANIC CHEMISTRY, 21s.
PART III. ORGANIC CHEMISTRY, 24s.

A Manual of Chemical Physiology, including its Points of Contact with Pathology.
By J. L. W. Thudichum, M.D.

8vo. with Woodcuts, 7s. 6d.

A Dictionary of Chemistry and the Allied Branches of other Sciences. By Henry Watts, F.C.S. assisted by eminent Scientific and Practical Chemists.

6 vols. medium 8vo. £8. 14s. 6d.

Second Supplement completing the Record of Discovery to the end of 1872.

[*In the press.*

A Course of Practical Chemistry, for the use of Medical Students. By W. Odling, F.R.S.

Crown 8vo. Woodcuts, 7s. 6d.

Select Methods in Chemical Analysis, chiefly Inorganic. By Wm. Crookes, F.R.S.

With 22 Woodcuts. Crown 8vo. 12s. 6d.

Todd and Bowman's Physiological Anatomy, and Physiology of Man.

Vol. II. with numerous Illustrations, 25s.

Vol. I. New Edition by Dr. LIONEL S. BEALE, F.R.S. *in course of publication*, with numerous Illustrations. Parts I. and II. in 8vo. price 7s. 6d. each.

Outlines of Physiology, Human and Comparative. By J. Marshall, F.R.C.S. Surgeon to the University College Hospital.

2 vols. cr. 8vo. with 122 Woodcuts, 32s.

The FINE ARTS and ILLUSTRATED EDITIONS.

Albert Durer, his Life and Works; including Autobiographical Papers and Complete Catalogues. By William B. Scott.

With 6 Etchings by the Author and other Illustrations. 8vo. 16s.

In Fairyland; Pictures from the Elf-World. By Richard Doyle. With a Poem by W. Allingham.

With 16 coloured Plates, containing 36 Designs. Second Edition, folio, 15s.

A Dictionary of Artists of the English School: Painters, Sculptors, Architects, Engravers, and Ornamentists; with Notices of their Lives and Works. By Samuel Redgrave.

8vo. 16s.

The New Testament, illustrated with Wood Engravings after the Early Masters, chiefly of the Italian School.

Crown 4to. 63s.

The Life of Man Symbolised by the Months of the Year.
Text selected by R. Pigot.
25 *Illustrations on Wood from Designs by John Leighton, F.S.A.* Quarto, 42s.

Lyra Germanica; the Christian Year and the Christian Life.
Translated by Miss C. Winkworth.
With about 325 *Woodcut Illustrations by J. Leighton, F.S.A. and other Artists.* 2 vols. 4to. price 42s.

Lord Macaulay's Lays of Ancient Rome. With 90 *Illustrations on Wood from Drawings by G. Scharf.*
Fcp. 4to. 21s.

Miniature Edition, with Scharf's 90 *Illustrations reduced in Lithography.*
Imp. 16mo. 10s. 6d.

Sacred and Legendary Art.
By Mrs. Jameson.
6 vols. square crown 8vo. price £5. 15s. 6d. as follows:—

Legends of the Saints and Martyrs.
New Edition, with 19 Etchings and 187 Woodcuts. 2 vols. 31s. 6d.

Legends of the Monastic Orders.
New Edition, with 11 Etchings and 88 Woodcuts. 1 vol. 21s.

Legends of the Madonna.
New Edition, with 27 Etchings and 165 Woodcuts. 1 vol. 21s.

The History of Our Lord, with that of his Types and Precursors.
Completed by Lady Eastlake.
Revised Edition, with 13 Etchings and 281 Woodcuts. 2 vols. 42s.

The USEFUL ARTS, MANUFACTURES, &c.

A Manual of Architecture: being a Concise History and Explanation of the Principal Styles of European Architecture, Ancient, Mediæval, and Renaissance; with a Glossary.
By Thomas Mitchell, Author of 'The Stepping Stone to Architecture.'
With 150 Woodcuts.   Crown 8vo. 10s. 6d.

History of the Gothic Revival; an Attempt to shew how far the taste for Mediæval Architecture was retained in England during the last two centuries, and has been re-developed in the present.
By Charles L. Eastlake, Architect.
With 48 Illustrations.   Imp. 8vo. 31s. 6d.

D

Industrial Chemistry; a Manual for Manufacturers and for Colleges or Technical Schools. Being a Translation of Professors Stohmann and Engler's German Edition of Payen's 'Précis de Chimie Industrielle,' by Dr. J. D. Barry. Edited, and supplemented with Chapters on the Chemistry of the Metals, by B. H. Paul, Ph.D.
8vo. with Plates and Woodcuts.
[*In the press.*

Gwilt's Encyclopædia of Architecture, with above 1,600 Woodcuts.
Fifth Edition, with Alterations and Additions, by Wyatt Papworth.
8vo. 52s. 6d.

The Three Cathedrals dedicated to St. Paul in London; their History from the Foundation of the First Building in the Sixth Century to the Proposals for the Adornment of the Present Cathedral. By W. Longman, F.S.A.
With numerous Illustrations. Square crown 8vo. 21s.

Hints on Household Taste in Furniture, Upholstery, and other Details. By Charles L. Eastlake, Architect.
New Edition, with about 90 Illustrations. Square crown 8vo. 14s.

Geometric Turning; comprising a Description of Plant's New Geometric Chuck, with Directions for its use, and a Series of Patterns cut by it, with Explanations. By H. S. Savory.
With 571 Woodcuts. Square cr. 8vo. 21s.

Lathes and Turning, Simple, Mechanical, and Ornamental. By W. Henry Northcott.
With 240 Illustrations. 8vo. 18s.

Handbook of Practical Telegraphy. By R. S. Culley, Memb. Inst. C.E. Engineer-in-Chief of Telegraphs to the Post-Office.
Sixth Edition, Plates & Woodcuts. 8vo. 16s.

Principles of Mechanism, for the use of Students in the Universities, and for Engineering Students. By R. Willis, M.A. F.R.S. Professor in the University of Cambridge.
Second Edition, with 374 Woodcuts. 8vo. 18s.

Perspective; or, the Art of Drawing what one Sees: for the Use of those Sketching from Nature. By Lieut. W. H. Collins, R.E. F.R.A.S.
With 37 Woodcuts. Crown 8vo. 5s.

Encyclopædia of Civil Engineering, Historical, Theoretical, and Practical. By E. Cresy, C.E.
With above 3,000 *Woodcuts.* 8vo. 42s.

A Treatise on the Steam Engine, in its various applications to Mines, Mills, Steam Navigation, Railways and Agriculture. By J. Bourne, C.E.
With Portrait, 37 *Plates*, and 546 *Woodcuts.* 4to. 42s.

Catechism of the Steam Engine, in its various Applications. By John Bourne, C.E.
New Edition, with 89 *Woodcuts.* Fcp. 8vo. 6s.

Handbook of the Steam Engine. By J. Bourne, C.E. forming a KEY to the Author's Catechism of the Steam Engine.
With 67 *Woodcuts.* Fcp. 8vo. 9s.

Recent Improvements in the Steam Engine. By J. Bourne, C.E.
With 124 *Woodcuts.* Fcp. 8vo. 6s.

Lowndes's Engineer's Handbook; explaining the Principles which should guide the Young Engineer in the Construction of Machinery.
Post 8vo. 5s.

Ure's Dictionary of Arts, Manufactures, and Mines. Sixth Edition, re-written and greatly enlarged by R. Hunt, F.R.S. assisted by numerous Contributors.
With 2,000 *Woodcuts.* 3 vols. medium 8vo. £4. 14s. 6d.

Handbook to the Mineralogy of Cornwall and Devon; with Instructions for their Discrimination, and copious Tables of Locality. By J. H. Collins, F.G.S.
With 10 *Plates*, 8vo. 6s.

Guns and Steel; Miscellaneous Papers on Mechanical Subjects. By Sir J. Whitworth, C.E. F.R.S.
With *Illustrations.* Royal 8vo. 7s. 6d.

Practical Treatise on Metallurgy, Adapted from the last German Edition of Professor Kerl's Metallurgy by W. Crookes, F.R.S. &c. and E. Röhrig, Ph.D.
3 vols. 8vo. with 625 *Woodcuts.* £4. 19s.

Treatise on Mills and Millwork. By Sir W. Fairbairn, Bt.
With 18 *Plates* and 322 *Woodcuts.* 2 vols. 8vo. 32s.

Useful Information for Engineers.
By Sir W. Fairbairn, Bt.
With many Plates and Woodcuts. 3 vols. crown 8vo. 31s. 6d.

The Application of Cast and Wrought Iron to Building Purposes.
By Sir W. Fairbairn, Bt.
With 6 Plates and 118 Woodcuts. 8vo. 16s.

The Strains in Trusses Computed by means of Diagrams; with 20 Examples.
By F. A. Ranken, C.E.
With 35 Diagrams. Square cr. 8vo. 6s. 6d.

Practical Handbook of Dyeing and Calico-Printing.
By W. Crookes, F.R.S. &c.
With numerous Illustrations and Specimens of Dyed Textile Fabrics. 8vo. 42s.

Mitchell's Manual of Practical Assaying.
Fourth Edition, revised, with the Recent Discoveries incorporated, by W. Crookes, F.R.S.
8vo. Woodcuts, 31s. 6d.

Occasional Papers on Subjects connected with Civil Engineering, Gunnery, and Naval Architecture.
By Michael Scott, Memb. Inst. C.E. & of Inst. N.A.
2 vols. 8vo. with Plates, 42s.

Loudon's Encyclopædia of Gardening: comprising the Theory and Practice of Horticulture, Floriculture, Arboriculture, and Landscape Gardening.
With 1,000 Woodcuts. 8vo. 21s.

Loudon's Encyclopædia of Agriculture: comprising the Laying-out, Improvement, and Management of Landed Property, and the Cultivation and Economy of the Productions of Agriculture.
With 1,100 Woodcuts. 8vo. 21s.

RELIGIOUS and MORAL WORKS.

An Exposition of the 39 Articles, Historical and Doctrinal.
By E. H. Browne, D.D. Bishop of Winchester.
New Edition. 8vo. 16s.

An Introduction to the Theology of the Church of England, in an Exposition of the 39 Articles. By Rev. T. P. Boultbee, LL.D.
Fcp. 8vo. 6s.

Historical Lectures on the Life of Our Lord Jesus Christ.
By C. J. Ellicott, D.D.
Fifth Edition. 8vo. 12s.

Sermons; including Two Sermons on the Interpretation of Prophecy, and an Essay on the Right Interpretation and Understanding of the Scriptures.
By the late Rev. Thomas Arnold, D.D.
3 vols. 8vo. price 24s.

Christian Life, its Course, its Hindrances, and its Helps; Sermons preached mostly in the Chapel of Rugby School.
By the late Rev. Thomas Arnold, D.D.
8vo. 7s. 6d.

Christian Life, its Hopes, its Fears, and its Close; Sermons preached mostly in the Chapel of Rugby School.
By the late Rev. Thomas Arnold, D.D.
8vo. 7s. 6d.

Sermons Chiefly on the Interpretation of Scripture.
By the late Rev. Thomas Arnold, D.D.
8vo. price 7s. 6d.

Sermons preached in the Chapel of Rugby School; with an Address before Confirmation.
By the late Rev. Thomas Arnold, D.D.
Fcp. 8vo. price 3s. 6d.

Three Essays on Religion: Nature; the Utility of Religion; Theism.
By John Stuart Mill.
8vo. price 10s. 6d.

Synonyms of the Old Testament, their Bearing on Christian Faith and Practice.
By Rev. R. B. Girdlestone.
8vo. 15s.

Reasons of Faith; or, the Order of the Christian Argument Developed and Explained.
By Rev. G. S. Drew, M.A.
Second Edition. Fcp. 8vo. 6s.

The Eclipse of Faith: or a Visit to a Religious Sceptic.
By Henry Rogers.
Latest Edition. Fcp. 8vo. 5s.

Defence of the Eclipse of Faith.
By Henry Rogers.
Latest Edition. Fcp. 8vo. 3s. 6d.

Sermons for the Times preached in St. Paul's Cathedral and elsewhere. By Rev. T. Griffith, M.A.
Crown 8vo. 6s.

The Life and Epistles of St. Paul. By Rev. W. J. Conybeare, M.A. and Very Rev. J. S. Howson, D.D.

LIBRARY EDITION, with all the Original Illustrations, Maps, Landscapes on Steel, Woodcuts, &c. 2 vols. 4to. 48s.
INTERMEDIATE EDITION, with a Selection of Maps, Plates, and Woodcuts. 2 vols. square crown 8vo. 21s.
STUDENT'S EDITION, revised and condensed, with 46 Illustrations and Maps. 1 vol. crown 8vo. 9s.

A Critical and Grammatical Commentary on St. Paul's Epistles. By C. J. Ellicott, D.D.

8vo. Galatians, 8s. 6d. Ephesians, 8s. 6d. Pastoral Epistles, 10s. 6d. Philippians, Colossians, & Philemon, 10s. 6d. Thessalonians, 7s. 6d.

The Voyage and Shipwreck of St. Paul; with Dissertations on the Ships and Navigation of the Ancients. By James Smith, F.R.S.
Crown 8vo. Charts, 10s. 6d.

Evidence of the Truth of the Christian Religion derived from the Literal Fulfilment of Prophecy. By Alexander Keith, D.D.
40th Edition, with numerous Plates. Square 8vo. 12s. 6d. or in post 8vo. with 5 Plates, 6s.

Historical and Critical Commentary on the Old Testament; with a New Translation. By M. M. Kalisch, Ph.D.

Vol. I. Genesis, 8vo. 18s. or adapted for the General Reader, 12s. Vol. II. Exodus, 15s. or adapted for the General Reader, 12s. Vol. III. Leviticus, Part I. 15s. or adapted for the General Reader, 8s. Vol. IV. Leviticus, Part II. 15s. or adapted for the General Reader, 8s.

The History and Literature of the Israelites, according to the Old Testament and the Apocrypha. By C. De Rothschild and A. De Rothschild.
Second Edition. 2 vols. crown 8vo. 12s. 6d.
Abridged Edition, in 1 vol. fcp. 8vo. 3s. 6d.

Ewald's History of Israel. Translated from the German by J. E. Carpenter, M.A. with Preface by R. Martineau, M.A.
5 vols. 8vo. 63s.

Commentary on Epistle to the Romans. By Rev. W. A. O'Conor.
Crown 8vo. 3s. 6d.

A Commentary on the Gospel of St. John. By Rev. W. A. O'Conor.
Crown 8vo. 10s. 6d.

The Epistle to the Hebrews; with Analytical Introduction and Notes. By Rev. W. A. O'Conor.
Crown 8vo. 4s. 6d.

Thoughts for the Age.
By Elizabeth M. Sewell.
New Edition. Fcp. 8vo. 3s. 6d.

Passing Thoughts on Religion.
By Elizabeth M. Sewell.
Fcp. 8vo. 3s. 6d.

Self-examination before Confirmation.
By Elizabeth M. Sewell.
32mo. 1s. 6d.

Preparation for the Holy Communion; the Devotions chiefly from the works of Jeremy Taylor.
By Elizabeth M. Sewell.
32mo. 3s.

Readings for a Month Preparatory to Confirmation, from Writers of the Early and English Church.
By Elizabeth M. Sewell.
Fcp. 8vo. 4s.

Readings for Every Day in Lent, compiled from the Writings of Bishop Jeremy Taylor.
By Elizabeth M. Sewell.
Fcp. 8vo. 5s.

Bishop Jeremy Taylor's Entire Works; with Life by Bishop Heber. Revised and corrected by the Rev. C. P. Eden.
10 vols. £5. 5s.

Hymns of Praise and Prayer.
Collected and edited by Rev. J. Martineau, LL.D.
Crown 8vo. 4s. 6d.

Thoughts for the Holy Week, for Young Persons.
By Elizabeth M. Sewell.
New Edition. Fcp. 8vo. 2s.

Spiritual Songs for the Sundays and Holidays throughout the Year.
By J. S. B. Monsell, LL.D.
Fourth Edition. Fcp. 8vo. 4s. 6d.

Lyra Germanica; Hymns translated from the German by Miss C. Winkworth.
2 series, fcp. 8vo. 3s. 6d. each.

Endeavours after the Christian Life; Discourses.
By Rev. J. Martineau, LL.D.
Fifth Edition. Crown 8vo. 7s. 6d.

An Introduction to the Study of the New Testament, Critical, Exegetical, and Theological.
By Rev. S. Davidson, D.D.
2 vols. 8vo. 30s.

Supernatural Religion; an Inquiry into the Reality of Divine Revelation.
New Edition. 2 vols. 8vo. 24s.

32　NEW WORKS published by LONGMANS & CO.

The Life of Christ.
For the use of Young Persons, selected from the Gospels and Chronologically arranged; with Supplementary Notices from parallel Passages.
By the Rev. R. B. Gardiner, M.A.
Crown 8vo. 2s.

Lectures on the Pentateuch & the Moabite Stone; with Appendices.
By J. W. Colenso, D.D. Bishop of Natal.
8vo. 12s.

The Pentateuch and Book of Joshua Critically Examined.
By J. W. Colenso, D.D. Bishop of Natal.
Crown 8vo. 6s.

The New Bible Commentary, by Bishops and other Clergy of the Anglican Church, critically examined by the Rt. Rev. J. W. Colenso, D.D. Bishop of Natal.
8vo. 25s.

TRAVELS, VOYAGES, &c.

The Valleys of Tirol; their Traditions and Customs, and How to Visit them.
By Miss R. H. Busk, Author of 'The Folk-Lore of Rome' &c.
With Frontispiece and 3 Maps. Crown 8vo. 12s. 6d.

Eight Years in Ceylon.
By Sir Samuel W. Baker, M.A. F.R.G.S.
New Edition, with Illustrations engraved on Wood by G. Pearson. Crown 8vo. Price 7s. 6d.

The Rifle and the Hound in Ceylon.
By Sir Samuel W. Baker, M.A. F.R.G.S.
New Edition, with Illustrations engraved on Wood by G. Pearson. Crown 8vo. Price 7s. 6d.

Meeting the Sun; a Journey all round the World through Egypt, China, Japan, and California.
By William Simpson, F.R.G.S.
With Heliotypes and Woodcuts. 8vo. 24s.

The Rural Life of England.
By William Howitt.
Woodcuts, 8vo. 12s. 6d.

The Dolomite Mountains. Excursions through Tyrol, Carinthia, Carniola, and Friuli.
By J. Gilbert and G. C. Churchill, F.R.G.S.
With Illustrations. Sq. cr. 8vo. 21s.

The Alpine Club Map of the Chain of Mont Blanc, from an actual Survey in 1863-1864.
By A. Adams-Reilly, F.R.G.S. M.A.C.

In Chromolithography, on extra stout drawing paper 10s. or mounted on canvas in a folding case, 12s. 6d.

The Alpine Club Map of the Valpelline, the Val Tournanche, and the Southern Valleys of the Chain of Monte Rosa, from actual Survey.
By A. Adams-Reilly, F.R.G.S. M.A.C.

Price 6s. on extra Stout Drawing Paper, or 7s. 6d. mounted in a Folding Case.

Hours of Exercise in the Alps.
By John Tyndall, F.R.S.

Third Edition, with 7 Woodcuts by E. Whymper. Crown 8vo. 12s. 6d.

Guide to the Pyrenees, for the use of Mountaineers.
By Charles Packe.

Second Edition, with Maps &c. and Appendix. Crown 8vo. 7s. 6d.

How to See Norway.
By J. R. Campbell.

With Map and 5 Woodcuts, fcp. 8vo. 5s.

Untrodden Peaks and Unfrequented Valleys; a Midsummer Ramble among the Dolomites.
By Amelia B. Edwards.

With numerous Illustrations. 8vo. 21s.

The Alpine Club Map of Switzerland, with parts of the Neighbouring Countries, on the scale of four miles to an Inch.
Edited by R. C. Nichols, F.S.A. F.R.G.S.

In Four Sheets, in Portfolio, 42s. or mounted in a Case, 52s. 6d. Each Sheet may be had separately, price 12s. or mounted in a Case, 13s.

The Alpine Guide.
By John Ball, M.R.I.A. late President of the Alpine Club.

Post 8vo. with Maps and other Illustrations.

Eastern Alps.
Price 10s. 6d.

Central Alps, including all the Oberland District.
Price 7s. 6d.

Western Alps, including Mont Blanc, Monte Rosa, Zermatt, &c.
Price 6s. 6d.

Introduction on Alpine Travelling in general, and on the Geology of the Alps.
Price 1s. Either of the Three Volumes or Parts of the 'Alpine Guide' may be had with this Introduction prefixed, 1s. extra.

Visits to Remarkable Places, and Scenes illustrative of striking Passages in English History and Poetry.
By William Howitt.

2 vols. 8vo. Woodcuts, 25s.

WORKS of FICTION.

Whispers from Fairyland.
By the Rt. Hon. E. H. Knatchbull-Hugessen, M.P. Author of 'Stories for my Children,' 'Moonshine,' 'Queer Folk,' &c.
With 9 Illustrations from Original Designs engraved on Wood by G. Pearson. Crown 8vo. price 6s.

Elena, an Italian Tale.
By L. N. Comyn.
2 vols. post 8vo. 14s.

Lady Willoughby's Diary during the Reign of Charles the First, the Protectorate, and the Restoration.
Crown 8vo. 7s. 6d.

Centulle, a Tale of Pau.
By Denys Shyne Lawlor, Author of 'Pilgrimages in the Pyrenees and Landes.'
Crown 8vo. 10s. 6d.

The Folk-Lore of Rome, collected by Word of Mouth from the People.
By R. H. Busk, Author of 'The Valleys of Tirol' &c.
Crown 8vo. 12s. 6d.

Cyllene; or, The Fall of Paganism.
By Henry Sneyd, M.A.
2 vols. pos 8vo. 14s.

Tales of the Teutonic Lands.
By Rev. G. W. Cox, M.A. and E. H. Jones.
Crown 8vo. 10s. 6d.

Becker's Gallus; or Roman Scenes of the Time of Augustus.
Post 8vo. 7s. 6d.

Becker's Charicles: Illustrative of Private Life of the Ancient Greeks.
Post 8vo. 7s. 6d.

Tales of Ancient Greece.
By the Rev. G. W. Cox, M.A.
Crown 8vo. 6s. 6d.

The Modern Novelist's Library.
Atherstone Priory, 2s. boards; 2s. 6d. cloth.
The Burgomaster's Family, 2s. boards; 2s. 6d. cloth.
MELVILLE'S Digby Grand, 2s. and 2s. 6d.
———— Gladiators, 2s. and 2s. 6d.
———— Good for Nothing, 2s. & 2s. 6d.
———— Holmby House, 2s. and 2s. 6d.
———— Interpreter, 2s. and 2s. 6d.
———— Kate Coventry, 2s. and 2s. 6d.
———— Queen's Maries, 2s. and 2s. 6l.
———— General Bounce, 2s. and 2s. 6d.
TROLLOPE'S Warden, 1s. 6d. and 2s.
———— Barchester Towers, 2s. and 2s. 6d.
BRAMLEY-MOORE'S Six Sisters of the Valleys, 2s. boards; 2s. 6d cloth.

Novels and Tales.
By the Right Hon. Benjamin Disraeli, M.P.

Cabinet Editions, complete in Ten Volumes, crown 8vo. 6s. each, as follows :—

Lothair, 6s. | Venetia, 6s.
Coningsby, 6s. | Alroy, Ixion, &c. 6s.
Sybil, 6s. | Young Duke, &c. 6s.
Tancred, 6s. | Vivian Grey, 6s.
Henrietta Temple, 6s.
Contarini Fleming, &c. 6s.

Cabinet Edition, in crown 8vo. of Stories and Tales by Miss Sewell :—

Amy Herbert, 2s. 6d. | Ivors, 2s. 6d.
Gertrude, 2s. 6d. | Katharine Ashton, 2s. 6d.
Earl's Daughter, 2s. 6d. |
Experience of Life, 2s. 6d. | Margaret Percival, 3s. 6d.
Cleve Hall, 2s. 6d. | Landon Parsonage, 3s. 6d.
Ursula, 3s. 6d.

POETRY and THE DRAMA.

Ballads and Lyrics of Old France; with other Poems.
By A. Lang.
Square fcp. 8vo. 5s.

Moore's Lalla Rookh, Tenniel's Edition, with 68 Wood Engravings.
Fcp. 4to. 21s.

Moore's Irish Melodies, Maclise's Edition, with 161 Steel Plates.
Super-royal 8vo. 31s. 6d.

Miniature Edition of Moore's Irish Melodies, with Maclise's 161 Illustrations reduced in Lithography.
Imp 16mo. 10s. 6d.

Milton's Lycidas and Epitaphium Damonis.
Edited, with Notes and Introduction, by C. S. Jerram, M.A.
Crown 8vo. 3s. 6d.

Lays of Ancient Rome; with Ivry and the Armada.
By the Right Hon. Lord Macaulay.
16mo. 3s. 6d.

Lord Macaulay's Lays of Ancient Rome. With 90 Illustrations on Wood from Drawings by G. Scharf.
Fcp. 4to. 21s.

Miniature Edition of Lord Macaulay's Lays of Ancient Rome, with Scharf's 90 Illustrations reduced in Lithography.
Imp. 16mo. 10s. 6d.

Southey's Poetical Works with the Author's last Corrections and Additions.
Medium 8vo. with Portrait, 14s.

Bowdler's Family Shakspeare, cheaper Genuine Edition.
Complete in 1 vol. medium 8vo. large type, with 36 Woodcut Illustrations, 14s. or in 6 vols. fcp. 8vo. price 21s.

Horatii Opera, Library Edition, with English Notes, Marginal References and various Readings. Edited by Rev. J. E. Yonge.
8vo. 21s.

The Æneid of Virgil Translated into English Verse. By J. Conington, M.A.
Crown 8vo. 9s.

Poems by Jean Ingelow.
2 vols. Fcp. 8vo. 10s.

FIRST SERIES, containing 'Divided,' 'The Star's Monument,' &c. 16th Thousand. Fcp. 8vo. 5s.

SECOND SERIES, 'A Story of Doom,' 'Gladys and her Island,' &c. 5th Thousand. Fcp. 8vo. 5s.

Poems by Jean Ingelow. First Series, with nearly 100 Woodcut Illustrations.
Fcp. 4to. 21s.

RURAL SPORTS, HORSE and CATTLE MANAGEMENT, &c.

Down the Road; or, Reminiscences of a Gentleman Coachman. By C. T. S. Birch Reynardson.
With Twelve Chromolithographic Illustrations from Original Paintings by H. Alken. Medium 8vo. [*Nearly ready.*

Blaine's Encyclopædia of Rural Sports; Complete Accounts, Historical, Practical, and Descriptive, of Hunting, Shooting, Fishing, Racing, &c.
With above 600 Woodcuts (20 from Designs by JOHN LEECH). 8vo. 21s.

A Book on Angling: a Treatise on the Art of Angling in every branch, including full Illustrated Lists of Salmon Flies. By Francis Francis.
Post 8vo. Portrait and Plates, 15s.

Wilcocks's Sea-Fisherman: comprising the Chief Methods of Hook and Line Fishing, a glance at Nets, and remarks on Boats and Boating.
New Edition, with 80 Woodcuts. Post 8vo. 12s. 6d.

The Ox, his Diseases and their Treatment; with an Essay on Parturition in the Cow. By J. R. Dobson, Memb. R.C.V.S.
Crown 8vo. with Illustrations, 7s. 6d.

A Treatise on Horse-Shoeing and Lameness. By J. Gamgee, Vet. Surg.
8vo. with 55 Woodcuts, 10s. 6d.

Youatt on the Horse. Revised and enlarged by W. Watson, M.R.C.V.S.
8vo. Woodcuts, 12s. 6d.

Youatt's Work on the Dog, revised and enlarged.
8vo. Woodcuts, 6s.

Horses and Stables.
By Colonel F. Fitzwygram, XV. the King's Hussars.
With 24 Plates of Illustrations. 8vo. 10s. 6d.

The Dog in Health and Disease.
By Stonehenge.
With 73 Wood Engravings. Square crown 8vo. 7s. 6d.

The Greyhound.
By Stonehenge.
Revised Edition, with 24 Portraits of Greyhounds. Square crown 8vo. 10s. 6d.

Stables and Stable Fittings.
By W. Miles, Esq.
Imp. 8vo. with 13 Plates, 15s.

The Horse's Foot, and how to keep it Sound.
By W. Miles, Esq.
Ninth Edition. Imp. 8vo. Woodcuts, 12s. 6d.

A Plain Treatise on Horse-shoeing.
By W. Miles, Esq.
Sixth Edition. Post 8vo. Woodcuts, 2s. 6d.

Remarks on Horses' Teeth, addressed to Purchasers.
By W. Miles, Esq.
Post 8vo. 1s. 6d.

The Fly-Fisher's Entomology.
By Alfred Ronalds.
With coloured Representations of the Natural and Artificial Insect.
With 20 coloured Plates. 8vo. 14s.

The Dead Shot, or Sportsman's Complete Guide; a Treatise on the Use of the Gun, Dog-breaking, Pigeon-shooting, &c.
By Marksman.
Fcp. 8vo. with Plates, 5s.

WORKS of UTILITY and GENERAL INFORMATION.

Maunder's Treasury of Knowledge and Library of Reference; comprising an English Dictionary and Grammar, Universal Gazetteer, Classical Dictionary, Chronology, Law Dictionary, Synopsis of the Peerage, Useful Tables,&c.
Fcp. 8vo. 6s.

Maunder's Biographical Treasury.
Latest Edition, reconstructed and partly rewritten, with about 1,000 additional Memoirs, by W. L. R. Cates.
Fcp. 8vo. 6s.

Maunder's Scientific and Literary Treasury; a Popular Encyclopædia of Science, Literature, and Art.
New Edition, in part rewritten, with above 1,000 new articles, by J. Y. Johnson.
Fcp. 8vo. 6s.

Maunder's Treasury of Geography, Physical, Historical, Descriptive, and Political.
Edited by W. Hughes, F.R.G.S.
With 7 Maps and 16 Plates. Fcp. 8vo. 6s.

Maunder's Historical Treasury; General Introductory Outlines of Universal History, and a Series of Separate Histories.
Revised by the Rev. G. W. Cox, M.A.
Fcp. 8vo. 6s.

Maunder's Treasury of Natural History; or Popular Dictionary of Zoology.
Revised and corrected Edition. Fcp. 8vo. with 900 Woodcuts, 6s.

The Treasury of Bible Knowledge; being a Dictionary of the Books, Persons, Places, Events, and other Matters of which mention is made in Holy Scripture.
By Rev. J. Ayre, M.A.
With Maps, 15 Plates, and numerous Woodcuts. Fcp. 8vo. 6s.

Collieries and Colliers: a Handbook of the Law and Leading Cases relating thereto.
By J. C. Fowler.
Third Edition. Fcp. 8vo. 7s. 6d.

The Theory and Practice of Banking.
By H. D. Macleod, M.A.
Second Edition. 2 vols. 8vo. 30s.

Modern Cookery for Private Families, reduced to a System of Easy Practice in a Series of carefully-tested Receipts.
By Eliza Acton.
With 8 Plates & 150 Woodcuts. Fcp. 8vo. 6s.

A Practical Treatise on Brewing; with Formulæ for Public Brewers, and Instructions for Private Families.
By W. Black.
Fifth Edition. 8vo. 10s. 6d.

Three Hundred Original Chess Problems and Studies.
By Jas. Pierce, M.A. and W. T. Pierce.
With many Diagrams. Sq. fcp. 8vo. 7s. 6d.
Supplement, 2s. 6d.

Chess Openings.
By F. W. Longman, Balliol College, Oxford.
Second Edition, revised. Fcp. 8vo. 2s. 6d.

The Theory of the Modern Scientific Game of Whist.
By W. Pole, F.R.S.
Fifth Edition. Fcp. 8vo. 2s. 6d.

The Cabinet Lawyer; a Popular Digest of the Laws of England, Civil, Criminal, and Constitutional.
Twenty-fourth Edition, corrected and extended. Fcp. 8vo. 9s.

Blackstone Economised; being a Compendium of the Laws of England to the Present Time.
By D. M. Aird, Barrister.
Revised Edition. Post 8vo. 7s. 6d.

Pewtner's Comprehensive Specifier; a Guide to the Practical Specification of every kind of Building-Artificer's Work.
Edited by W. Young.
Crown 8vo. 6s.

Hints to Mothers on the Management of their Health during the Period of Pregnancy and in the Lying-in Room.
By Thomas Bull, M.D.
Fcp. 8vo. 5s.

The Maternal Management of Children in Health and Disease.
By Thomas Bull, M.D.
Fcp. 8vo. 5s.

KNOWLEDGE for the YOUNG.

The Stepping-Stone to Knowledge; or upwards of 700 Questions and Answers on Miscellaneous Subjects, adapted to the capacity of Infant minds.
18mo. 1s.

Second Series of the Stepping-Stone to Knowledge: Containing upwards of 800 Questions and Answers on Miscellaneous Subjects not contained in the First Series.
18mo. 1s.

The Stepping-Stone to Geography: Containing several Hundred Questions and Answers on Geographical Subjects.
18mo. 1s.

The Stepping-Stone to English History; Questions and Answers on the History of England.
18mo. 1s.

The Stepping-Stone to Bible Knowledge; Questions and Answers on the Old and New Testaments.
18mo. 1s.

The Stepping-Stone to Biography; Questions and Answers on the Lives of Eminent Men and Women.
18mo. 1s.

The Stepping-Stone to Irish History: Containing several Hundred Questions and Answers on the History of Ireland.
18mo. 1s.

The Stepping-Stone to French History: Containing several Hundred Questions and Answers on the History of France.
18mo. 1s.

The Stepping-Stone to Roman History: Containing several Hundred Questions and Answers on the History of Rome.
18mo. 1s.

The Stepping-Stone to Grecian History: Containing several Hundred Questions and Answers on the History of Greece.
18mo. 1s.

The Stepping-Stone to English Grammar: Containing several Hundred Questions and Answers on English Grammar.
18mo. 1s.

The Stepping-Stone to French Pronunciation and Conversation: Containing several Hundred Questions and Answers.
18mo. 1s.

The Stepping-Stone to Astronomy: Containing several Hundred familiar Questions and Answers on the Earth and the Solar and Stellar Systems.
18mo. 1s.

The Stepping-Stone to Music: Containing several Hundred Questions on the Science; also a short History of Music.
18mo. 1s.

The Stepping-Stone to Natural History: Vertebrate or Backboned Animals. Part I. Mammalia; Part II. Birds, Reptiles, Fishes.
18mo. 1s. each Part.

The Stepping-Stone to Architecture; Questions and Answers explaining the Principles and Progress of Architecture from the Earliest Times.
With 100 Woodcuts. 18mo. 1s.

INDEX.

Acton's Modern Cookery	39
Aird's Blackstone Economised	39
Alpine Club Map of Switzerland	33
Alpine Guide (The)	33
Amos's Jurisprudence	10
———— Primer of the Constitution	10
Anderson's Strength of Materials	20
Armstrong's Organic Chemistry	20
Arnold's (Dr.) Christian Life	29
———————— Lectures on Modern History	2
———————— Miscellaneous Works	12
———————— School Sermons	29
———————— Sermons	29
———— (T.) Manual of English Literature	12
Arnould's Life of Lord Denman	7
Atherstone Priory	39
Autumn Holidays of a Country Parson	13
Ayre's Treasury of Bible Knowledge	38
Bacon's Essays, by *Whately*	10
———— Life and Letters, by *Spedding*	10
———— Works	10
Bain's Mental and Moral Science	11
——— on the Senses and Intellect	11
Baker's Two Works on Ceylon	32
Ball's Guide to the Central Alps	38
——— Guide to the Western Alps	38
——— Guide to the Eastern Alps	38
Becker's Charicles and Gallus	34
Black's Treatise on Brewing	39
Blackley's German-English Dictionary	15
Blaine's Rural Sports	36
Bloxam's Metals	20
Boultbee on 39 Articles	28
Bourne's Catechism of the Steam Engine	27
———— Handbook of Steam Engine	27
———— Treatise on the Steam Engine	27
———— Improvements in the same	27
Bowdler's Family *Shakspeare*	35
Bramley-Moore's Six Sisters of the Valley	39
Brande's Dictionary of Science, Literature, and Art	22
Bray's Manual of Anthropology	22
——— Philosophy of Necessity	11
Brinkley's Astronomy	17
Browne's Exposition of the 39 Articles	28
Brunel's Life of *Brunel*	7
Buckle's History of Civilisation	3
———— Posthumous Remains	12
Bull's Hints to Mothers	39
——— Maternal Management of Children	39
Burgomaster's Family (The)	39

Burke's Rise of Great Families	8
———— Vicissitudes of Families	8
Busk's Folk-lore of Rome	34
——— Valleys of Tirol	32
Cabinet Lawyer	39
Campbell's Norway	33
Cates's Biographical Dictionary	8
———— and *Woodward's* Encyclopædia	5
Changed Aspects of Unchanged Truths	13
Chesney's Indian Polity	3
———— Modern Military Biography	3
———— Waterloo Campaign	3
Clough's Lives from Plutarch	4
Colenso on Moabite Stone &c.	32
———'s Pentateuch and Book of Joshua	32
———— Speaker's Bible Commentary	32
Collins's Mineralogy of Cornwall	27
———— Perspective	26
Commonplace Philosopher in Town and Country, by A. K. H. B.	13
Comte's Positive Polity	8
Comyn's Elena	34
Congreve's Essays	10
———— Politics of Aristotle	10
Conington's Translation of Virgil's Æneid	36
———— Miscellaneous Writings	14
Contanseau's Two French Dictionaries	14
Conybeare and *Howson's* Life and Epistles of St. Paul	29
Cotton's Memoir and Correspondence	7
Counsel and Comfort from a City Pulpit	13
Cox's (G. W.) Aryan Mythology	4
———— Crusades	6
———— History of Greece	4
———— Tale of the Great Persian War	4
———— Tales of Ancient Greece	34
———— and *Jones's* Teutonic Tales	34
Crawley's Thucydides	4
Creasy on British Constitution	3
Cresy's Encyclopædia of Civil Engineering	27
Critical Essays of a Country Parson	14
Crookes's Chemical Analysis	24
———— Dyeing and Calico-printing	28
Culley's Handbook of Telegraphy	26
Cusack's Student's History of Ireland	3
D'Aubigné's Reformation in the Time of Calvin	6

42 NEW WORKS PUBLISHED BY LONGMANS & CO.

Davidson's Introduction to New Testament 31
Dead Shot (The), by *Marksman* 37
De Caisne and *Le Maout's* Botany 23
De Morgan's Paradoxes 13
De Tocqueville's Democracy in America 9
Disraeli's Lord George Bentinck 7
——— Novels and Tales 35
Dobson on the Ox 36
Dove's Law of Storms 18
Doyle's Fairyland 24
Drew's Reasons of Faith 29

Eastlake's Gothic Revival 25
——— Hints on Household Taste 26
Edwards's Rambles among the Dolomites 33
Elements of Botany 22
Ellicott's Commentary on Ephesians 30
——————————— Galatians 30
——————————— Pastoral Epist. 30
——————————— Philippians, &c. 30
——————————— Thessalonians 30
——— Lectures on Life of Christ 29
Epochs of History 6
Evans's Ancient Stone Implements 22
Ewald's History of Israel 30

Fairbairn's Application of Cast and Wrought Iron to Building 28
——— Information for Engineers 28
——— Treatise on Mills and Millwork 27
Farrar's Chapters on Language 13
——— Families of Speech 13
Fitzwygram on Horses and Stables 37
Forsyth's Essays 9
Fowler's Collieries and Colliers 38
Francis's Fishing Book 36
Freeman's Historical Geography of Europe 5
From January to December 14
Froude's English in Ireland 2
——— History of England 2
——— Short Studies 12

Gairdner's Houses of Lancaster and York 6
Gamgee on Horse-Shoeing 36
Ganot's Elementary Physics 19
——— Natural Philosophy 19
Gardiner's Buckingham and Charles 3
——— Life of Christ 32
——— Thirty Years' War 6
Gilbert and *Churchill's* Dolomites 32
Girdlestone's Bible Synonyms 29
Goodeve's Mechanics 20
——— Mechanism 20
Grant's Ethics of Aristotle 10
Graver Thoughts of a Country Parson 14
Greville's Journal 1
Griffin's Algebra and Trigonometry 20
Griffith's Sermons for the Times 29
Grove on Correlation of Physical Forces 18
Gwilt's Encyclopædia of Architecture 26

Hare on Election of Representatives 14

Harrison's Political Problems 8
Hartwig's Aerial World 21
——— Polar World 21
——— Sea and its Living Wonders 21
——— Subterranean World 21
——— Tropical World 21
Haughton's Animal Mechanics 19
Hayward's Biographical and Critical Essays 7
Heer's Switzerland 22
Helmholtz's Scientific Lectures 18
Helmsley's Trees, Shrubs, and Herbaceous Plants 23
Herschel's Outlines of Astronomy 17
Holland's Recollections 7
Howitt's Rural Life of England 32
——— Visits to Remarkable Places 33
Humboldt's Life 7
Hume's Essays 11
——— Treatise on Human Nature 11

Ihne's History of Rome 5
Ingelow's Poems 36

Jameson's Legends of Saints and Martyrs 25
——— Legends of the Madonna 25
——— Legends of the Monastic Orders 25
——— Legends of the Saviour 25
Jenkin's Electricity and Magnetism 20
Jerram's Lycidas of Milton 35
Jerrold's Life of Napoleon 1
Johnston's Geographical Dictionary 17

Kalisch's Commentary on the Bible 30
Keith's Evidence of Prophecy 30
Kenyon's (Lord) Life 7
Kerl's Metallurgy, by *Crookes* and *Röhrig* 27
Kirby and *Spence's* Entomology 21
Knatchbull-Hugessen's Whispers from Fairy-Land 34

Landscapes, Churches, &c. by A. K. H. B. 13
Lang's Ballads and Lyrics 35
Latham's English Dictionary 14
Laughton's Nautical Surveying 18
Lawlor's Centulle 34
Lawrence on Rocks 22
Lecky's History of European Morals 5
——— Leaders of Rationalism 5
——— Leaders of Public Opinion 7
Leisure Hours in Town, by A. K. H. B. 13
Lessons of Middle Age, by A. K. H. B. 13
Lewes's Biographical History of Philosophy 5
Liddell and *Scott's* Greek-English Lexicons 15
Life of Man Symbolised 25
Lindley and *Moore's* Treasury of Botany 23
Lloyd's Magnetism 20
——— Wave-Theory of Light 20

NEW WORKS PUBLISHED BY LONGMANS & CO.

Longman's Chess Openings	39
———— Edward the Third	3
———— Lectures on History of England	3
———— Old and New St. Paul's	26
Loudon's Encyclopædia of Agriculture	28
———— Gardening	28
———— Plants	22
Lowndes's Engineer's Handbook	27
Lubbock's Origin of Civilisation	22
Lyra Germanica	25, 31
Macaulay's (Lord) Essays	2
———— History of England	2
———— Lays of Ancient Rome	25, 35
———— Miscellaneous Writings	12
———— Speeches	12
———— Works	2
McCulloch's Dictionary of Commerce	16
Macleod's Principles of Economical Philosophy	10
———— Theory and Practice of Banking	38
Markham's History of Persia	4
Marshall's Physiology	24
———— Todas	22
Marshman's History of India	3
———— Life of Havelock	8
Martineau's Christian Life	31
———— Hymns	31
Maunder's Biographical Treasury	38
———— Geographical Treasury	38
———— Historical Treasury	38
———— Scientific and Literary Treasury	38
———— Treasury of Knowledge	38
———— Treasury of Natural History	38
Maxwell's Theory of Heat	20
May's History of Democracy	2
———— History of England	2
Melville's Digby Grand	39
———— General Bounce	39
———— Gladiators	39
———— Good for Nothing	39
———— Holmby House	39
———— Interpreter	39
———— Kate Coventry	39
———— Queen's Maries	39
Mendelssohn's Letters	8
Menzies' Forest Trees and Woodland Scenery	23
Merivale's Fall of the Roman Republic	4
———— Romans under the Empire	4
Merrifield's Arithmetic and Mensuration	20
———— Magnetism	18
Miles on Horse's Foot and Horse Shoeing	37
———— on Horse's Teeth and Stables	37
Mill (J.) on the Mind	10
——— (J. S.) on Liberty	9
———— Subjection of Women	9
———— on Representative Government	9
———— Utilitarianism	9
———'s Autobiography	6
———— Dissertations and Discussions	9
———— Essays on Religion &c.	29
———— Hamilton's Philosophy	9
———— System of Logic	9
Mill's Political Economy	9
———— Unsettled Questions	9
Miller's Elements of Chemistry	23
———— Inorganic Chemistry	20

Minto's (Lord) Life and Letters	6
Mitchell's Manual of Architecture	25
———— Manual of Assaying	28
Modern Novelist's Library	34
Monsell's 'Spiritual Songs'	31
Moore's Irish Melodies, illustrated	35
———— Lalla Rookh, illustrated	35
Morell's Elements of Psychology	11
———— Mental Philosophy	11
Morris's French Revolution	3
Müller's Chips from a German Workshop	12
———— Science of Language	12
———— Science of Religion	5
New Testament Illustrated with Wood Engravings from the Old Masters	24
Northcott on Lathes and Turning	26
O'Conor's Commentary on Hebrews	30
———— Romans	30
———— St. John	30
Odling's Course of Practical Chemistry	24
Owen's Comparative Anatomy and Physiology of Vertebrate Animals	20
Owen's Lectures on the Invertebrata	20
Packe's Guide to the Pyrenees	33
Pattison's Casaubon	7
Payen's Industrial Chemistry	26
Pewtner's Comprehensive Specifier	39
Pierce's Chess Problems	39
Pole's Game of Whist	39
Prendergast's Mastery of Languages	15
Present-Day Thoughts, by A. K. H. B.	13
Proctor's Astronomical Essays	17
———— Moon	17
———— Orbs around Us	17
———— Other Worlds than Ours	17
———— Saturn	17
———— Scientific Essays (New Series)	20
———— Sun	17
———— Transits of Venus	17
———— Two Star Atlases	18
———— Universe	17
Public Schools Atlas	16
———— Modern Geography	16
———— Ancient Geography	16
Ranken on Strains in Trusses	28
Rawlinson's Parthia	4
———— Sassanians	4
Recreations of a Country Parson	13
Redgrave's Dictionary of Artists	24
Reilly's Map of Mont Blanc	37
———— Monte Rosa	37
Reynardson's Down the Road	36
Rich's Dictionary of Antiquities	15
River's Rose Amateur's Guide	22
Rogers's Eclipse of Faith	29
———— Defence of Eclipse of Faith	29
———— Essays	9

NEW WORKS PUBLISHED BY LONGMANS & CO.

Roget's Thesaurus of English Words and Phrases ... 14
Ronald's Fly-Fisher's Entomology ... 37
Rothschild's Israelites ... 30
Russell on the Christian Religion ... 6
———— English Constitution ... 2
————'s Recollections and Suggestions ... 2

Sandars's Justinian's Institutes ... 10
Sanford's English Kings ... 2
Savory's Geometric Turning ... 26
Schellen's Spectrum Analysis ... 18
Scott's Albert Durer ... 24
———— Papers on Civil Engineering ... 28
Seaside Musing, by A. K. H. B. ... 13
Seebohm's Oxford Reformers of 1498 ... 3
———— Protestant Revolution ... 6
Sewell's History of the Early Church ... 5
———— Passing Thoughts on Religion ... 31
———— Preparation for Communion ... 31
———— Principles of Education ... 14
———— Readings for Confirmation ... 31
———— Readings for Lent ... 31
———— Examination for Confirmation ... 31
———— Stories and Tales ... 35
———— Thoughts for the Age ... 31
———— Thoughts for the Holy Week ... 31
Sharp's Post-office Gazetteer ... 16
Shelley's Workshop Appliances ... 20
Short's Church History ... 5
Simpson's Meeting the Sun ... 32
Smith's Paul's Voyage and Shipwreck ... 30
———— (*Sydney*) Essays ... 12
———— ———— Life and Letters ... 7
———— ———— Miscellaneous Works ... 12
———— ———— Wit and Wisdom ... 12
———— (Dr. R. A.) Air and Rain ... 18
Sneyd's Cyllene ... 34
Southey's Doctor ... 13
———— Poetical Works ... 35
Stanley's History of British Birds ... 21
Stephen's Ecclesiastical Biography ... 7
———— Freethinking and Plainspeaking ... 9
Stepping Stones (the Series) ... 40
Stirling's Secret of Hegel ... 11
———— Sir *William Hamilton* ... 11
Stonehenge on the Dog ... 37
———— on the Greyhound ... 37
Sunday Afternoons at the Parish Church of a University City, by A. K. H. B. ... 13
Supernatural Religion ... 31

Taylor's History of India ... 3
———— Manual of Ancient History ... 6
———— Manual of Modern History ... 6
———— (*Jeremy*) Works, edited by *Eden* ... 31
Text-Books of Science ... 19
Thirlwall's History of Greece ... 4

Thomson's Laws of Thought ... 11
Thorpe's Quantitative Analysis ... 20
———— and *Muir's* Qualitative Analysis ... 20
Thudichum's Chemical Physiology ... 23
Todd (A.) on Parliamentary Government ... 2
———— and *Bowman's* Anatomy and Physiology of Man ... 24
Trench's Realities of Irish Life ... 12
Trollope's Barchester Towers ... 39
———— Warden ... 39
Tyndall's American Lectures on Light ... 20
———— Belfast Address ... 19
———— Diamagnetism ... 20
———— Fragments of Science ... 19
———— Hours of Exercise in the Alps ... 33
———— Lectures on Electricity ... 20
———— Lectures on Light ... 20
———— Lectures on Sound ... 20
———— Heat a Mode of Motion ... 20
———— Molecular Physics ... 20

Ueberweg's System of Logic ... 11
Ure's Dictionary of Arts, Manufactures, and Mines ... 27

Warburton's Edward the Third ... 6
Watson's Geometry ... 20
Watts's Dictionary of Chemistry ... 24
Webb's Objects for Common Telescopes ... 18
Weinhold's Experimental Physics ... 19
Wellington's Life, by *Gleig* ... 8
Whately's English Synonymes ... 14
———— Life and Correspondence ... 6
———— Logic ... 10
———— Rhetoric ... 10
White and *Donkin's* English Dictionary ... 15
———— and *Riddle's* Latin Dictionaries ... 15
Whitworth on Guns and Steel ... 27
Wilcocks's Sea-Fisherman ... 36
Williams's Aristotle's Ethics ... 10
Willis's Principles of Mechanism ... 26
Willoughby's (Lady) Diary ... 34
Wood's Bible Animals ... 22
———— Homes without Hands ... 21
———— Insects at Home ... 21
———— Insects Abroad ... 21
———— Out of Doors ... 21
———— Strange Dwellings ... 21

Yonge's English-Greek Lexicons ... 16
———— Horace ... 36
Youatt on the Dog ... 37
———— on the Horse ... 36

Zeller's Socrates ... 5
———— Stoics, Epicureans, and Sceptics ... 5

Spottiswoode & Co., Printers, New-street Square, London.

www.ingramcontent.com/pod-product-compliance
Lightning Source LLC
Chambersburg PA
CBHW032045230426
43672CB00009B/1477